WHICH
COMMANDMENTS
SHOULD
I OBEY?

HOW TO WALK DAILY
IN THE COMMANDMENTS

A 365 DAILY SEARCH FOR
HIS COMMANDMENTS IN SCRIPTURE

by
Debra Stuart Sanford

CCB Publishing
British Columbia, Canada

Which Commandments Should I Obey?:
A 365 Daily Search for His Commandments in Scripture

Copyright ©2015 by Debra Stuart Sanford
ISBN-13 978-1-77143-226-9
First Edition

Library and Archives Canada Cataloguing in Publication
Sanford, Debra Stuart, author
Which commandments should I obey? : a 365 daily search for his commandments
in scripture / by Debra Stuart Sanford. -- First edition.
Issued in print and electronic formats.
ISBN 978-1-77143-226-9 (pbk.).--ISBN 978-1-77143-227-6 (pdf)
Additional cataloguing data available from Library and Archives Canada

Book design by Kevin O'Keefe.

This book may be ordered from: **www.AlephTavScriptures.com**

Publisher: CCB Publishing
               British Columbia, Canada
               www.ccbpublishing.com

DEDICATION

THIS book is dedicated to my children who are a gift from Heaven: Jennifer, Jessica, Jason, Jordan, Justin, and also the children that have been added to me: Josh, Michael, Joshua, Chloe, Madelyn, and Tobey Samuel. I feel blessed everyday to have been given such treasures.

ACKNOWLEDGEMENTS

I want to personally thank my husband, William Sanford, for his constant encouragement. Without his support and loving devotion this book would have not been published.

Which Commandments Should I Obey?

HAVE YOU EVER WONDERED, "WHAT COMMANDMENTS SHOULD I OBEY?"

I have wondered this myself as I read what Yahshua said in John 14:15 "If you love me, you will keep my commandments." What commandments was He talking about? The ones he taught his disciples? The 10 commandments? I often read the 10 commandments and wondered if I was keeping all the commandments. One day I asked myself, "How do I keep the Sabbath day holy? What does this really mean?" I began to read the scriptures to find the answer. I wanted to keep His commandments, so I could obey Him and show Him how much I loved Him. His Word tells us in Jeremiah 29:13, "You will seek Me and find Me when you search for Me with all your heart." I asked Father to show me His commandments, so I would not be blinded, but live in the Light of His Presence. This led me on my journey to discover how to keep Sabbath and all the other commandments that Father has given us. It is a glorious journey! I found that keeping His Commandments brought me life. His Ways had been hidden from me, because I was following the traditions of men instead of searching for Truth in His Word. There it was right in my hands, but I never saw it until He opened my eyes to the Truth. Finding Truth is like finding "a pearl of great price." Gathering all His treasures from His Word will bring you tremendous joy and contentment. You will know you are living a life that really shows that you do love Him. Father wants His people to know what he desires from them. Deut. 30:11 tells us that these commandments are "not too hard for you to keep," but we have to know what they are before we can keep them. Thus,

4

I studied the commandments, and I wrote down what I felt Father was saying to me about each commandment that I found. There are other commandments, but I used the commandments more relevant to my life. I realized that these words could stir any of His covenant people, especially the exiles of the House of Israel that have been scattered across the nations. So many of those in exile do not even know what commandments to obey. I wanted to share the Truth that I had found with others, so they would also know the joy of keeping the commandments. As you begin your search for Truth, this book can be the beginning of your journey. Each day has one commandment for you to mediate on for that day and night. As you meditate on the commandment, search your heart to find evidence that you are obeying that commandment. Your life will be changed. We have this promise in His Word: Joshua 1:8 "Do not let this Book of the Law depart from your mouth; meditate on it day and night, so that you may be careful to do everything written in it. Then you will be prosperous and successful."

*I used the Hebrew names for God (Elohim) and the Lord (YHUH) and Jesus (Yahshua) to honor our Hebrew heritage. Jesus' disciples called him Yahshua, so I want to also call him by this name also. The scribes of the Scriptures took out YHUH's memorial name and replaced it with "the Lord," so no one would profane His Name. I want to honor His Name and use it correctly as He intended for us to use it.

Which Commandments Should I Obey?

Contents

A *365* Daily Search

7

Which Commandments Should I Obey?

A *365* Daily Search

Which Commandments Should I Obey?

A *365* Daily Search

Which Commandments Should I Obey?

A *365* Daily Search

Which Commandments Should I Obey?

Which Commandments Should I Obey?

A *365* Daily Search

1

You should begin your day at sunset.

Gen 1:3 And Elohim (God) said, "Let there be light," and there was light. 4 Elohim saw that the light was good, and He separated the light from the darkness. 5 Elohim called the light "day," and the darkness He called "night." And there was evening, and there was morning-the first day.

My beloved, I gave you Light, so your planet would grow and you would not be in total darkness. I divided the Light with the moon, so you would have a time of darkness to sleep and rest your body and heal, so you would not be sick or tired. When I divided the Light, I set up days and nights and seasons and months. I gave you a day that starts at evening and lasts until the next evening. Whenever the sun sets, then a new day begins. The Evil One took away My divine calen-dar and set up his own calendar focusing on the sun. He has the day beginning when the sun rises and ends when it is dark. The Evil One has perverted Truth and taken away My perfect times that I have set up. His goal is to destroy all Truth in My Words, so he can deceive the nations. Think of how he has deceived man and how he is taking all Truth away. Think of his ways and how he wants to take all My Ways from you, so you do not even know Me at all. Only My chosen ones will cling to My Words and My Ways. Only My chosen ones will not bend, but stay firm as the Evil One challenges them. The days grow dark. Search My Words for Truth-not the traditions of men that the Evil One has perverted, but the Truth from My Words. If you will cling to Me and My Words, I will bring Truth to your house and blessings to you and your family.

2

Man should take a wife, be fruitful and multiply.

Gen 1:26 Then Elohim said, "Let us make man in our image, in our likeness, and let them rule over the fish of the sea and the birds of the air, over the livestock, over all the earth, and over all the creatures that move along the ground." 27 So Elohim created man in his own image, in the image of Elohim He created him; male and female He created them. 28 Elohim blessed them and said to them, "Be fruitful and increase in number; fill the earth and subdue it. "

My beloved, I made man and I told him to be fruitful-to have children-and may the earth be filled with your children. The Evil One did not like that I made man in My image as My chosen child to inherit My kingdom in the last days of Earth. He made a plan to deceive man and cause him to sin. He started in the garden and deceived Eve and Adam. He continues to this day to lie to My children and steal their blessings by deceiving them and making them sin. Be on guard! Do not allow him to deceive you by telling you not to have children or to abort a child or to cut off your sperm, so you can no longer have any more children. He will try to keep you from bearing fruits of righteousness-your children. He tries to stop you from being born, so less Light will come to the world and expose the Truth. He tries to keep the Truth hidden, so you are blind and walk in darkness. You do not know Me unless you find the Truth, because I AM Truth. I do love you, and if you search for Me you will find Me and find Truth. You must not walk in darkness while on this planet, but you must walk in Light and be surrounded by Me. I will guide you into blessings and deliver you from the curses of your ancestors who sinned. Awake! Arise and be free.

3

You should remember the Shabbat day to keep it set apart.

Gen 2:2 By the seventh day Elohim had finished the work He had been doing; so on the seventh day he rested from all his work. 3 And Elohim blessed the seventh day and made it sacred, because on it He rested from all the work of creating that He had done. Ex 20:8 Remember the Sabbath day to set it apart for Elohim.

My beloved, I created all the heavens and earth and it was good-perfect- complete. I set aside the seventh day as a day for man to rest from this work and enjoy the creation I had made for him. His body needs rest, and he must heal during his rest. He becomes strong when he takes time to rest. The Evil One wants to take away this day of rest, but do not allow him to do this. Instead fight hard to keep your Sabbath rest and abide in Me during this time. Some of you say, "My job demands that I work on the Sabbath," then find a new job. Call on My name and I will help you find a new job. Teach your children to rest on Sabbath. Make Sabbath a family day where all the children stay at home and love each other and draw close to each other as a family. The members of a family make each other strong or destroy the unity of the family. Teach your children to love each other and be friends to each other. Do not compare your children to each other, but love each of them equally. Only then you will have a loving family, and you will dwell in peace. Draw together as one and be as one-praying together over every decision, so you will make the right choices as led by My Spirit. Blessings will come to your house, and your house will be a blessing to others. Rejoice in the Sabbath, and remember that it is set apart, so do not sin against it.

4

Man should take a Wife by the Sacrament of Marriage.

Gen 2:24 For this reason a man will leave his father and mother and be united to his wife, and they will become one flesh. Matt 19:5 Yahshua said, "For this cause a man shall leave his father and mother, and shall cleave to his wife; and the two shall become one flesh." 6 "Consequently they are no longer two, but one flesh. What therefore Elohim has joined together let no man separate."

My beloved, I made man and he was alone in the garden. He cared for the garden, but he did not have a help mate. I put him to sleep and divided him into two unique beings that are as one flesh when united in marriage. I found it to be good in My sight-the same being yet different and complete. They communicated with each other and helped each other, and I delighted in them. I wanted all of My beings to have such a help mate, so I made them able to reproduce and have children and this also delighted Me. I want you to find joy with a mate and marry and have children. Every man should choose a wife and go to her father's house and ask her father for permission to have his daughter in marriage. It is hard for a man to give up his daughter, but he will give her up only if the man can prove to him that he can care for this daughter and treat her with respect. Once he gives his permission to the man, the man must go prepare a place for the daughter. A man should leave his mother and father and prepare his own house. This does not mean he has to move far away, but only to another house which could be on the same land or in the same town or wherever I lead him to go. A man must cherish his wife and protect her and love her, so she will not miss her father's house where she was well cared for by her father and mother. A man must consider her feelings and not be harsh with her. Man should be kind and loving like I AM kind and loving, and then the wife will cling to him and they will be as one flesh.

5

You should circumcise your male child on the eighth day.

Gen 17:10 Every male among you shall be circumcised. 11 You are to undergo circumcision, and it will be the sign of the covenant between Me and you. 12 For the generations to come every male among you who is eight days old must be circumcised, including those born in your household or bought with money from a foreigner-those who are not your offspring.

My beloved, I made a covenant with Abraham. The sign of those who keep the covenant is circumcision when the male child is eight days old. There is a reason that I chose this sign. I chose it to protect My People against disease, because it kept them clean and was easier for men to cleanse themselves. I also chose the sign, because the pagan gods worshipped the penis as a symbol of fertility. I wanted My people to worship only Me and look to Me to give them life-not a pagan god. If a man marks his penis as a sign between him and Me, then he clings to Me and worships only Me and no other gods. I will bless him with many children. There is a release of blood-a sacrifice to Me, and a mark of the covenant between us. Sealing of any covenant should be done with blood. If you say that you were a baby and do not even remember this covenant, it was your parents who chose for you to walk in My covenant. Each man must choose to walk in My covenant. Abraham was an older man when he made his covenant with Me. You may not have been circumcised as a child, but you may have to choose for yourself as a man to make the sacrifice, so you can join in My covenant. You may think that since your heart is circumcised you do not have to have an outer sign, but I want all men who love Me to have the sign of My covenant on them. Listen for My voice and I will guide you. You may say that you do not have the money for circumcision, but if you call on My name, I will provide the money for you. You must obey My will for you.

6

You should bury your dead. You should bury the guilty man on the day of his execution.

Gen 23:3 Then Abraham rose from beside his dead wife and spoke to the Hittites. He said, 4 "I am an alien and a stranger among you. Sell Me some property for a burial site here so I can bury my dead." Deut 21:22 If a man guilty of a capital offense is put to death and his body is hung on a tree, 23 you must not leave his body on the tree overnight. Be sure to bury him that same day, because anyone who is hung on a tree is under Elohim's curse. You must not desecrate the land YHUH (the Lord) your Elohim (God) is giving you as an inheritance.

My beloved, I asked My children to be covered with dirt after they have died. I wanted their bodies to go back to the dirt from which they came. I do not want you to burn your body, and then bury it as the pagans do. I want you to do as your ancestors did. I want you to bury the dead body. You do not have to have a family burial site, but you can if you want. It may not be convenient for all family members to be buried on the same plot of land. You must think of what is most important. One day you will all be together again in My Kingdom if you have followed My ways and been obedient to My laws. If you sentence a person to hanging as his punishment for murdering someone, then take the body down before sunset and bury him. You have already had the family suffer from his death, so do not humiliate the family also. The man was wicked, but the rest of the family may not be sinful. If you execute a person with a weapon, then bury the body as soon as possible. Do not keep the body laying out on display, but cover the body with dirt. The pagans leave their dead out on display as a sign of victory, but this is not My way. Try to walk in My ways, because they are loving and kind and fair to others. Justice must reign supreme, and the guilty must be punished.

7

You should determine the appointed times by observing New Moons.

Ex 12:2 You are to begin your calendar with this month (moon); it will be the first month of the year for you. (Aviv). Is 66:23 And it shall come to pass, that from one new moon to another, and from one Sabbath to another, shall all flesh come to worship before Me, said YHUH.

My beloved, when I took My children out of Egypt, I started a new calendar for them based on the new moons. Every cycle of the moon is a month. If you kept this calendar and not a calendar based on the sun, you would not have to make any adjustments such as leap year and some months being longer than others. I made the earth to be set on a moon calendar, but man wanted to worship the sun as his god. He based all things in his life on the sun. Your life should revolve around Me and not the sun. I control the sun, the rain, the clouds, and all forces of nature. I send storms and disaster to punish My people or peoples of disobedience. I control all things, so look to Me for wisdom and advice. I will guide you down the path you must follow. I still want you to follow My calendar, so you can keep up with My feast days. I want you to know the day of My celebrations, so you can celebrate with Me and rejoice with all My people. The leaders in Israel have taken My feast days and set them on the sun calendar, so the times of the feasts are off a few days. You can calculate My feast days yourself. Learn about the moons and how to celebrate based on the moons, because this is the way I set up your planet. Look to the sky for the times and season and watch for My return. The moons will help you know the time of My arrival, so watch for Me.

8

You should eat the meat cooked in the fire on Passover. You shall eat the meat with bitter herbs and unleavened bread.

Ex 12:8 That same night they are to eat the meat roasted over the fire, along with bitter herbs, and bread made without yeast.

My beloved, on the fourteenth day on the first month you should keep the Passover Meal. If you do not know when this day is, you must ask someone who teaches the Laws given to Moses and he will tell you when this day is so you can celebrate with all My people. It is a time of remembrance of what I did for your ancestors. It is a time when I passed over your ancestors' home while they were in Egypt and spared the firstborn male's life. I brought your ancestors out of the bondage of slavery and into a life of blessing under the protection of My right hand. So many times, I spared the lives for your ancestors as Moses interceded for them in the desert. I have given you and your ancestors so much-a life in Me with an inheritance in My kingdom. Rejoice during Passover and cook the lamb in the fire. Also include bitter herbs to remember the suffering of your ancestors. The unleavened bread helps you remember that they left in haste and could not allow their bread to leaven and had to eat it unleavened. Remember how they left with the wealth of Egypt on their shoulders and how I protected them from Pharaoh and his army. I delivered them with great miracles and destroyed all the gods of Egypt, so My people could see there is only one Elohim. Celebrate Passover and remember the night I passed over your ancestors.

9

You should not eat the Passover meat raw or boiled. You should burn up any meat left in the morning.

Ex. 12:9 Do not eat the meat raw or boiled in water, but roast it over the fire-head, legs and inner parts. 10 Do not leave any of it till morning; if some is left till morning, you must burn it. 14 This is a day you are to commemorate; for the generations to come you shall celebrate it as a festival to YHUH-a lasting ordinance.

My beloved, I told My People to keep My Passover, because it is very special to Me. I delivered My People at this time from a wicked nation that had enslaved them for years. I covered them with My blood and saved them from destruction. When you keep My Passover do not eat the meat raw or boiled in water, but cook the meat over a fire and allow the smoke to cook the meat. I want My People to eat all the meat at the feast, but if any is left over after the feast then burn it up in the fire as a fragrant aroma to Me. Lift up My Name during this time and thank Me for delivering your people from the bondage of slavery. I made you My Slaves and gave you instructions how to serve Me. I want you to serve Me with all your heart and listen to My Voice, and do whatever I tell you to do. I AM a good and kind Master. I will take care of you and make sure that you have all that you need. If you are a disobedient slave and do not follow your Master's voice, then you will suffer under My Punishment. Think of ways that you can please Me and show My Love to others. Tell others of My Passover and how they can enter into My Feast Days. Honor Me by obeying all My Laws. You are My Ambassadors. You should shine your light to those around you, and be a sign to the nations that I have given you a great blessing. You have seen a great Light. Rejoice that I have given you so much!

10

You should remove all yeast from your home before Passover. You should not eat leavened bread after Passover has begun and for seven days.

Ex 12:14 This is a day you are to commemorate; for the generations to come you shall celebrate it as a festival to YHUH-a lasting ordinance. 15 For seven days you are to eat bread made without yeast. On the first day remove the yeast from your houses, for whoever eats anything with yeast in it from the first day through the seventh must be cut off from Israel.

My beloved, I told My people to keep Passover in the first month of the year on the fourteenth day of the Hebrew calendar-the one I designed for My people from the beginning. The Evil One keeps trying to destroy My calendar and anything that I give My people. What I give is good and he wants to destroy all that is good. He hates My people, because they are made in My image. One day they will rule the universe as My sons and daughters. I asked My children to keep the Passover feast by not eating any bread with yeast in it. I want you to keep this feast also, because you will remember how I passed over your ancestors and did not kill their first born. I also helped them escape bondage and destroyed all the gods of Egypt. The people of Egypt were shown that I AM the one Elohim. If you keep My Passover, I will bless you for your obedience. What you must do is simple. You must not eat yeast in any food for seven days, and you must not have any yeast in your house. You will say, "I have taken all the sin out of my house. I will cleanse myself and fast for seven days. I will praise YHUH in thanksgiving for all He has done for Me and My ancestors." I will smile on you, because you are obedient. Celebrate with your meal of roasted lamb and bitter herbs, and whatever foods you may like for your family. You must keep My laws I have established for all My people no matter where you live.

11

You should not work on the first day or the seventh day of Feast of Unleavened Bread.

Ex.12:6 On the first day hold a sacred assembly, and another one on the seventh day. Do no work at all on these days, except to prepare food for everyone to eat-that is all you may do. 19 For seven days no yeast is to be found in your houses. And whoever eats anything with yeast in it must be cut off from the community of Israel, whether he is an alien or native-born.

My beloved, the first day and the last day of the Feast of Unleavened Bread are to be set apart and you should do not work on them, except to prepare food for your family. On these days rejoice and be glad that I love you so much. Declare with uplifted voices that you are thankful for all My Blessings. Don't go to work on these days, but rest and enjoy the day. Rest and dwell in peace and love those around you. If you must work because you are required to do services for others, then continue to rejoice and be glad that I have given you so much. Do not eat any yeast from the first day of the Feast of Unleavened Bread until the end of the day on the seventh day. You must focus on removing the sin from your body. You must wash yourself clean by sacrificing your flesh and staying away from anything with yeast in it. If you are not aware of the foods with yeast in it, then look carefully and guard over yourself during this time so your sacrifice can be pleasing in My Sight. There are many who will think that you are foolish because you keep My Feast Days, but it is a sign to the nations of your dedication to Me and My Laws. You will walk uprightly and not give into temptation. You will be free to walk without the burden of sin on you. You are delivered from bondage and now you are able to serve Me with your whole heart, soul, mind, and strength. Rejoice as you serve Me.

12

***You should keep Feast of Unleavened Bread every year
no matter what country you live in.***

**Ex 12:17, 20 Celebrate the Feast of Unleavened Bread, because it
was on this very day that I brought your divisions out of Egypt. Celebrate this day as a lasting ordinance for the generations to come. Eat
nothing made with yeast. Wherever you live, you must eat unleavened
bread. (Matt 26:17-19, Luke 2:41-42, Luke 22:8, Acts 20:6)**

My beloved, everyone who loves Me will keep My Laws. Everyone who wants
to serve Me will keep My laws. If you love Me and want to serve Me, then you
must look to Me and ask Me to guide you and help you. No matter where you
live, even if you live in exile, keep My Feast Days and I will bless you. Keep My
Feast Days as a memorial, so you will remember what I did for My People on
each feast. Be sure to teach your children what I have done for you. If you honor
My Feast Days, then I will honor you and raise you up and show you how good I
can be to you. If you honor My Feast Days, then I will draw you closer to Me and
tell you secret things, so you can be at one with Me. If you love Me, you will want
to please Me. If you do not realize the importance of the feast days that they are
a shadow of the things to come, then you must learn about these things. Some
feast days have already been fulfilled and others are waiting to be fulfilled. Watch
for what events happen around My Feast Days. You can see ahead if you use My
Feast Days as stepping stones. I have given you little sign markers along the way
to direct your path to the Truth. If you look carefully for the signs and ask Me
to guide you so you can walk into all Truth, then the doors will open on all sides
for you to see the Truth. I will allow you to see hidden things, so you can grasp
onto who I AM and how I will form you into My Image. You will emerge into a
glorious being. Rejoice and be glad that I have given you so much!

13

You should teach the deliverance of Israel from Egypt during Passover.

Ex 13:8 On that day tell your son, 'I do this because of what YHUH did for me when I came out of Egypt.' 9 This observance will be for you like a sign on your hand and a reminder on your forehead that the law of YHUH is to be on your lips. For YHUH brought you out of Egypt with His mighty hand. 10 You must keep this ordinance at the appointed time year after year.

My beloved, when you are sitting at your Passover table, tell your children why you celebrate Passover. Tell them how I destroyed all the gods of Egypt, and how I did many miracles to deliver My people from bondage. Tell them how I passed over your ancestors houses, because they had placed the blood of the lamb on their doorposts making the Hebrew letter for life. You must realize that I had planned from the beginning to deliver you. I wanted to let Egypt know that I AM the only Elohim. I wanted to bring with Me all My people and not leave one behind. Tell your children of My mercy and compassion with your ancestors. My people tested Me in the desert by their complaining against Me, because they had no faith in My ability to care for them. Do not test Me this day. Do not complain, but rejoice in any situation you find yourself. Rejoice and be glad, because I have given so much to you. Celebrating the Passover is a sign that you are My people, because you are obedient to Me and you do all I command you. My people read My laws and observe My festivals. Some say, "If you are in Israel, only then you should keep Passover." I say wherever you live, you can celebrate the Passover with your family. Remind them of My wondrous works and My love for My people and how I remember My covenant with them and deliver them from their enemies.

14

You should not remove the Passover lamb from your house until morning. You should not break any bone of the Passover lamb.

Ex 12:46 It must be eaten inside one house; take none of the meat outside the house. Do not break any of the bones. 47 The whole community of Israel must celebrate it.

My beloved, Do not eat the Passover lamb outside of your house. It is a family meal that is shared together. Do not break any bones of the lamb. I AM the Passover Lamb and I paid the sacrifice for you, so that you could have eternal life with Me. My bones were not broken, but My blood was spilled out. I went to the grave and to the land of the living held captive in the underworld. I released a host of My People. They were allowed to escape to My kingdom-all My beloved children-Abraham, Isaiah, Jacob and all their descendants were given freedom. It was a day of great rejoicing. Remember these things at your Passover table. Remember all the miracles that I have done for you and your people. All your ancestors rejoiced over the many miracles that I have done for them. Do not lose sight of these miracles, but teach them to your children and show them that I AM almighty. I can do anything for them, if they call on My Name. Teach your children how to have faith in Me. They will watch your example, so live by faith and walk in My Ways. You will see how I bless your house, and I will bless your children. You will rejoice over My many blessings. You will rejoice that I love you so much.

15

You should not allow any uncircumcised person to eat the Passover lamb.

Ex 12:48 "An alien living among you who wants to celebrate YHUH's Passover must have all the males in his household circumcised; then he may take part like one born in the land. No uncircumcised male may eat of it."

My beloved, I told My people not to allow anyone that is not circumcised to eat a piece of the Passover lamb. This meal is just for My people–those who want to obey Me and walk in My ways. You may say, "I am a believer and I want to walk in your ways, but I am not circumcised. Should I be denied the Passover Meat?" I must say, "Yes, for now you are denied," because circumcision is a sign of My obe-dient ones. It is also a sign to the world of My Mark. What other people are given a mark on their flesh as a sign to their god? Only My Chosen Ones have a mark on their flesh. You must rest and believe in Me and My ways. You must humble yourself and be obedient. Do not allow any uncircumcised person at your Pass-over meal. This is the only meal that I ask this to happen. It is a remembrance of your ancestors and what I did for them. Treat My Table as set apart prepared for Me and My Presence. Treat My Table as a place to glorify My Name and honor Me. Do not drag in the world to My Table. Only My Set Apart Ones should come to My Table. These are the ones who pull away from the world and want to keep My Laws and walk in My Ways. You are not like the other peoples of the world. Keep yourself clean and in harmony with Me. Keep yourself free from the entanglements of the world, then you can rejoice in My Presence and I can show you secret things that will help you draw closer to Me.

16

You should consecrate (set apart) every first born male to YHUH.

Ex 13:1 YHUH said to Moses, 2 "Consecrate to Me every firstborn male. The first offspring of every womb among the Israelites belongs to Me, whether man or animal." Luke 2:22 When the time of their purification according to the Law given to Moses had been completed, Joseph and Mary took Him (Yahshua, Jesus) to Jerusalem to present Him to YHUH (as it is written in the Law of YHUH, "Every firstborn male is to be consecrated to YHUH"), and to offer a sacrifice in keeping with what is said in the Law of YHUH: "a pair of doves or two young pigeons."

My beloved, all firstborn males are Mine, because I passed over the first born while in Egypt and spared them death and counted them as Mine. To redeem the firstborn, you were required to go to the Temple and pay an offering to buy him back or either dedicate him to the priesthood. I have delivered you from Egypt, but you are still My people. I want you to be consecrated unto Me, because you are My firstborn among men. You are to be separated from the rest of the world. You are to be My set apart people. Many dedicate their children to Me in the church before the assembly, but then they do not teach My children My laws or My ways. They do not teach their children to seek Me and find Me and be led by Me, so their children wander around and have no foundation. When the dark days come, they will sink and have no sure footing. If you really want to consecrate your children to Me, then you must make a sacrifice every day to teach your children My words and My ways. You must live righteous lives before them-an example of love and kindness. You must be able to make whatever sacrifice has to be made to keep your family on the right path. If I call you to come out of Babylon, then do so quickly for the sake of your children.

Which Commandments Should I Obey?

17

You should listen to the voice of YHUH.

Ex 15: 25 There YHUH made a decree and a law for them, and there He tested them. 26 He said, "If you listen carefully to the voice of YHUH your Elohim and do what is right in His eyes, if you pay attention to His commands and keep all His decrees, I will not bring on you any of the diseases I brought on the Egyptians, for I am YHUH, who heals you." Ex 19:5 Now if you obey Me fully and keep my covenant, then out of all nations you will be my treasured possession. Although the whole earth is mine, 6 you will be for Me a kingdom of priests and a sacred nation.

My beloved, listen to My voice and do as I tell you and you will do well. You will prosper and be blessed. You will be lifted up and I will send you good things. If you listen to Me, I will guide your steps and you will see ahead clearly. You will not fall into traps or entanglements of the Evil One, but you will be free from all bondage. You will live your life rejoicing and resting in peace in My presence. You have been given My laws. I have written them down for you. You know what they are, if you read them and meditate on them. If you ignore My laws, then you will be punished and your children will suffer because of your rebellion. Not all have the seed of righteousness within them. Not all can serve Me or even want to serve Me. Stay away from those people. Stay away from those who do not love Me and follow in My ways. You will see if you allow such people in your life, you will not prosper and grow. Darkness will hinder your relationship with Me. If you dwell in darkness and associate with those in darkness, then you will be hindered and you will suffer loss. You must draw close to Me. Listen to My voice. I AM calling all My children to come to Me. The days are growing dark and the end of the days of this planet is almost here. Rejoice that I come quickly, but be ready and stay alert. Keep awake, because I come soon to get My children who are faithful. Are you faithful? Are you listening to My voice and obeying Me? If you are, I will heal you and bless you greatly.

18

You should know YHUH Exists and believe in Him.

Ex 20:2 "I am YHUH your Elohim, who brought you out of the land of Egypt, out of the house of slavery." (Believe in Me!) James 2:22 And the scripture was fulfilled that says, "Abraham believed YHUH, and it was credited to him as righteousness," and he was called YHUH's friend. Heb 11:6 And without faith it is impossible to please Him, for he who comes to YHUH must believe that He does exist, and that He is a rewarded of those who seek Him out.

My beloved, I AM YHUH-believe in Me. This is the first commandment that I gave My people. This is the first commandment that you must keep to be able to keep all the rest of My commandments. You must believe I AM the only Elohim and there is no other god. You must trust in Me to deliver you from the bondage of sin just like I delivered My people from the bondage of slavery. Every man that comes to Me and opens his arms to Me and accepts Me as his only true Elohim will be saved from eternal damnation-eternal darkness. He will be no more. You must humble yourself and trust only in Me, so you do not put yourself up as a "god" and want to do as you please. Only I know what is best for you. Only I know where you need to be going and when. You must trust Me to guide your feet and get you there on time. If you constantly want your own way, then you will suffer loss. I try to give you peace and happiness, but you reject the good things I want to give you when you reject My laws and My ways. If you long for the things of the world, you will die with the world. You must long for Me and follow My voice, and then in the darkest of days you will be led by Me to safety, and I will cover you in My arms. You are precious to Me, and the evil one wants to deceive you, and then destroy you. Beware of his evil plan, and cling to Me for salvation.

19

You should not serve any god but YHUH. You should not entertain the idea that there is any god but the Eternal One.

Ex 20:3 "You shall have no other gods before Me."

My beloved, you are to have no gods before Me. You are not to put anything else before Me. You are not to want to please anyone else instead of Me. You should only want to serve Me and no one else including yourself. Do not be selfish and think only of yourself and what you want, but look at the needs of others and take care to meet their needs instead of your own. I do not mean take the food, shelter, or clothes away from you or your family, but if you have abundance, then give of your abundance to others. Do not seek more and more and be greedy. Greedy people do not enter the kingdom of heaven, but they are cast away from Me. Only those who love others will enter My kingdom. My beloved, serve only Me, and then you will walk in love. Being a servant to Me is easy. I AM not a hard task master, but I want to give you only the best gifts on the earth. You must prove your loyalty and faithfulness to Me, because only faithful servants are rewarded. You must show your faithfulness to Me by being obedient. When I call, answer Me and do as I say to do. If you do not understand exactly what to do, then wait and I will show you a sign. I will help you know exactly what to do, because you seek Me for advice and you know My leading. In the last days those who love the world will die in the world, but those who love Me will rule eternally with Me in My kingdom, because I AM the only Elohim of this world.

20

You should not worship an idol.

Ex 20:4 You shall not make for yourself an idol in the form of anything in heaven above or on the earth beneath or in the waters below. 5 You shall not bow down to them or worship them; for I, YHUH your Elohim, am a jealous Elohim, punishing the children for the sin of the fathers to the third and fourth generation of those who hate Me, 6 but showing love to a thousand generations of those who love Me and keep my commandments.

My beloved, do not worship other gods. Don't make for yourselves any statue to worship. Do not set up an altar with an image or statue on it. I AM an invisible Elohim, and I do not want any visible image of Me for you to worship. No man has seen My face, and no man will see My face. You are a people of faith. You do not need an image of Me to worship. You can set up an altar in your home in remembrance of Me, but do not place an image on it. This is what the pagans do, and you are not a polluted people. You do not stare at the picture or statue or image and say this is my god. I AM a jealous Elohim. I place My blessings, on those who serve Me. I place My stamp/seal of approval on those who are faithful. I lift up those people of Mine who worship Me in spirit and truth. You may say you do not worship an idol and do not have any other gods in your house, but if you have any statutes of pagan gods or statues that you do not know the origin, then you must remove all statues from your house. Do not look to the sky for your guidance. Do not worship the sun, moon, or stars. Do not worship angels. You may be worshipping demons and not be aware of it. My angels will not allow you to worship them. Beware of what is in your home, and remove any questionable objects, because they carry spirits. Be careful! The evil one will try to come into your home in any possible way, so beware!

21

You should not utter the Name of YHUH in vain.

Ex 20:7 You shall not misuse the name of YHUH your Elohim, for YHUH will not hold anyone guiltless who misuses His name.

My beloved, do not use My name unless in worship or to call out to Me. Do not use My name lightly. It is a sacred name and has been hidden, so man cannot trample upon it. I want no man to say My name in an oath. Do not swear by Me, but if you do, you must keep the oath and you cannot break it. If you say you will do something for someone, then you must do it. Do not break a promise. If you do, you are not full of truth. You lie. You are not honest. Think before you speak and do not say, "Yes, I will" until you have counted the cost. You must be cau-tious. Look at what you must do and decide if you have the time and resources to do it. You must be faithful and loyal to the words you speak, and then men will view you as an honest person, and you will have value. You will be a light for Me-an example of My loyalty to others. Keeping your word is not hard. You must do all you say you will do. If you are married or a daughter that lives in her father's house, then the husband or father can break the oath for you if it is unreasonable. The husband or father is a covering for the woman, because she is the weaker vessel and she may make a mistake. I gave authority to the husband or father to override her oaths. Be careful to weigh your words, and say what you know you can do. Be faithful to Me and honor My name. Let it be sacred on your lips, and rejoice that you have an Elohim who loves you so much.

22

You should show respect and honor your parents. You should not strike a parent.

Ex 20:12 Honor your father and your mother, so that you may live long in the land YHUH your Elohim is giving you. Ex 21:15 Anyone who attacks his father or his mother must be put to death. Ex 21:17 Anyone who curses his father or mother must be put to death.

My beloved, honor your father and mother and love them. Obey their commands and be humble towards them. They have lived longer than you and have more wisdom than you. If your parents are not following My ways and not keeping My commandments, then you must put Me and My ways first. You should always treat your parents with respect, because they raised you and cared for you while you were small. You are the seed of their body-part of their flesh, and you must honor and show respect for those of your own blood-your ancestors. Your ancestors may not have served Me, but My seed of righteousness passed through them to you. Be thankful for your ancestors. Do not shun your family's name or bring dishonor to your family name. Your ancestors may have been sinners, but they are not forsaken by Me. I have kept them and not wiped them out. I have carried them over distant seas to come to a new land and escape their enemies. I have made them strong, so they could endure the trip. They had to start again and prosper, so they could have children and establish themselves in a new land. I have given you much. You should thank your parents for all their righteousness towards you, if they trust in My name. Always care for them and do good things for them, and I will bless you with a long life.

23

You should not steal personal property.

Ex 20:15 You shall not steal.

My beloved, do not take anything that is not yours. If you find something that is not yours, then try to find the owner. If no owner is found, then keep it in your possession until you can find the owner. Someone is sad, because they have lost this item. Do not covet what someone has so much that you steal the item from him. If you want the item, then ask the owner if he will sell it to you. If the owner is not willing to sell it to you, then look for a similar item and buy it. You must realize that this item is not meant to be in your possession. I bring to you all that you need. Do not try to collect up numerous items for yourself, because this is selfish and greedy. You must keep only the things that you need, and give away the other things that you do not need. You must hold onto what I want you to have. Listen to My Voice, and only buy what I tell you to buy. If you listen to My Voice, you can save your money and have extra money when you need it. You must do what I tell you to do not what the world tells you to do. The world says to accumulate possessions, but I tell you not to accumulate possessions for yourself. Give to others and only keep in our house exactly what you need. If you will do this, then your burden will be light. You will rejoice over what I give you and still be able to give to others. You must love only Me and not the world, and then I can bless you greatly.

24

You should not covet (crave) what belongs to another.

Ex 20:17 You shall not covet your neighbor's house. You shall not covet your neighbor's wife, or his manservant or maidservant, his ox or donkey, or anything that belongs to your neighbor.

My beloved, do not long for what others have. Be satisfied with what I have given you. All wealth comes from Me. I give to who I please. If you do not have something, it is because you have not asked Me. I will give it to you. If you have asked Me and you still do not have it, maybe you asked selfishly or in greed. I saw your heart, and I knew you needed to be humbled not exalted with more wealth. If you think only of yourself, then you will not be given anything until you humble yourself and want to serve only Me. If you humble yourself and want to be My servant and follow My ways and not your ways, then I will bless you. All blessings come from Me. I open all doors. Do not look at the things of the world and desire it. Do not desire large mansions, expensive cars, rare jewels, or designer clothing. What value does all of this have? It will burn along with the rest of mankind. Long for the gifts of the spirit and righteousness. If you are lusting after another man's wife or another woman's husband, repent quickly. You could cause them to commit adultery, and this is evil. Woe to the man or woman who makes a husband or wife commit adultery. Woe to the one who brings sin on a family. Listen to My words and keep your heart from lust. Wait on Me to bring you a mate. If you rush out to the world, then you will suffer loss. Only what I bring you can give you satisfaction.

25

You should not make a graven image or have it made by others to worship.

Ex 20: 23 Do not make any gods to be alongside Me; do not make for yourselves gods of silver or gods of gold.

My beloved, My people were worshipping other gods. They said that these other gods were the ones who prospered them. They were an abomination to Me. I guided and protected them, and they said false gods were the ones who cared for them. I had enough of their wickedness. Their sins against Me multiplied until they were no longer able to remain in My land. I drove them out into captivity, and they did not repent. They continued to worship other gods. Whatever nation they fled to, they worshipped their gods. I kept a few people for Myself-only those whose hearts were grieved by being in a foreign land with foreign gods. I looked for the few among My people who really wanted to serve Me. I delivered them from their enemies, and I brought them back to My land and cared for them. Today I AM still looking for the few who really want to serve Me and walk in all My ways. If you want to follow Me and keep all My commandments, then I will bless you and cover you with My hand. Others may want to worship idols of Mary or the saints. They may want to light candles to their gods. If you follow My ways, I will bless you. Do not seek after the ways of men, but ask Me, "How can I serve you?" I will bless you by showing you My ways.

26

You should not kidnap anyone.

Ex 21:16 Anyone who kidnaps another and either sells him or still has him, when he is caught must be put to death.

My beloved, you should never force someone to do something against his will. You must not take someone and hold him and not let him go. You must always ask a person if he wants to come with you. If he says "No," then you must not force him to go. If you force a person to go with you or capture a person, then you will be punished. You must not capture a person and sell him as a slave. You must not violate the rights of others. If a person is poor and says, "I will work for you if you pay my debts," then the person will work for you until his debt is paid because that is your agreement. If the person is poor, you cannot force the person to work for you against his will. Maybe the poor person says, "I will work for you if you provide Me food, clothes, and shelter," then you have taken on the responsibility of this person. You must never forsake him or his family. You must not violate the rights of others, but you must be kind and loving to others, even the poor. If you are fighting for custody of your children, then you cannot take them even if they want to go with you. You must prove to the court that you are worthy and can raise them. You must have custody of them before you take them, or you will suffer through the court system. You must think clearly and know that I will give you your children, if they are in a bad place or in harm. Many times you do not know what is best because you do not see clearly, but I will help you with all your problems.

27

You should pay for any loss you caused anyone to suffer.

Ex 21:18 If men quarrel and one hits the other with a stone or with his fist and he does not die but is confined to bed, 19 the one who struck the blow will not be held responsible if the other gets up and walks around outside with his staff; however, he must pay the injured man for the loss of his time and see that he is completely healed.

My beloved, if you fight with someone and injure him, then you must pay for his medical bills and time away from work. If you were only defending yourself in a fight, then you owe no compensation. You must tell the person that you do not want to fight and try to get the person to stop trying to hit you. If you do not say these things, then you have not tried to stop the fight. If you damage a person while in a car or with any other object even though it was accidental or on purpose, then you must pay for his medical bills and time away from work. If the accident was his fault, then he must compensate you for the damages. If the person is poor and cannot pay you, then I will provide for you so you can have all you need. If you know someone who is hurting because of an accident or fight, then go to him and pray for him that he will be healed. Ask him to repent and do what is right. Anytime you must pay restitution to someone, it is because you have sinned. You must realize that all sins must be paid back, so you can fully pay your debt of sin while you are on earth. I will not allow My children's debt of sin to add up. I make them pay for all their sins before they die, so they can enter eternal life with all their debts paid. No one can enter My Kingdom of Light without making restitution to others.

28

You should pay for any damage your animals cause.

Ex 21:28 If a bull gores a man or a woman to death, the bull must be stoned to death, and its meat must not be eaten. But the owner of the bull will not be held responsible. 29 If, however, the bull has had the habit of goring and the owner has been warned but has not kept it penned up and it kills a man or woman, the bull must be stoned and the owner also must be put to death. (Ex 22:5)

My beloved, if you have animals, then keep them locked up or on a leash. If you do not care for your animals properly and they damage a neighbor's yard or possessions, then you must make restitution. If your dog digs holes in a neighbor's yard and destroys his plants, then you must replace the plants and fill in the holes. If your dog attacks another dog and harms it, then you need to pay for any medical bills caused by your dog. If the animal attacks a person and causes him harm, then you are responsible for the medical bills and any time lost from work. If the animal kills someone, then you must kill the animal. If the animal has killed before and you let the animal live, then you are responsible for the person and his blood is on your hands. Do not value an animal over the life of a person. You must be careful with your animals. If an animal looks sick and he is not acting normal, then lock him up and care for him so he does not harm someone while he is ill. If you do not care for your animals but neglect them, then I will judge you for this. You must feed your animals and provide for them a clean place to live. If you decide you no longer need an animal, do not throw it out of your house into the streets. Find a place for it to be fed and cared for, then you will do well in my sight.

29

You should pay for any loss you caused someone to suffer due to your neglect of your property.

Ex 21:33 If a man uncovers a pit or digs one and fails to cover it and an ox or a donkey falls into it, 34 the owner of the pit must pay for the loss; he must pay its owner, and the dead animal will be his.

My beloved, you must take care of your property, so there are no dangerous places that could cause harm to others. Fill in holes and make your land level. Fence off land that needs to be enclosed for animals. Make sure there are no dangerous areas for children to play in like old refrigerators or an open swimming pool with no gates around it. You must keep your little ones safe, and do not allow them to play without supervision. You must guard over and protect the lives of others who are on your property. If someone is hurt on your property because of your carelessness, then you are responsible for their medical bills and time lost from work. Look around your house and see if you have rotten or unsecure boards that might harm others when they walk. Pick up objects left on the ground, so no one trips over them. Sometimes accidents do happen in your home, but it may not be because of your neglect. If you are not neglectful and have secured your home safely for others, then you are not held responsible for the damages of others. If you are blamed for the accident but you know it was not your fault, then reason with the person. If necessary go to another brother with the complaint. If the person is not a believer, then talk with a judge about it. Make sure to clear your name, so you can have peace and be free from turmoil.

30

You should pay back double for any possessions you steal.

Ex 22:1 If a man steals an ox or a sheep and slaughters it or sells it, he must pay back five head of cattle for the ox and four sheep for the sheep. 2 If a thief is caught breaking in and is struck so that he dies, the defender is not guilty of bloodshed; 3 but if it happens after sunrise, he is guilty of bloodshed. A thief must certainly make restitution, but if he has nothing, he must be sold to pay for his theft.4 If the stolen animal is found alive in his possession-whether ox or donkey or sheep-he must pay back double.

My beloved, if someone breaks into your house at night, you must defend yourself. If the thief is killed, then you were only protecting your family. If a man breaks in your house during the day, you can see his face and identity him. You do not have to kill him, because you know when you have beaten him enough or he can see your weapon and can flee from your house. If you have no weapon, you are able to call the police and identity the person. The police can take care of locating him. If you are worried about robberies, then you must put your house in My Hands and I will protect you from all dangers. I will send angels to your house, so you are protected. You do not have to worry or fear. If you live in a neighborhood where the crime rate is high, then move as soon as you can to another place so you can raise your children in another place. If you do not have money to move, call on My name so I can place you in a good place. Do not hold onto a neighborhood, but hold onto Me and let Me guide you to a safe place. I want all my children who serve Me to live in safety so I can bless them with peace. If you catch a thief, then he is required to pay you back double for what he has taken from you. Maybe he will learn that stealing is not profitable, but hard work can bring him profit.

31

You should pay for any property you destroyed with fire.

Ex 22:6 If a fire breaks out and spreads into thorn bushes so that it burns shocks of grain or standing grain or the whole field, the one who started the fire must make restitution.

My beloved, you must make restitution for anything you have destroyed by fire whether it was an accident or not. If you are burning leaves and your neighbor's house catches on fire, then you must pay for the damages. If you are in a forest and you are not careful with your fire and your fire spreads and destroys property, then you must make restitution. If you are cooking at someone else's home and a fire breaks out in their home and causes damage, then you are held responsible and must pay for the damages. If insurance covers the house except for the deductible, then you must pay the deductible. Do not walk away and not make restitution for anything you do to others or their property. This is not right in My eyes. You must pay for any loss you have caused to others. You cannot ignore the situation and do nothing. You must restore what has been destroyed, so you can be at peace with the person. I do not want My Children to be people who do not pay their debts. I do not want My Children to ignore the needs of others especially if the problem was caused by you. Even if your child who may not know exactly what they are doing causes the harm to property, you must make restitution because the children are your responsibility until they are twenty years of age or married.

32

You should pay double for anything stolen while under your care. You should have to appear before a judge to determine your innocence.

Ex 22:7-13 If a man gives his neighbor silver or goods for safekeeping and they are stolen from the neighbor's house, the thief, if he is caught, must pay back double. In all cases of illegal possession of an ox, a donkey, a sheep, a garment, or any other lost property about which somebody says, This is mine, both parties are to bring their cases before the judges. The one whom the judges declare guilty must pay back double to his neighbor.

My beloved, if someone says to you, "Will you care for my pet while I am gone?" or "Will you keep my car at your house while I am on vacation?" or "Will you care for my children while I am out of town?" or any other such situation where someone asks you to watch over their possessions while they are gone, then you are responsible for the care of these possessions. If anyone steals the man's possession while they are in your care, then you must report the matter to the police immediately and have them file a report, so they can catch the thief as soon as possible. If the thief is caught, then he must make restitution to the person. He must give back the possessions and pay double the value of the possessions as a fine. If he does not have the stolen items, then he must also add the value of the possessions to the restitution. If the thief cannot be found, then you must explain this to the person who asks you to care for the items. If the items were well cared for and locked away and the thief broke in and stole them, then you are innocent. If you failed to lock them away or did not watch over the possessions as you said you would do, then you are guilty. You must state before Me that you were innocent in the matter. If two people both claim the same object, then they must settle it in court to regain possession of the object.

33

You should pay for anything borrowed and loss or stolen.

Ex 22: 14 If a man borrows an animal from another man and it is injured or dies when its owner is not present, the man must pay for it. 15 But if that happens when the owner is present, the man need not repay. If it is a rented animal, the loss is covered by the rental price.

My beloved, if you borrow something form someone, then you are responsible for the item. If something happens to it so that it breaks or is lost or it is damaged, then you must pay for the loss. You must pay for the value of the item, so the person can be able to replace it. If you borrow a saw from a neighbor and it breaks, and then you have it repaired or replace the saw, he will be able to have the saw in good working order. If you borrow a car and it breaks down or runs out of gas or has a flat tire, you are responsible for bringing it back to your neighbor in good working order. If you borrow anything, you must think, "This possession is not mine and I must care for it very carefully." If you care for it carefully, then you can bring it back to your neighbor in the way you borrowed it. If you borrow an object and it doesn't work when you borrow it, then quickly go back to you neigh-bor and tell him that it does not work, so he will not blame you for breaking it. It is best to examine it in the presence of your neighbor, so you can know it works before you borrow it. It is best not to borrow from others if possible, but If you are poor and have to borrow, then remember to regard whatever is borrowed as your own. If you borrow clothes, you must care for them and wash or dry clean them before returning them or ask how the clothes should be cared for so you do not damage the clothes you borrowed. If you do damage the clothes, then pay the full value of the clothes to the owner. This will be pleasing in my sight.

34

You should not allow anyone practicing witchcraft to live among you.

Ex 22:18 Do not allow a sorceress to live.

My beloved, do not allow anyone who practices magic or witchcraft to live in your house. Do not become friends with anyone who wants to be part of an occult. Do not take part in any of their activities. If you do not become friends with them to begin with, then you will not have to be concerned about going to any place with them that may not please Me. If you have a friend and he says that he has begun to take part in the occult, then try to convince your friend not walk into such darkness. If your friend will not listen, then no longer be a friend to him, because he has turned against Me and does not want to follow My ways. If your friend will not listen to you, then your fiend does not value your wisdom and is not loyal to you. The friend was not a good friend to you from the beginning. If you are married and your mate says he wants to become part of an occult and practice the dark arts, then you must explain to him the dangers of his actions and how I will punish him for walking into darkness. If he will not listen, then put him in My Hands and I will punish him and humble him until he can see the error of his ways. If you love your mate, then fast and pray that he will see clearly and not be destroyed by his rebellion towards Me. I will hear your prayer and redeem him.

35

You should not eat the flesh of a beast that is torn or died of natural causes.

Deut 14:21 Do not eat anything you find already dead. You may give it to an alien living in any of your towns, and he may eat it, or you may sell it to a foreigner. But you are a people sacred to YHUH your Elohim. (Ex 22:31)

My beloved, you are My sacred people, so keep yourself clean. Do not eat meat that has not been slaughtered by one who knows how to kill an animal and drain the blood from it. You must not eat an animal you find dead in the woods or an animal killed by a car or torn by wild animals. You should make sure the animal is healthy and does not have a disease, because you may also pick up the disease and become ill. Guard well over what you eat and do not eat any unclean foods, so you can continue to stay well. Think of this before you take a bite of any food. Look at what is in the food. Does it contain chemicals that are not natural, like man-made preservatives or any kind of sugar that is not natural? Think about what goes into your body and guard over yourself and your children. Monitor what comes into your house, so you can only buy what is good for you to eat and stay away from all the unclean foods that are spoken of in My Words. Today there are other unclean foods, because the Evil One wants to pollute your food and make you sick and diseased. If you obey Me and eat what I tell you to eat, then I will bless you and keep you from all diseases.

36

You should not repeat a false or slanderous report. You should not lie to protect a wicked man or woman.

Ex 23:1 Do not spread false reports. Do not help a wicked man by being a malicious witness. Ex 20:16 You shall not give false testimony against your neighbor.

My beloved, do not lie about someone, because you are angry with the person or the person has harmed you in some way and you want to harm them. If you lie about anything your soul will become dark and you will want lie again and again until you have no conscious, and you cannot repent of your sins. If you lie, then repent quickly so you can turn from your evil ways and no darkness will come into and remain in you. If a rebellious man continues to push away repentance, then soon it will be too late for him and there will be no repentance. If you go to court make sure you tell the truth to the judge and jury. Make sure you do not protect those who are guilty. If you protect the guilty, even if they are your family, they will sin again unless they are punished and humbled. If they are punished they may turn to Me and repent of their sins while they are suffering in jail. Remember to always pursue the Truth, and you will be blessed. Liars are an abomination to Me, and they will receive no blessing from My kingdom. If your heart is turned towards Me, then you will walk in Truth, and there will be no darkness in you that would allow you to lie to others.

37

You should not join a majority, multitude or mob to do evil. You should not lie to pervert justice.

Ex 23:2 Do not follow the crowd in doing wrong. When you give testimony in a lawsuit, do not pervert justice by siding with the crowd, 3 and do not show favoritism to a poor man in his lawsuit.

My beloved, when you are called to be a witness in a court or an officer comes to your house to collect evidence for a case, always tell the truth. Do not protect someone who has committed a crime by presenting a false testimony. This is evil in My sight. If a person breaks the law, then the person must pay for the crime. You must never protect even a loved one from going to jail, if the person deserves the penalty. If you sit on a jury do not follow the crowd, but really look at the evidence and decide what is right in My sight. If you are on the jury for a person that you know, then quickly release yourself from the jury, so you will not show any favoritism. You should not favor a poor person, because he has had a hard life and release him from his sentence. No matter if a person is poor or has been abused in any way, if he has broken the law he must pay the penalty. The person knows what is right and wrong. If the one is a child or has the mental capacity of a child, then you must realize that the child may not have known the law. The parents are responsible for any crime the child or mentally handicapped has done, and they must pay the price of restitution but not any prison sentence. The parents must guard over the child closer, and not give the child the opportunity to break the law again.

38

You should testify truthfully. You should testify in Court if you possess evidence.

Lev 5:1 If a person who is a witness sworn to testify, sins by refusing to tell what he has seen or heard about the matter, he will be held responsible.

My beloved, when you go to court to testify, always tell the truth. Do not lie to cover the sins of another, because those sins will fall on you and your family. It is very important for the guilty person to be punished for his sins. If he is not punished, then his sins will pile up against him and he will not be able to enter into My kingdom. If a man is punished, then he may repent and turn away from this wickedness and serve Me with all his heart. If you know of a crime and you do not go to the proper authorities to let the truth be known, then I will hold you responsible for not bringing the truth to light. The sin of this person will come on you, because you did not bring the truth to the proper authorities. If you allow an innocent man to go to jail, then you will have double the punishment on you, and I will set the innocent man free and release him from his sentence. If a man goes to jail for a crime he did not commit and he has sinned in the past and has not been punished for it, then he is justified in serving his time in jail so he can pay back for the times he has sinned and not been punished. Be strong and be brave. I will help you tell the truth in court and no man can harm you, if you stand up and do what is right.

39

You should assist anyone who has a legitimate need.

Ex 23:4 If you come across your enemy's ox or donkey wandering off, be sure to take it back to him. 5 If you see the donkey of someone who hates you fallen down under its load, do not leave it there; be sure you help him with it.

My beloved, if you hate someone and you see him in need of help, you must help him. This is pleasing in My sight. If you see someone who hates you or has been mean to you in the past, help the person if he needs help. You most put aside your hatred and love him even when he does not love you. If you see him stranded on the side of the road, then pick him up and get him help or call in help for him. Do not laugh and be happy for his misery. If he has lost a loved one, do not be happy but send your words of sympathy to him. If you see him lose a job or home or suffer other troubles, do not be happy but extend your hand of help. This will do more for you than to hold onto hatred. If the person hates you, your love will heal what has been broken. If you are prejudice because of the color of his skin or country he came from, then repent and love all types of people. Extend your hand to those in need no matter who they are or what feelings they may have towards you. You help others because you love Me and whatever you do towards others will be accounted to you as righteousness. All your good deeds are recorded, and so are your sins. You must pay for your sins, and then they are cancelled. I AM just and fair, and I balance the scales. Love others and do good things for them, and I will bless you.

40

You should not accept a bribe or gift to give false testimony.

Ex 23:8 Do not accept a bribe, for a bribe blinds those who see and twists the words of the righteous.

My beloved, do not accept a bribe. Do not accept money to do anything that is against My laws or is against the laws of the land. Do not love money so much that you will do anything to have some money. This makes you a weak, easily influenced, powerless person. If you stand up for justice and what is right, then you are strong and powerful and able to tear down walls of darkness. The Evil One looks for the weak to deceive and he gives him money, power, influence, and fame to do his will, but in the end this person will suffer great loss. You should be very careful not to desire the things of the world so much that you would do whatever it takes to get it. Once you have the things of the world, you will never be satisfied. You will always long for more. If you desire Me, I will bring you satisfaction. I will bring you all that you need. I will cover you with My Hand and protect you and provide for you. You do not have to fear for your future. I know all your needs and if you follow My ways and keep my commands, then I will bless you greatly. Do not be afraid, but just trust in Me. The Evil One deceives and lies, but I bring Truth and comfort and complete satisfaction.

41

You should rest on the Sabbath day.

Ex 31:15-16 For six days work is to be done, but the seventh day is a day of Sabbath rest sacred to YHUH. Whoever does any work on the Sabbath day is to be put to death. The people of Israel are to observe the Sabbath, celebrating it for the generations to come as a lasting covenant. Ex 31:12 Then YHUH said to Moses, 13 "Say to the Israelites, You must observe my Sabbaths. This will be a sign between Me and you for the generations to come, so you may know that I am YHUH, who makes you sacred." (Luke 23:55)

My beloved, I made all of creation in six days and on the seventh day I rested from creating. I made the seventh day a special day, and I blessed it. When I made man I told him that every seventh day is blessed, and he must rest. Adam and Eve always kept the Sabbath day as a day of rest. They celebrated Me on the Sabbath. Many continued to keep the Sabbath day set apart as sacred, if they loved Me and served Me. Then evil men came along and changed the Sabbath day and made Sunday the LORD's day set apart to Me. I never asked man to change My Day of rest to another day. This is what evil men do when they want to set themselves up as gods, so do not fall into their trap. My laws are forever and never change. My laws are perfect. I set aside the day for man to rest. I AM ruler of all things and I have decided the seventh day is My set apart day. Who is man to change it? They tell you that I rose from the dead on Sunday, but this is not true. The women who loved Me came to find Me on the first day of the week and did into find Me. This does not mean I rose on Sunday. No, it means that I rose after three full days in the grave. The women kept the Sabbath day sacred, so they would not make themselves unclean by coming to My tomb on Sabbath. They came very early on Sunday. I rose on the very end of Sabbath day and went to reign in My Kingdom. You should not be tricked by evil men, but keep My day I set aside as sacred. Do not be as the pagans and celebrate Sunday to their sun god. This is an abomination to Me. Sabbath is a sign between Me and My Children forever.

42

You should not labor to kindle a fire to cook in your dwellings on the Shabbat.

Ex 35:1 Moses assembled the whole Israelite community and said to them, "These are the things YHUH has commanded you to do: 2 For six days, work is to be done, but the seventh day shall be your sacred day, a Sabbath of rest to YHUH. Whoever does any work on it must be put to death. 3 Do not light a fire in any of your dwellings on the Sabbath day."

My beloved, do not do any work on My Sabbath day. Do not go outside and do your yard work or any other kind of work that would cause you to exert your body. If you say, "I enjoy yard work. It is not work to Me," then you must consider what I consider work and this is work. Your body is being used to lift and to do work. You must rest on this day and not think about your work or even do any of your paper work from your job. Put your job aside for one day and put cleaning your house aside for one day and let there not be any cooking for one day. Just rest and be at peace. Enjoy your family and do not go out to shop or buy groceries, but plan ahead so you can rest and not be going here and there. If you must buy medicine or if you have an emergency, then you must take care of it. Your normal Sabbath day is the seventh day–not Sunday the first day. Read My Word and see the Truth for yourself, so you will not be deceived by the Evil One. The Evil One wants to take everything that is good away from you. Sabbath is a sign to Me and to others that you follow the Truth, and you are not listening to the lies of others. Keeping Sabbath is following My ways. You will be looked on as different, but you are My People set apart from the rest of the nations, so keep My Sabbath.

43

You should not break a law even if it was done unintentionally.

Lev 5:17 If a person sins and does what is forbidden in any of YHUH's commands, even though he does not know it, he is guilty and will be held responsible.

My beloved, if you commit a sin and you do not know that you have done wrong, then you are still guilty and must pay the penalty for the sin. If later you find out that you have sinned, then you can ask for forgiveness because you did not know you did wrong. You still must make restitution for your sins. The Evil One lies to you and he has perverted the religions, so there is little truth in them. Only My words hold the Truth. You must study My words, so you will know what is right and what is wrong. You must learn and be led by My Spirit to teach you Truth. Do not depend on a pastor or priest to teach you My commandments. Read them for yourselves, and let Me show you the way. The Evil One covers the Truth and deceives many. He has changed My calendar and My feast days and he has even perverted My words through wrong translations of the scriptures. He wants only to take away all Truth and deceive the nations, but My Children will search for Truth and they will love Me with all their heart and soul and strength. My people will not be deceived by the Evil One, but they will be able to see his deception and know him for who he is–a liar and deceiver. My people will seek Me to find the Truth while the rest of the world is covered in darkness. Awake, My little ones, and do not allow your eyes to be blinded any more. Pull away from the things of the world-from Babylon. Do not desire what they have, but desire only Me and the gifts I can give. I will bless you, and your children will be saved from destruction.

44

You should add 1/5th (20%) value to restitution of anything stolen.

Lev 6:1 YHUH said to Moses: 2 "If anyone sins and is unfaithful to YHUH by deceiving his neighbor about something entrusted to him or left in his care or stolen, or if he cheats him, 3 or if he finds lost property and lies about it, or if he swears falsely, or if he commits any such sin that people may do-- 4 when he sins and becomes guilty, he must return what he has stolen or taken by extortion, or what was entrusted to him, or the lost property he found, 5 or whatever it was he swore falsely about. He must make restitution in full, add a fifth of the value to it and give it all to the owner."

My beloved, if you steal from someone, you must make restitution. You must give to the person the value of the item plus one-fifth of the value of the item. If you steal a car, then you must give back the car plus one-fifth of the market value for the car to make restitution. The same applies for money or any other item you may have stolen. If you do this, then I will forgive you, because you have balanced the scale with your neighbor. If you force your neighbor to pay you money through extortion, then you must also pay him back what you took from him by threatening him and add one-fifth. If you lie to someone you must also make restitution, but this is harder because you do not have an item to set a value on. You must do something for the person that you lied to, so he can forgive you, and you will be released from your sin. If you do not make restitution for your sins, then you will have to pay the penalty for your sins. I AM just and fair, but I expect all My Children to pay the penalty for their sins and I will forgive them. I love you and if you pay for all your sins here on Earth, then you will be able to come and live in My Kingdom eternally. You wonder why some people suffer so much in their last days of life. It is to pay for past sins before they are released from this planet and their time of testing is over.

45

You should not eat the fat or blood of any animal.

Lev 7:22 YHUH said to Moses, 23 "Say to the Israelites: Do not eat any of the fat of cattle, sheep, or goats. 25 Anyone who eats the fat of an animal from which an offering by fire may be made to YHUH must be cut off from his people. 26 And wherever you live, you must not eat the blood of any bird or animal."

My beloved, do not eat the fat or blood of any animal. Both of these are not digestible by your body and will cause your body to break down. Look at the foods that you eat and check for fat content and do not eat foods that are filled with fats, because it wears on your blood flow. Consider what your body needs to have your blood flowing freely through your arteries and veins. It is a strain on your heart and this can cause health problems. When you prepare meat cut off all the fat on the meat and throw it away. Do not use it as seasoning in other foods, because you are still eating the fat. If you do not monitor what you eat, you will become ill and be in pain. You must have self-control. Do not pretend like you can eat all foods. I AM your Creator and I have set aside certain foods for you to eat, and other meats are for the animals so they can eat. You must realize that I know what is best for your body. I know what to feed you to help you stay healthy. There are many toxins in your food. The Evil One tries to poison you through poisoning the food supply. He wants to kill all My people. He wants to reduce the world population, so he can have more control over the people. He wants all people to worship him, and he will do this by controlling the food supply and the currency. You must listen to Me and eat wisely, because you are My set apart people.

46

You should only eat animals that have both split hoofs and chew the cud.

Deut 14:3-8. Do not eat any detestable thing. These are the animals you may eat: the ox, the sheep, the goat, the deer, the gazelle, the roe deer, the wild goat, the ibex, the antelope and the mountain sheep. You may eat any animal that has a split hoof divided in two and that chews the cud.

My beloved, I AM your creator and I created food for you to eat, but not all animals were created for you to eat. I gave Moses very strict guidelines to follow for you, so you would eat only the clean animals. If you eat meat from an animal that chews the cud and has a split hoof, then you are eating meat created for your body to digest and it is not detestable to you. If you eat a meat that is not from an animal that is clean, then you are polluting your body. You are eating unclean detestable food. Examine carefully what you eat. Look at the pig. I did not create the pig for you to eat, but to clean up the earth. The pig eats all sorts of garbage and his meat carries what he has been eating. When you eat this unclean animal, you are bringing toxins into your body and you are defiling your body. If you eat only what I tell you to eat, then you will stay healthy. You wonder why so many people get sick. That is because they do not eat the foods I tell them to eat. If you keep My commandments, you will be blessed. If you disobey Me, you will be punished by sickness or disease. You need to give up your bacon and ham. Do not season your food with bacon or ham. Check every label and see if the contents contain pork, pig, bacon, or ham, and do not eat it. Then you will be obedient and I will bless you.

47

You should not eat unclean birds (scavengers and predators).

Deut 14:11 You may eat any clean bird. 12 But these are the kinds of birds you are not to eat: eagles, owls, hawks, falcons; buzzards, vultures, crows; ostriches; seagulls, storks, herons, pelicans, cormorants; hoopoes; and bats.

My beloved, be careful to examine what birds of the air that you eat. You must not eat any scavenger birds that hunt for food or that eat the remains of dead animals. The earth must be cleaned up, so I made creatures to clean up the earth by eating the remains of dead animals. If a bird is not clean, do not eat it. Birds such as an owl, bat, vulture, buzzard, eagle, or other hunters, you should stay away from them. You may eat a chicken or quail and enjoy them. You may also eat their eggs and enjoy them. There are other smaller birds that you many eat, but they are too small to give you much meat. You may eat a turkey and it is larger so you have more meat. You must examine carefully the birds you eat and if you are not familiar with the habits of a bird, then research it first before you eat it. I will always provide clean food for you to eat when you are hungry. Call on My name and I will bring it to your door. In the last days you will have to depend on Me to bring you all your food. I will be faithful to only bring you clean food that will benefit your body and not make you sick. If you trust in Me, I will teach you My ways and you will know what is clean and unclean and what is detestable and what is not detestable.

48

You should eat only insects with four jointed legs and that leap on earth.

Lev 11:20 All flying insects that creep on all fours shall be an abomination to you. 21 Yet these you may eat of every flying insect that creeps on all fours: those which have jointed legs above their feet with which to leap on the earth. 22 These you may eat: the locust after its kind, the destroying locust after its kind, the cricket after its kind, and the grasshopper after its kind. 23 But all other flying insects which have four feet shall be an abomination to you.

My beloved, examine all winged creatures before you eat them. You must look to see if they have jointed legs above the feet like knees, and if they have four legs and not many legs or no legs. You must not eat worms, ants, roaches, or an insect that does not hop and have four legs joined at the knees. In your country you do not eat such things as cricket and grasshoppers, but these are also given to you as food. What you consider unclean or detestable is not unclean or detestable. If I have given it to you as food, then accept it as a blessing. If a swarm of grasshoppers come to you, then gather them as food and consider them a blessing. You can cook them and eat them as you would cook any other meat. It takes more of them for a meal, but the meat is still beneficial to you. I AM your Creator and I know what is best for you. I would rather you eat grasshoppers or crickets instead of shrimp, crabs, and lobsters that are detestable to Me. I have not given them to you as food, but the Evil One has said, "This is good food. Eat it. The laws given to Moses have passed away. Eat and celebrate." If you listen to his words, then destruction will come to you and your body will be sick, and you will suffer for your disobedience. If you say these words are too hard, then call on Me and I will help you.

49

***You should not touch any feces or the carcass of any
unclean animal. You should not eat or carry a carcass
of a beast that died naturally.***

Lev 5:2 Or if a person touches anything ceremonially un-
clean-whether the carcasses of unclean wild animals or of unclean
livestock or of unclean creatures that move along the ground-even
though he is unaware of it, he has become unclean and is guilty. 3 Or if
he touches human uncleanness-anything that would make him un-
clean-even though he is unaware of it, when he learns of it he will be
guilty.

My beloved, if an animal dies, you do not know if the animal died of an illness
or disease, so do not touch it and do not eat it. You do not know if the animal is
contaminated or not. If you touch the dead animal and it has a disease, then you
could contract the disease and it could be a fatal disease. Also if you touch any
human waste, then wash your hands as soon as you can with soap and water,
because sickness or disease could be in the human waste or in animal waste. Do
not defile yourself by touching it. I know that you may use the animal waste as a
fertilizer, but do not touch it with your hands. This will make you unclean. You
are going to have to watch over your family during the coming days, because
sickness will become more viable and disease will be rampant. You must wash
your hands with soap and keep yourself away from those who have a sickness.
You must take care of yourself and not eat unclean food. Go to your local farmer
and buy foods and ask him about the pesticides he uses and how he cares for his
plants. Try your best to eat as few toxins as possible, so your body will be healthy
and can fight off disease. I will keep you from sickness and disease if you obey Me
and follow all my laws, and then you will be blessed.

50

You should not eat swarming things that crawl on their belly or on many feet or swarm in the water or walk on paws making you unclean.

Lev 11: 27 Of all the animals that walk on all fours, those that walk on their paws are unclean for you; whoever touches their carcasses will be unclean till evening. 29 Of the animals that move about on the ground, these are unclean for you: 41 And every creeping (swarming) thing that creeps on the earth shall be an abomination. It shall not be eaten. 42 Whatever crawls on its belly, whatever goes on all fours, or whatever has many feet among all creeping things that creep on the earth, these you shall not eat, for they are an abomination.

My beloved, be careful to examine all that you eat very carefully. Do not eat an animal that walks on paws such as a dog, cat, leopard, tiger, or lion, because these are hunters and they do not eat clean food. If you eat these animals, the meat would not be beneficial for your body and would cause you to become sick. Do not eat any animal that travels on its belly or any reptile. Do not eat snakes, lizards, alligator or crocodiles. These animals also eat detestable food that is not good for you. They may eat an animal that has a disease and then if you eat it, you would also contract the disease. I AM your Creator and I know what is best for you to eat. I made some foods for you to eat, but some things are not for you to eat. In the Garden of Eden I gave Adam and Eve trees to eat from, and other tress to not eat from. When Eve disobeyed and ate from the Tree of Good and Evil, then she was filled with sin and she was punished for her disobedience. When you eat an unclean animal you become unclean and filled with sin, and you are punished because you are disobedient. You may say, "I did not know this law," but you are punished whether you did not know the law or not, because the meat will not digest in your body as it should and will break down your immune system and make you more susceptible to disease. Guard over yourself.

51

You should quarantine those who have an infectious skin disease.

Lev 13:9 When anyone has an infectious skin disease, he must be brought to the priest. Num 5:1 YHUH said to Moses, 2 "Command the Israelites to send away from the camp anyone who has an infectious skin disease or a discharge of any kind, or who is ceremonially unclean because of a dead body. 3 Send away male and female alike; send them outside the camp so they will not defile their camp, where I dwell among them."

My beloved, guard over your skin and wash it carefully with soap, so you can remain clean. If you notice a rash or a spot that does not heal, then have someone anoint you with oil and pray for you, so I can hear your prayers and heal you. I do not want you to be sick or have a disease. If you are prayed for and it does not go away, then fast and pray and repent of your sins, so I can heal you. If you have unforgiveness in your heart, then seek Me so you can forgive the person and be free from the bondage of sin. Disease should not be able to stay on you, if you are walking in righteousness. What if there is a curse on your family and there is a genetic disease that runs in your family line, then fast and pray for Me to have mercy on you and end the curses on your family for your sake and your children after you. If you are grieved because you have sinned and want to walk in righteousness, then I will hear your prayers and remove your sickness from you. If you see a skin disease on you, you may also search for herbs to take care of the itch until it has been removed from your skin. Come to Me when you have any sickness, and I will heal you if you are right with Me.

52

You should not wear clothing contaminated with mildew.

Lev 13:47 If any clothing is contaminated with mildew 49 and if the contamination in the clothing, or leather, or woven or knitted material, or any leather article, is greenish or reddish, 52 He must burn up the clothing, or the woven or knitted material of wool or linen, or any leather article that has the contamination in it, because the mildew is destructive; the article must be burned up.

My beloved, be careful and examine your clothes, so you do not wear clothes that contain mildew. Some clothes are made of synthetic fibers and mildew cannot grow in these fibers, but in natural fibers such as cotton, wool, linen, or leather the mildew can grow and become harmful to you. If you see mildew on your clothes, wash them and bleach out the mildew. If you can bleach out the mildew, then you have saved the garment, but if you cannot bleach it out, then discard the garment. Throw it away or if you can burn it, then do so. Mildew is toxic and will harm you. Some mildew is worse than others. If it is green or red, it is more toxic then black, but all forms of mildew are bacteria that grow and can cause sickness and disease. You should keep yourself far from mildew whether in your house or clothes. Mildew grows in moist areas so dry your clothes as soon as you wash them, and do not throw them in a basket wet and leave them in a warm place. If you have sweated in the clothes and don't hang the clothes to dry, mildew may begin and spread. You should care for the clothes that I give you. It is wasteful not to take care of your clothes. I want you not to be wasteful or lazy, but be frugal and maintain your household well. Then I will bless you for being righteous and not sinful.

53

You should not dwell in a house that has mildew.

Lev 14:33 YHUH said to Moses and Aaron, 34 "When you enter the land of Canaan, which I am giving you as your possession, and I put a spreading mildew in a house in that land, 35 the owner of the house must go and tell the priest, 'I have seen something that looks like mildew in my house.' 44 the priest is to go and examine it and, if the mildew has spread in the house, it is a destructive mildew; the house is unclean. 45 It must be torn down-its stones, timbers and all the plaster-and taken out of the town to an unclean place.'"

My beloved, if you live in a house with mildew, then call on My Name, so I can show you how to kill the mildew. Do not live in a house with mildew, because it is harmful to you. A curse is on the house, and you must cleanse it to remove all the mildew. If you live in an older house, then mildew could be in the walls or attic or even the vents. You must check carefully and remove all the mildew, because it will make you sick. You need to cleanse the house, and then anoint your house with oil and bless the house and ask Me to keep your house free from mildew. There are other times you may want to leave a house. If a house is invested with insects, such as termites, roaches, rats, or snakes, kill the insects or rodents and then remove all of their caresses, because you do not want to breathe in their remains. If you have an infectious disease in your house, you may want to leave the house for a few days so you will not contract the disease. If you have no place to go, then keep the diseased person in one room and do not let him come out, and no one should come in until the person is well. If the person gets up and says, he is no longer ill, then rejoice because he has been released from his sickness. The family should celebrate their happiness together.

54

Men should bathe with water if they have any type of discharge. Men and women should bathe after sexual relations.

Lev 15:2 When any man has a discharge from his body, his discharge is unclean. 16 When a man has an emission of semen, he must bathe his whole body with water, and he will be unclean till evening. 17 Any clothing or leather that has semen on it must be washed with water, and it will be unclean till evening. 18 When a man lies with a woman and there is an emission of semen, both must bathe with water, and they will be unclean till evening.

My beloved, if a man has a discharge, this means he has an inflection somewhere in his body and he could be contagious. So that no one else contracts the disease, those around him were asked to wash themselves with soap to keep the disease from traveling to another person. The man must wash himself and all the clothes he has been wearing and any materials or fabrics that he has leaked on. He must keep himself clean for the sake of the people around him. If a man has a seminal discharge, then he must bathe and wash himself and any other material that he may have leaked on. A man is unclean until the sun sets. What does this mean "unclean"? He was not allowed in My Presence in My Tabernacle. He must wait until he has washed and the sun has set. What does this mean today? I do not walk in your midst as I did in the desert, but I do sent My Spirit to dwell inside of you. I do expect you to keep yourself clean and guard against sickness and disease. If a man and woman have intercourse, they must bathe and wash all materials they were lying on during intercourse. If you will do this, then all will go well with you. I smile upon a husband and wife becoming one through intercourse, but I hate adultery or fornication. Keep yourself pure and do not fall into sexual sin. Stand firm in My Words and do not allow the evil one to deceive you by numbing you to sin. Read My Words and let it be alive in your heart.

55

Women should bathe with water from any kind of discharge or during menstruation and not allow their blood to touch others.

Lev 15:19 When a woman has a discharge, if her discharge in her body is blood, she shall continue in her menstrual impurity for seven days; and whoever touches her shall be unclean until evening. 24 And if a man actually lies with her, so that her menstrual impurity is on him, he shall be unclean seven days, and every bed on which he lies shall be unclean. 25 Now if a woman has a discharge of her blood many days, not at the period of her menstrual impurity, or if she has a discharge beyond that period, all the days of her impure discharge she shall continue as though in her menstrual impurity; she is unclean.

My beloved, if a woman has a discharge, this is a sign that she could have an infection within her body. She could be contagious, so others must stay away from her, and her discharge must not get on others. They could also contract the disease. If a woman is in her menstrual period, then she must bathe daily to cleanse herself. She must wash all materials on which her blood flowed onto it. She must not lie next to someone if she is having a heavy flow, so she will not get her blood on another person. It is very important for the woman's blood not to touch another person and contaminate the person with her blood. Wash all materials that are stained with her blood whether from a regular menstrual period or another flow of blood. Blood carries the person's diseases and can contaminate those who touch it. If a person carries a disease, then the person should use extra caution not to spill blood or any bodily fluids on others. If any body fluid comes on you such as urine, spit, or any salvia, then cleanse yourself quickly with water and soap. Your skin is a protective covering, but it is a membrane and does absorb any substance that touches it. Your skin also may get cuts that are open and if bodily fluids come in contact with the cut, it is easily contaminated. Teach your children to wash themselves carefully, especially their hands to cut back on diseases.

56

You should slay cattle, deer and fowl so the blood is drained from the flesh. You should cover the blood of animals with dirt.

Lev 17:13 So when any man from the sons of Israel, or from the aliens who sojourn among them, in hunting catches a beast or a bird which may be eaten, he shall pour out its blood and cover it with earth. 14 For as for the life of all flesh, its blood is identified with its life. Therefore I said to the sons of Israel, "You are not to eat the blood of any flesh, for the life of all flesh is its blood; whoever eats it shall be cut off."

My beloved, do not eat the blood from animals, but drain it out on the ground, and then cover the blood with dirt so no wild animals or insects will be attracted to the blood. When you slaughter an animal you must hang the animal up and slit its throat and drain all the blood out of the animal. If you go to a grocery store and see meat and blood is all in it, then this meat is not good for you. Go to a butcher who you can ask how he kills his meat and how he drains the blood from the animal, or you can have an animal slaughtered from a local farmer so you know the animal is well and has been fed properly. You can talk to the man who raises the cattle yourself and cut costs on processing, packaging, and shipping. You can select your own meat and know you have chosen an animal that will not bring sickness into your house. Search for this type of animal. In the days to come sickness will abound, and you will have to take extra steps to care for your family. Listen to My Voice and I will guide you. I will show you what foods to eat and how to guard yourself against sickness and disease. There are some who delight in drinking blood and want to do as the pagans do. They are polluting their blood, and they are walking further into darkness. Stay away from these people, because they will take you into sin, and you will feel the presence of darkness and not light. If you love Me, you will obey my commands and keep them with all your heart, so you will not sin against Me.

57

***You should not practice the religious practices or
customs of any idolater.***

Lev 18:1 YHUH said to Moses, 2 "Speak to the Israelites and say
to them: 'I am YHUH your Elohim. 3 You must not do as they do in
Egypt, where you used to live, and you must not do as they do in the
land of Canaan, where I am bringing you. Do not follow their practices. 4 You must obey my laws and be careful to follow my decrees. I am
YHUH your Elohim. 5 Keep my decrees and laws, for the man who
obeys them will have life through them. I am YHUH.'"

My beloved, do not follow the ways of the world. Do not follow the ways of men.
Do not follow religious ceremonies, if they are not written in My words. Examine
My words closely and throw off your man-made traditions. Throw away what
your parents taught you unless it is written in My words. I gave My laws to Moses.
Study them and find truth. I have not changed My laws, but I have kept them
through the ages preserved so all could know Me and find Me. Do not think I
have changed My perfect laws or thrown them away just because I came to walk
among you. The Evil One would like for you to believe that My laws are not for
today, but see the Truth and live. Life is in My laws and all who abide in them
will prosper and have an abundant life. If you are not sure what laws are Mine,
fast and pray and I will bring Truth to your door. I will bring you abundant life.
Do not even look into their ways, but stay far away from the pagans or anyone
who wants to pervert My ways. If you cannot keep the ten commandments, then
you cannot follow Me. First is to know Me, and next is to put Me first in all things
and have no other idols before Me. If you keep My Sabbath sacred on the seventh
day by not working or making anyone else work and loving those around you
and treating them with kindness, then you can live a life filled with My blessings.

58

You should not indulge in familiarities with relatives, such as kissing, embracing, flirting, which may lead to incest.

Lev 18:6 No one is to approach any close relative to have sexual relations. I am YHUH.

My beloved, do not flirt or cause any of your relatives to become aroused by the way you are acting. Do not kiss or embrace in a sexual manner any of your relatives whether through blood or through marriage. Your in-laws are also forbidden to you. You must not look on your sister's husband or brother's wife with desire. You must not look on your mother in-law or father in-law with desire. You must keep yourself pure. Think of the hurt feelings you would cause if you continued in this way or the jealously you would cause. Do not say, "We are just kidding around" when you are flirting with someone and you know you are causing the person to become jealous or hurt by your actions. If you have a person who is causing you to become jealous, then go to the person and talk with him or her about how you feel and ask him or her to stop their actions towards the person you love. If the person will not listen, then cut the person off from any of your family activities. Do all you can to preserve your family. The Evil One wants to destroy families, because I created a family as a warm loving environment to raise children and protect them from the world. If you allow the Evil One to come in and destroy your family, then you have lost a gift from Me. Do not allow the gift I have given you to be stolen, but preserve your family.

59

You should not have sexual relations with close relatives.

Lev 18:7 Do not dishonor your father by having sexual relations with your mother. She is your mother; do not have relations with her. 8 Do not have sexual relations with your father's wife; that would dishonor your father. 9 Do not have sexual relations with your sister, either your father's daughter or your mother's daughter, whether she was born in the same home or elsewhere.

My beloved, do not have sexual relations with anyone unless you are married to him or her. Do not look upon others in a sexual way if you have a husband or wife. You must not desire anyone but the one you are married to. If you look at pictures of other naked men or women, this is an abomination to Me. If you try to cause someone to be aroused by your words even through you don't touch his or her body, this is an abomination to Me. If you try to go to someone and secretly have sexual relations with him or her, this is an abomination to Me. If you go to a prostitute and pay for sex, this is an abomination to Me. If you have sexual relations with anyone but your mate, then you are an abomination. You must keep your mind pure by keeping away from pornography, movies, TV, and all other sources that would cause you to become aroused. You must focus on Me and keep My laws in your heart so you will not sin. I want you to have a good marriage and I delight when you and your mate join together in sexual relations and enjoy each other. This union keeps you as one and keeps the Evil One from coming in to steal from you. You must delight in the mate I have given you. If your mate commits adultery and leaves you, then I will care for you and be your husband. I will give you all you need, and you will never have to worry.

60

You should not have intercourse with a woman in her menstrual period.

Lev 18:19 Do not approach a woman to have sexual relations during the uncleanness of her monthly period.

My beloved, keep yourself pure and only have sexual relations with your mate. Husbands do not force yourself on your wife when she is in her menstrual period. This is an abomination to Me. Be patient with your wife and allow her a week, so that her blood may flow from her body and she can be cleansed. If you have sexual relations with her, then your penis will force the blood back up inside of her, and this will cause disease and she could become infertile. You must protect your wife and not force yourself on her during this time. You must caress her and hold her close to you during this time, because the menstrual period can start with cramps and she may not feel well. You should treat your wife tenderly, because she is a gift that I have given to you, so do not destroy the gift by forcing yourself on her during her menstrual period. Wives, you should also treat your husbands with kindness during this time and even though you do not feel well, you should not say or do mean things to your husband. You must always honor your husband and encourage your husband. He needs to hear your praise not your complaints. He needs to have you honor him to your friends. Never tear down your husband or any member of your family to others. Always build up every member of your family and encourage them, so they can feel your love. When they go into the world, your love will be a shield around them, and I will protect them from all things.

61

You should not commit any homosexual or lesbian acts.

Lev 18:22 Do not lie with a man as one lies with a woman; that is detestable.

My beloved, if you are a man do not desire a man, and if you are a woman do not desire a woman. I have made you man and woman, so your union will complete each other and you will be one. This is the only sexual act that I delight in. Any homosexual act or lesbian act is an abomination to Me. If you say, "I was born like this," then you were born under a curse from the sins of your ancestors. Pray and fast and seek Me to be released from the spirit that haunts you and torments you, so you will not live in bondage all your life. You must recognize this for what it is: deception. If you want to remain in deception, then you will not enter My Kingdom of heaven. If you really love Me, you will stop your acts of perversion and you will want to walk in My ways. It is better to walk in My ways and be sexually unsatisfied. What is more important-what you want or what I want? I have a reason for every law. The Evil One wants to pervert the marriage bed, and he wants more people not to marry or stay in their marriage covenant. Do not be deceived. I want you to marry and remain in covenant and not enter into sexual sins, but to have children and raise them to serve Me and honor Me and My laws. If you really love Me, you will seek such a union and be faithful to your mate and remain in union as long as you both live. This is My way for the sake of your children, so you can show them love and faithfulness to each other.

62

You should not have intercourse with an animal.

Lev 18:23 Do not have sexual relations with an animal and defile yourself with it. A woman must not present herself to an animal to have sexual relations with it; that is a perversion. 30 Keep my requirements and do not follow any of the detestable customs that were practiced before you came and do not defile yourselves with them. I am YHUH your Elohim.

My beloved, do not desire to mate with an animal or do not use an animal for sexual pleasure while your mate is away. This is perversion to Me and evil in My sight. This is the reason I drove out nations and crushed empires because of their sexual perversion. If your nation has these perverted sexual acts in your midst, then beware because your nation will be punished. If you see children being aborted, and homosexual and lesbian couples not being rebuked for their sins, and sexual perversion with animals, then you know judgment is coming quickly. You will see disasters start to come to the nation to wake them up to repent, but if they are blinded, then the government will crumble and new men will come to take over the nation. Only then will the people see their sins and repent. If you see the warning signs, then ask Me if you should stay in a nation or leave and go to a place where sin is not so rampant. I told the Israelites to kill all the inhabitants of such sinful nations-men, women, children, and animals. All were sexually perverted-all had been defiled. Even the animals had been used for sexual pleasure and carried the diseases that sexual perversion brings. Look at the large number of sexually transmitted diseases in your nation. This is a sign of the wickedness that has come upon your nation. If you say you are a Christian and yet you have not kept yourself sexually pure-think again-repent and walk in My ways, and then you will be pleasing in My sight.

63

You should not make any figures for ornament for worship. You should not turn one's attention to idolatry.

Lev 19:4 Do not turn to idols or make gods of cast metal for yourselves. I am YHUH your Elohim.

My beloved, do not make any gods or do not make any ornaments to worship. Do not make anything that would hinder you from serving Me. Do not make anything that would draw your attention away from Me and to yourself. If you delight in covering yourself in fine gold and jewels, then repent because you are setting yourself up as an ornament or casting yourself as "god" for others to wor-ship. If you are worshipping your beauty or you are making yourself beautiful by your expensive ornaments or you value yourself so much that you have to cover yourself in gold and jewels, then repent. Let your body be a symbol of My Spirit working within you. If you want others to look at you, then show them your lov-ing kindness. Show others how you worship Me by putting Me first. You are My beloved and I will cover you in precious jewels-the jewels of the spirit- and you will shine because you are My future bride-the only one I take unto Myself–the one who I prepare mansions for in My sacred kingdom. Rejoice and be glad that I delivered you from slavery so once again you could live. I know you are in exile now and driven away from My sacred land of Israel, but soon I will cleanse My bride and bring you home out of your prostitution and into a life of loyalty to Me. You will be faithful once again and a light to all the nations.

64

You should not lie. You shall not steal, neither deal falsely, neither lie one to another.

Lev 19:11 Do not lie to one another, seeing that you have put off the old man with his deeds. (Col 3:9 , Prov 12:22, Prov 13:5)

My beloved, I want you to always tell the Truth. I want you to be honest in all you do. If you see a wicked man and you know that he is lying, you must expose his sin and do what is right in My eyes. You will see that the people of the world like to lie, and they do not think it is wrong. They cover their sins by lying. My people do not cover their sins, but they confess their sins to Me and repent of their sins. If you walk in the way of Truth, then you will not have to be concerned about things going wrong in your life. You must always speak the Truth to others. If you are honest and do good things for others, then you will be looked upon as a righteous man. You will be an example to Light to others. If you walk in the Light, then you will be able to share with others the Truth and they will receive it. The people of the world   hide their sins as much as they can. They walk behind a veil of darkness. They do not want to repent and draw closer to Me. They want to serve themselves and not Me. If you really love Me, you will want to speak the Truth always. You will want to be a person that others look to as honest and kind. Do not allow the people of the world to turn you away from Me. Keep your eyes on Me, and I will direct your path. Keep your eyes on Me and I will show you the way to go. Being a set apart people is not easy, but the rewards in My Kingdom are great. Remember that you are here to serve only Me and My People worship Me in Spirit and Truth. Guard over your words and remain in communion with Me.

65

You should not swear falsely by the name of YHUH.

Lev 19:12 Do not swear falsely by my name and so profane the name of your Elohim. I am YHUH. Num 30:2 When a man makes a vow to YHUH or takes an oath to obligate himself by a pledge, he must not break his word but must do everything he said.

My beloved, you are formed in My Image. What you say is an extension of Me. If you swear to do something, then as My Child and Heir, you must do what you said that you will do. You are swearing falsely, if you say you will do something and then you do not do it. You must do all that you said you would do. You must be righteous in all your ways. People look on and judge you by the words you speak. They see if you are honest and fair. They see if you will follow through with what you say that you will do. They watch how you speak about other people and how you treat them. All of this is an extension of Me. How you treat others reflects on My Image, because you call yourself a child of the King. You must not carry My Name and not walk in My Ways. If you say that you are My Child and call Me Father, then you must act like My Child. What would My Child act like? Look at My Son and see what he did. Walk in his ways and you will be an example of righteousness for others. You will draw men to Me by the love you give to others. If you walk in My Ways and treat your words as sacred, then you will see your life changing before your eyes. I will bless your words and bring your words to pass. Right now I cannot trust your words, because they are tainted by the world. Do not condemn your brother and say you speak in love when you know that My words say to love your brother and be kind to him. Love those around you, and I will bless you for your loving kind words.

66

You should not withhold the wages of someone who has worked for you.

Lev 19:13 Do not defraud your neighbor or rob him. Do not hold back the wages of a hired man overnight. Deut 24:14 Do not take advantage of a hired man who is poor and needy, whether he is a brother Israelite or an alien living in one of your towns. 15 Pay him his wages each day before sunset, because he is poor and is counting on it. Otherwise he may cry to YHUH against you, and you will be guilty of sin.

My beloved, always pay someone who works for you on the day that he finishes the job. Do not hold back his wages, because this is an abomination to Me. If the person has signed a contract with you saying that it is okay for you to pay him every week or every two weeks, then you must pay him as the contract says. You must not delay his pay even a day, because the worker is counting on his pay and needs it to feed his family and pay his bills. It is shameful to hold back money for someone who works for you. Now if a man comes to you and says he will do a certain job for you such as roof your house and he has no money for materials to roof the house, then take the man to buy the materials for the roof-whatever he may need, but do not give the man any money to go buy the materials himself. The man may be tempted to take your money, and your money for your roof will be gone. If you buy the materials yourself and do not pay the man his labor fees until he is finished, then you will not lose your money. If the man is honest, he will work hard and finish the job, and you will have a nice roof. Make sure before the man even starts the roof that you have the man sign a contract and state his labor fees. Then you will have in writing your agreement, so if there is ever a problem you can present to the court your agreement. The man will work harder if his signature Is on the agreement, and he will be satisfied with the labor fees he receives. Remember my words of wisdom, and you will not suffer loss.

67

You should not curse a deaf person. You should not put a stumbling block in front of the blind.

Lev 19:14 You shall not curse a deaf man, nor place a stumbling block before the blind, but you shall revere your Elohim; I am YHUH. Matt 9:27 As Yahshua went on from there, two blind men followed Him, calling out, "Have mercy on us, Son of David!" 28 When He had gone indoors, the blind men came to Him, and He asked them, "Do you believe that I am able to do this?" "Yes, Master," they replied. 29 Then He touched their eyes and said, "According to your faith will it be done to you"; 30 and their sight was restored.

My beloved, do not be mean and harsh to the handicapped, but have compassion on them. If you see one who has trouble walking, then help him to a place where he can sit. If you see one who is deaf and is having trouble hearing what is said, then help him understand the words. If you see an aged person, guide him carefully because his sight may be failing him. You must have mercy on the weak and feeble, because one day you may be weak and feeble and how you treat the weak and feeble today is how you will be treated when you are weak and feeble. If your children see you have compassion on your aged parents and care for them tenderly, then they will treat you as the example you have set for them. Your children will put you in a nursing home, if you have put your parents in a nursing home. Watch how you treat others, because your children are watching your example. If you are harsh to the handicapped and say, "You are cursed because of the sins of your parents" and you have no compassion on them, then I also will have no compassion on you. The amount of mercy that you show to others is the amount of mercy I will show to you. If you say that mercy is not one of your gifts, then you should pray to Me to give you the ability to have mercy and compassion to others, because I AM merciful and compassionate to all mankind, but I AM just and fair and will punish all men for their sins.

68

You should not corrupt justice. You should not show partiality to the wealthy or influential or favor to a poor man in a lawsuit because he is poor.

Lev 19:15 Do not be unjust in judging-show neither partiality to the poor nor deference to the mighty, but with justice judge your neighbor. Ex 23:3 and do not show favoritism to a poor man in his lawsuit.

My beloved, judge your neighbor fairly. Do not judge him according to his wealth or education or power or influence. Do not judge him according to this position. Do not be partial to the rich and ignore the poor, but treat all men fairly. If you do, you will have My mind, because I look at all men the same. I judge all men fairly. I do not have different scales for the poor and for the rich, but every man is judged according to his deeds. I weigh his scales and if his good deeds outweigh the bad deeds, then he is counted righteous if he calls on Me as his Elohim. If the bad outweighs the good, then he is not righteous and does not love Me or he would serve Me and want to please Me by obeying Me. If a man loves Me, he will try to do only good to others and he will be righteous and his deeds will reflect that. If a man sins, then he must pay here on Earth for his sins. He must balance his scales, but if he is wicked then he will go to outer darkness. He will go to the place of the dead where no one ever returns. Many cry out not to go there, but their sins have been many. They did not repent and turn from their wickedness. Judge a man by his heart. Look inside the man and find the good inside. If the man is rich or poor does not matter. If he serves Me and wants to please Me, then he is on the path of righteousness. Judge fairly and do not carry a grudge against someone, but give every man an equal chance, and then all will go well with you.

69

You should not slander your neighbor.

Lev 19:16 Do not go around spreading slander among your people, but also don't stand idly by when your neighbor's life is at stake; I am YHUH.

My beloved, do not speak against your neighbor or falsely accuse him of a crime. Be kind to your neighbor and show your love to him. Do not allow jealously to cloud your vision, but let love abound. Do not covet what your neighbor has, but rejoice when he prospers. Rejoice when he has victory. Rejoice when I bless him, then I will see your humility and bless you also. Do not gossip and speak evil things that you do not know. Do not slander your brother or any member of your family, but always speak good things in public about your family and privately rebuke your family members if they are in sin. No one is perfect and all will make mistakes, even you. I did not create you to be perfect, but to be righteous. Every choice you make must be based on My Words, and your heart will lead you. If your heart is pure and wants to obey Me and serve Me, then I will guide you and you will not go astray. If I guide you, you will always be on the right path at the right time. If you love Me, you will long to do what is right. If you enjoy hearing gossip and spreading it, then you are sinful. If you love to slander others, then you are sinful. If you are angry with someone, forgive him and go to your brother and resolve your differences, but do not keep a grudge against him so that you want to speak something evil against him all the time. If you do this, then you have not forgiven him. If you can say kind words about someone who has wronged you, then you know you have forgiven him.

70

You should not stand by idly when a human life is in danger. You should not withhold aide from your neighbor.

Lev 19:16 Do not go around spreading slander among your people, but also don't stand idly by when your neighbor's life is at stake; I am YHUH.

My beloved, if you see that your neighbor needs help, then go to him and help. Him. You are not allowed to see someone struggling and you not help him, if you are capable of lending your hand to him. This would be merciless to stand and watch as your neighbor struggles and needs you to help him. Do not despise your neighbor no matter who he is. He may hate you, but your love will overcome him and he will see the light and love inside of you. Do not look at your neighbor with evil contempt in your heart. Let your heart be filled with love for your neighbor even if he has done things in the past that have not been kind. Forgive him, so you can be forgiven. Forgive him, so there is no hatred in your heart. You must be a creature of love and compassion, because you are My Child and you bear My Name. You must be at one with Me and love all men no matter who they are. Give generously to those around you. Walk in peace with all men, and then you will have peace in your heart continually. Man looks for someone who is loves others and is kind. Be the light to the nations that I created you to be. One day you will stand before Me and be counted worthy to be called My Child.

71

You should not hate or despise your neighbor. You should rebuke someone who has done evil regardless of his age.

Lev 19:17 You shall not hate your neighbor in your heart; but rebuke your neighbor frankly, so that you won't carry sin because of him.

My beloved, do not hold hatred in your heart. You can hate the sin your brother is in, but do not hate your brother. Go to your brother and tell your brother of his wrong doings and pray with your brother so he can repent. Do not approach your brother in a haughty matter, but approach him with loving kindness and concern for his wellbeing. If he does not repent of his sin, he is headed for outer darkness. You are responsible for telling your brother he is in sin. If you do not tell your brother, then I hold you responsible, because you saw his sin and did not point it out. Of course you should go to him privately and discuss his sin in a place where he is not humiliated, so he will listen and not hate you in his heart. If you confront him of his sin with others around, then you do not have love in your heart for him, but only a self-righteous attitude. You will never help your brother in this matter. You must go to him privately with love in your heart for him, and then he will listen. If he is blinded and cannot see clearly, then leave him because he cannot see his sin and he must pay the penalty for his sin. Many of My People are paying for past sins. In their punishment they cry out to Me, and I hear their voice and bring repentance to them and strength, so they can turn away from their sins. I want My People to walk in righteousness, but as their sins pile up they are blinded and cannot see clearly. Keep yourself pure, so you are free from deception and you will not fall under My Hand of punishment.

72

You should not take vengeance upon your neighbor.
You should not bear a grudge against the sons of your
neighbor.

Lev 19:18 Do not seek revenge or bear a grudge against one of your people, but love your neighbor as yourself. I am YHUH. Matt 5:43 "You have heard that it was said, 'You shall love your neighbor and hate your enemy.' 44 But I say to you, Love your enemies and pray for those who persecute you, 45 so that you may be sons of your Father who is in heaven; for He makes his sun rise on the evil and on the good, and sends rain on the just and on the unjust."

My beloved, do not hold hatred in your heart against a brother, but love him as you would love yourself. You would care for yourself and keep yourself well fed and give yourself good things, then do so for others. If you keep hatred in your heart, it will eat at you and tear at you and break down your body. Love brings healing to your body and hatred tears it down and eats into your bones. If you love yourself and want to do good to yourself, then love others. If is more blessed to love then to hate. I AM not an Elohim of hatred, but an Elohim of love. Do not hold a grudge against your brother. If he has sinned against you, then go to him and talk to him about his sin-how he has wronged you-then maybe he will repent and make restitution to you. If the person will not repent, you still must forgive him and not hold hatred in your heart. If you say, "I cannot forgive him, because his sin is too great," then ask Me to help you forgive him. I want all My Children to forgive others and put those who have sinned in My Hands, so I can judge them and past sentence on them and punish them for their sins. If you hold onto your hatred and not deliver them into My Hands, then I cannot pass judgment on them. If you punish them, then the punishment stands because you have chosen to judge them and pass judgment on them and have not delivered them into My Hands. I AM the Supreme Judge. Only I know what punishment should be given to bring repentance, so trust My Ability to judge and bring correction.

73

You should not cross breed animals of any kind.

Lev 19:19 Keep my decrees. Do not mate different kinds of animals. Do not plant your field with two kinds of seed. Do not wear clothing woven of two kinds of material.

My beloved, I told My People not to cross breed animals, because it makes a weaker breed and causes birth defects. The two are not meant to become one. The ancients who were here before you crossbred animals, humans, and all sorts of life. They were looking for perfection-a stronger more intelligent breed, but they found only destruction. The Evil One again is looking for a superior race of people, but only My People are Superior and no one can replace them. You carry My Spirit-a precious gift that is given only to My Children-My Priests who will rule nations as led by My Spirit. Angels look on in amazement at the work I have done. I have given you My Spirit, so you can hear My Voice and be comforted in times of trouble. You must stir yourself up and use the gifts I have given you to show love and kindness to others. Do not be deceived. People do not love Me. Only My Children love Me. You will continue to run into barriers, because the world does not love Me. I will open wide the doors for you, and show you a way around the barriers. Your path ahead is smooth and as long as you follow Me and allow Me to guide you, then you will prosper and all will go well with you. You must totally depend on Me to guide you, and have faith in Me that I have a plan for you. You must not give up or waiver, but you must continue on My road of righteousness and you will do well-you and your family.

74

You should not tattoo any part of your body. You should not cut yourself or pierce the flesh.

Lev 19:28 Do not cut your bodies for the dead or put tattoo marks on yourselves. I am YHUH. Deut 14:1 You are the children of YHUH your Elohim. Do not cut yourselves or shave the front of your heads for the dead, 2 for you are a people sacred to YHUH your Elohim. Out of all the peoples on the face of the earth, YHUH has chosen you to be His treasured possession.

My beloved, do not pierce your flesh so you can adorn yourself with jewelry. Do not gash your flesh or tattoo your flesh. Do not mar your flesh in any way to carry symbols or signs. I have made you in My image and you are not to mark your body in any way, because you are sacred-set aside-separate from the other peoples. You are My chosen ones. Keep yourself sacred. If you already have a tattoo, then find out how you can have it removed so your flesh will not be marked. Do not cut yourself when you are angry or sad. Do not try to punish yourself by causing yourself harm. If is an abomination to Me for you to harm your flesh in any way. I want you to keep yourself healthy and clean. I want you to eat only clean foods-not any forbidden foods. I want you to stay clean and keep away from the world. Do not look into anything dirty or pagan, but focus only on My words. Keep your eyes on Me and what I AM doing in your life. I will help you by guiding your feet by the path I want you to take. Only the people of the world want to mark up their bodies and cut their bodies. The evil one tells them that it is beautiful, because he wants to mar My image. He wants to defile My sacred ones, but if you love Me you will not even want to enter into any of these things. You will want to follow Me and walk in all My ways.

Which Commandments Should I Obey?

75

You should honor the Old and the Wise.

Lev 19:32 Stand up in the presence of the aged, show respect for the elderly. You are to fear your Elohim. I am YHUH!

My beloved, show respect for the aged or those older than you. Listen to the elderly for they have wisdom. They have lived many more years than you and their life experience has taught them much. You can learn from them, if you will only listen. If you show disrespect for the aged, I will punish you. If you mock the elderly or exalt yourself above them, I will punish you. You begin your life here as a helpless infant and you end your life here as a helpless adult. You will soon be one of the elderly and the measure of mercy you show now to the aged will be the measure of mercy that is shown to you when you are old. Look at yourself and see how fast your life passes. These elderly people cannot believe that they have aged so fast. They still feel young in their heart even though their flesh is wearing away. Do not be afraid of death. I will take you by the hand and lift you out of your flesh and take you to My Kingdom. You do not have to fear the future, if you are keeping My laws and walking in love and compassion. If you are not, then you will be punished before you die. This is why so many suffer before they die, so all their sins can be paid for before they stand before Me. You want to stand before Me having paid all your sins, so you can enter into My kingdom. Do not be afraid of the future, but cherish everyday with those you love and live your life as I would live Mine, and then you will be satisfied and blessed.

76

You should ensure that scales and weights are correct.
You should not use false measurements or false weights
in order to deceive.

Lev 19:35 Do not use dishonest standards when measuring length, weight or quantity. I am YHUH your Elohim, who brought you out of Egypt. Deut 25:13 You shall not have in your bag differing weights, a heavy and a light. 14 You shall not have in your house differing measures, a large and a small. 15 You shall have a perfect and just weight, a perfect and just measure, that your days may be lengthened in the land which YHUH your Elohim is giving you. 16 For all who do such things, and deal dishonestly, are an abomination to YHUH your Elohim.

My beloved, be honest in all you do. Treat others fairly. Do not try to make a profit illegally or unfairly at someone else's expense. Do not deal with your brother dishonestly. This is an abomination to Me and I will cut your life short. I will not allow anyone who takes advantage of others and brings financial harm to him and ruins his life to live for very long. You must help others not hurt others. You must treat others the way you would like to be treated. Do not do whatever you want to do to make a profit. Set a fair market price and stick to it. Do not accept bribes in business, so you have to defraud someone. Always try to give your customer a good price, so he can go to others and tell them about your honesty and fairness. Then you will have a reputation for being just and fair and your business will prosper. I will bless you for your fairness. If you see a man being unfair to you or someone else, then go to him privately and tell him of his sins, so he can repent and treat others fairly. If he will not listen, then cry out to Me and I will deal with him. You must not enter into a business unless you know the person is honest and will not take advantage of others. In times of disaster, do not double your price to make a profit from those who are hurting and are in need. How you deal with others is how I will deal with you, so be careful to treat all men honestly and fairly.

77

You will be held responsible and punished for sexual sins.

Lev 20:10 The man who commits adultery with another man's wife, he who commits adultery with his neighbor's wife, the adulterer and the adulteress, shall surely be put to death. 13 If a man lies with a man as one lies with a woman, both of them have done what is detestable. They must be put to death; their blood will be on their own heads. 15 If a man has sexual relations with an animal, he must be put to death, and you must kill the animal. 18 If a man lies with a woman during her monthly period and has sexual relations with her, he has exposed the source of her flow, and she has also uncovered it. Both of them must be cut off from their people.

My beloved, do not have sexual intercourse with anyone but the person you are married to. You must keep yourself pure. If someone comes to you and asks you to have sexual relations, rebuke him for his sins and stay far away from him. He is a sinner and is not walking down the path of righteousness. There is no way you should have sexual intercourse before you are married, even if the person says that he loves you and wants to marry you. This does not mean that he will keep his promise. You have already made yourself unclean by having sexual intercourse before your wedding day. Do not be deceived. You should keep yourself clean before Me. Do not be like the world and make yourself unclean by going after the lust of the flesh and pleasing yourself no matter what My commands are. Stay far away from these people. They will be punished for their sexual sins and any sin where they expose their nakedness to someone other than their mate. You must not expose your nakedness to anyone. It is an abomination to Me. Your body should be viewed by only your mate. You should not say you are only modeling or this is part of my job. You must get a new job, if you want to be pleasing in My sight. Guard your purity. Keep yourself clean and pure for your mate, so all will go well for you and you will be given children and your life will be filled with blessings. If you have already had sexual intercourse before you are married, then repent and remain pure until you are married. I will forgive you, if you turn from your sin and never have sexual intercourse again until you are married and joined in covenant together as one.

78

You should not profane (disrespect) the Divine Name of
YHUH. You should not blaspheme the name of YHUH.

Lev 22:31 "Keep my commands and follow them. I am YHUH. 32
Do not profane my sacred name. I must be acknowledged as sacred
by the Israelites. I am YHUH, who makes you sacred   33 and who
brought you out of Egypt to be your Elohim. I am YHUH." Ex 22:28
"Do not blaspheme YHUH or curse the ruler of your people."

My beloved, hold My name sacred above all other names. Show honor and
respect for My name, because I brought your ancestors out of Egypt and carried
you in My arms in the desert. I gave you a great land-rich and filled with treasures. I gave you many ancestors-a multitude of peoples. I rebuked your ancestors
and scattered them across the nations, because they served other gods. Wake up
and do not live as your ancestors lived. Wake up and repent-not only for yourself
but for your ancestors, so all curses can be broken from you and the darkness
will be lifted from you. Pray to Me and cling to Me and hear My voice, so you
can again return to the Land that I have given you. You are a wealthy people,
but you have been driven from your home because of your sin. Do not love the
things of the world but love only Me, and I will restore your blessings wherever
you live. Keep My Feast Days and honor My ways. Be loving and kind to others.
Always be helpful and give to others, then you will receive My blessings. You will
be filled with good things- you and your children. Teach your children to honor
and respect My name. If you keep all My commands and do not reject Me, then
you honor Me and you respect Me. If you turn away from Me, then you bring
cruses on yourself. You must wake up and repent. The days grow short. The end
is near. Be alert and do not be caught sleeping when I return.

79

You should rest and do no work on Shavuot (Pentecost).

Lev 23:15 From the day after the Sabbath, the day you brought the sheaf of the wave offering, count off seven full weeks. 16 Count off fifty days up to the day after the seventh Sabbath and then present an offering of new grain to YHUH. 21 On that same day you are to proclaim a sacred assembly and do no regular work. This is to be a lasting ordinance for the generations to come, wherever you live. (Acts 2:1-4)

My beloved, you should keep My Feast Days. Even if the temple is destroyed you should always keep My Feast Days as a sign of your obedience to Me. You should keep the Day of Pentecost by resting and doing no regular work such as going to your job or doing any outside chores that you normally do such as mowing your lawn or repairing your house. You must rest and pray that YHUH's Spirit will come upon you with fire like I sent to all the believers in Antioch. Call on My name to stir My Sprit within you, so you can speak in the voice of the spirit-tongues of the heavenly language-so your spirit can pray for what you need. Rejoice that I have sent My Sprit to come live within you-to comfort you-and guide you. I would not leave you alone. You are sealed with My Spirit, so the evil one cannot overtake you. He can oppress you with darkness and deceive you, so you are blinded and cannot think clearly or see the path ahead, but he cannot overtake you because you are sealed with My Spirit. No one can harm you. If you keep My Feast Days, I will bless you; I will send blessings to your house. You may not have fields or vineyards, but I will bring good health, many children, children who love and respect you, children who respect and honor Me, wisdom, and knowledge of the Truth to your house. You will rejoice and be glad that I have counted you worthy to call you a child of the Most High.

80

You should rest and do no work on Rosh Hashanah (Feast of Trumpets). You should sound the shofar on Rosh Hashanah.

Lev 23:23 YHUH said to Moses, 24 "Say to the Israelites: 'On the first day of the seventh month you are to have a day of rest, a sacred assembly commemorated with trumpet blasts. 25 Do no regular work, but present an offering made to YHUH by fire.'" (1 Thess 4:13-18)

My beloved, keep My Feast Days. Do not work on the Feast of Trumpets, but rest and blow your shofar. Celebrate with singing and dancing and know I AM coming soon. I will come at the sound of the trumpets. My angels will sound My coming for the world to know that its King has arrived-a King of judgment who will pass judgment on the entire world. I will lift My Children off this planet and burn the planet with fire to cleanse the planet from all its sin and make it undefiled once again. Then I will place My Children back on this planet, so they can live here eternally under My kingship. The planet will be ruled by Me and everyone will keep My laws or die. Do not want to know what laws I will place on those who live under My kingship? The same laws that I gave Moses-the same perfect laws that I have had in place from the beginning of this planet. I have given you a good way to live your life. If you follow My laws, you will have a good life and if you don't, then sin will destroy you and My judgment will come upon you because you have rejected Me and sinned against Me. You have chosen death for yourself-not life. Choose life and blessings not curses and death. Choose Me and cling to Me. Choose the One who created you and made you into My image to serve Me, and then you will have a life filled with joy and prosperity.

81

You should fast on Yom Kippur (Day of Atonement).
You should rest and do no work on Yom Kippur.

Lev 23:26 YHUH spoke to Moses, saying, 27 "On exactly the tenth day of this seventh month is the day of atonement; it shall be a sacred convocation for you, and you shall humble your souls and present an offering by fire to YHUH. 31 You shall do no work at all. It is to be a perpetual statute throughout your generations in all your dwelling places. 32 It is to be a Sabbath of complete rest to you, and you shall humble your souls; on the ninth of the month at evening, from evening until evening you shall keep your Sabbath." (Lev 16:29-31)

My beloved, I ask you to fast only one day a year-only on the Day of Atonement. It is a very sacred day when you fast and pray to ask Me to forgive your sins for the past year-you and your family. You should humble yourself before Me and eat no food, but pray and rejoice in My presence. If you will do this, I will shine My face on your family. I will make My face shine on you and bring favor to you, because you are obedient even in a foreign land with a foreign people. Others may mock you for keeping My Feast Days, but they will be punished for their mockery against My Words. They will pay for the punishment of their arrogance against you. Forgive them and put them in My Hands, and then I will deal with them. Do not be deceived. My temple is destroyed, but My laws still stand in the hearts of men. Do not try to shun My laws, but try to cling to them. They are your very life. They will bring you blessings, if you keep them. They are a sign to others that you are a set apart people-separated unto Me. You may be looked upon as different and you are. You are not like the world, so you should not celebrate as the world does. The evil one tries to deceive you and tell you that no one should keep My Feast Days anymore, because he knows that keeping My Feast days will bring you a blessing, and he wants no one to be blessed.

82

You should rest and do no work on the first and eighth day of Sukkot (Feast of Tabernacles).

Lev 23:33 Again YHUH spoke to Moses, saying, 34 "Speak to the sons of Israel, saying, 'On the fifteenth of this seventh month is the Feast of Tabernacles for seven days to YHUH. 35 On the first day is a sacred convocation; you shall do no laborious work of any kind, and on the eighth day hold a sacred assembly and present an offering made to YHUH by fire. It is the closing assembly; do no regular work.'" (Ex 34:16)

My beloved, I told My people to hold a feast to remember when they were slaves in Egypt and how they were brought out with a mighty hand. I did not want My people to become arrogant, but to remember who they were and how I rescued them from the pit of Egypt. They were dirty and abused and I picked them up, washed them off, and gave them power over nations. I have done this for you too. I have picked you up from this dirty world, and cleansed you by My Spirit, and taught you My laws and My ways, and have refreshed you with My Presence. I have given you good gifts, and My love has been poured upon you. I ask you to keep My laws as a sign of your obedience to Me. If you keep all My laws, I will bless you and prosper you. I will show you the way to go. I will lift up your children and guide them, because you have taught them to trust Me and to do My will. My people spent a week praising Me, feasting, dancing, and singing. They were a sign to the nations of My wondrous love for them. Now I only see crying in Israel. My people are torn with violence. My children weep and do not rejoice, because of the sin in the country. Soon I will bring a leader who serves Me to lead them in repentance. He will bring them off their knees, and will stand them up. They will become strong and powerful, because their trust is in Me- not man. Their eyes search longingly for Me to return.

83

You should take choice fruits and branches and rejoice before YHUH during Sukkot. You should dwell in sukkot each of the seven days of Sukkot.

Lev 23:40 On the first day you are to take choice fruit from the trees, and palm fronds, leafy branches and poplars, and rejoice before YHUH your Elohim for seven days. 41 Live in sukkot for seven days: All native-born Israelites are to live in sukkot 43 so your descendants will know that I had the Israelites live in sukkot when I brought them out of Egypt. I am YHUH your Elohim. (Deut 6:13-15, John 7:2-15)

My beloved, I asked My Children to remember how their ancestors lived in shelters for 40 years in the desert. I took care of them during the heat of the day and the cold of the night. They were wrapped in My Presence. They were in My Hands of protection. They were greatly loved by Me. I lifted them up and carried them in My Arms. I want you to remember all the miracles that I did for your ancestors while they walked in the Wilderness by staying seven days in a shelter that you make for this season. You can make the shelter any way that you want as long as you can dwell in it for seven days. Bring fruits and branches into the shelter and adorn it, so you can be joyful while you are there. You will remember the times your ancestors had no home and they depended only on Me to care for them. As you remember their journey you will remember that I care for you now while you are in exile. I take care of you every day. You may not be able to go to Jerusalem during the feast days, but you can rejoice wherever you are and praise Me for all the good things I do for you. You may be separate and alone on My feast days and have no one to celebrate with. You may not have singing and dancing with those who love Me, but you have My Presence and you can sing and dance to Me and I will rejoice in it. Sing praises to My Name that I have given you so much, and I will bless you greatly for keeping all My Feast Days and being such an obedient servant.

84

You should not take advantage of another man when selling property. You should not remove landmarks (property boundaries). You should not swear falsely in denial of another's property rights.

Lev 25:14 If you sell land to one of your countrymen or buy any from him, do not take advantage of each other. 17 Do not take advantage of each other, but fear your Elohim. I am YHUH your Elohim. Deut 19:14 Do not move your neighbor's boundary stone set up by your predecessors in the inheritance you receive in the land YHUH your Elohim is giving you to possess.

My beloved, be fair to others when you sell your house, land, or business, and do not try to make a large profit. Try to sell to your brother in a way that you would want him to sell to you. Are there things that need to be repaired in the house? Make sure you repair your house, and do not try to deceive someone by telling him that the house is in perfect order when it is not. You would be very disappointed if you bought a house and you had to have the house repaired or the appliances did not work. You must remember to treat your brother fairly. If you try to deceive others, then someone will deceive you. The way you treat others will be the way you are treated. I know that in a market where houses are going up and down that you are not sure what a fair price is. Remember that you should ask the same price as the neighbors in your community, because the house will be judged by the fair market value. If you want to sell your house, you must come to Me and submit the house to Me and put it in My hands and I will sell it for you. I will bring the right buyer to you with a fair price for your house. You must trust Me, and I will help you. You must not be afraid to sell your home if I ask you to move to another place. I will help you sell the house and find another home and a job. If you are obedience, then I will go before you and remove all obstacles, because I love you and I will give you all you need.

85

You should not humiliate a poor brother with oppressive, degrading or unnecessary tasks.

Lev 25:39 If one of your countrymen becomes poor among you and sells himself to you, do not make him work as a slave. 40 He is to be treated as a hired worker or a temporary resident among you; he is to work for you until the Year of Jubilee. 41 Then he and his children are to be released, and he will go back to his own clan and to the property of his forefathers. 42 Because the Israelites are my slaves, whom I brought out of Egypt, they must not be sold as slaves. 43 Do not rule over them ruthlessly, but fear your Elohim. (Lev 5:47-53)

My beloved, if a man has no money and many debts, he can sell himself to someone to be his slave. In this country people do not do this, because the government takes care of them so there is no need to work. This is an abomination to Me. I want all men and women to work hard and release themselves from the bondage of debt. If you buy slaves, go to a nation that does not serve Me and choose people who do not serve Me. When they work for you, you can require them to keep your ways of worship, and they may begin to serve Me and follow in My ways. Do not allow the slaves to bring in their idols or any charm or magical potent into your house, but demand that all pagan worship be stopped. You must insist on this with all your slaves, or they will bring pagan worship into your home and put your house under a curse. You must be careful not to buy a believer as a slave, but if you do, then treat him like a hired man and give him wages or have his wages apply to his purchase price. In this way you will treat your brother fairly. You may need slaves if you work on a large farm or plantation. Treat your slaves with love. Do not treat them harshly, but treat them with respect as you would treat a brother. In the days to come as the land becomes poor and the people are desperate for food, many will come to you to work for you as your slaves just so they can have shelter, clothes, and food. Do not rejoice in their misfortune, but let your love shine on them all the days, and then I will bless you.

86

You should not bow, even to worship YHUH, before any idol or image.

Lev 26:1 Do not make idols or set up an image or a sacred stone for yourselves, and do not place a carved stone in your land to bow down before it. I am YHUH your Elohim.

My beloved, do not bow down to any god or idol or statue. This is an abomination to Me. Do not set up for yourself statues to Me. I want no statue or idol set up for Me. I want you to worship the invisible Elohim-the one who created you from dirt-the one who placed you on this planet and placed My seed of righteousness in you, so you would desire to serve only Me. If you do go to a church, do not bow to any statute. If you go to these places and there are temples there to other gods, do not enter them. Do not go searching for temples or other gods to visit or to investigate. Focus your eyes on Me, so I can bring you revelation. You must stay far away from other gods and their practices. When you worship Me, prostrate yourself before Me. You need no signs, symbols, statues, or idols to help you worship Me. Strip your house of such things, so you can be free from any curses that may be on them. You say, "But I have a picture of Yahshua to look at" and I say, "No you don't." That picture is not what I look like, so tear it up and focus on Me. You say you have a statute of Mother Mary, but I say, "No you don't." My mother was made of dirt like you, so do not worship her or any other saints. Do not pray to Mary or any saint, but pray only to Me, because only I can help you. The others are sleeping waiting for My return when the dead shall rise and I will meet them in the air.

87

You should give a tenth of what YHUH gives you back to Him.

Lev 27:31 One tenth of all the produce of the land, whether grain or fruit, belongs to YHUH. 32 If a man wishes to buy any of it back, he must pay the standard price plus an additional 20 percent. 33 One of every ten domestic animals belongs to YHUH. When the animals are counted, every tenth one belongs to YHUH.

My beloved, I have asked you to give a tenth to Me from all you make each year. I asked My people who lived on My land to take the tenth animal that passes under the shepherd's staff as they come into the fold to be set apart and separate unto Me. This animal was to be given to Me as a sacrifice in My temple and also a tenth of their grain and wine, so My people could sit in My presence and eat and celebrate the blessings I have given them. The priests would have their share of the offering, and they would be taken care of by My people. Now the temple is gone, but I still ask you to give Me a tenth of all the money you take home after your taxes are taken out, because this is what you make. You should give this money to the poor, needy, orphans, widows, and any Torah teacher who is walking in righteousness and needs a means of support. I want all those lacking and without of My people to receive help, and if you give a tenth to them, then all will have their needs met. Do not be fearful if you are in debt and you are struggling to pay your bills every month. Focus on getting out of debt. Take another job and do not spend any money until you are free from your creditors. Use all your money to pay your bills, and do not buy anything else until you have paid off your creditors. Soon you will be free of bondage and can pay Me a tenth of what you earn, so those around you who are struggling will be able to have their needs met. If you are in bondage to lenders, release yourself as soon as you can, so you can be delivered from the world system.

88

You should be counted as an adult at twenty years old and be held responsible for your sins.

Num 14:29 In this desert your bodies will fall-every one of you twenty years old or more who was counted in the census and who has grumbled against me. 30 Not one of you will enter the land I swore with uplifted hand to make your home, except Caleb son of Jephunneh and Joshua son of Nun.

My beloved, I counted all the men twenty years old as responsible for their choices, and they were held accountable for their sins. A man is head of his house and he is responsible for all those in his house, even his wife. A man is a covering for his wife and children. He must be strong and stand firm in righteousness, so he can lead his family down the path I have chosen for them. A man is held responsible for the sins of his children and wife. A man must rebuke his wife and children and tell them of their sins and punish his children if he knows they are in sin. A man should not listen to a wife who wants to lead the family away from Me and into other religions. A man should not allow a wife to over spend and put the family in debt. A man must watch over the wife and remind her of her duties to her family, if she becomes lazy or if she becomes a busy body. A wife must submit to her husband when he points out her sin, and she should repent and walk in My ways. A wife should support her husband when he corrects and punishes his children, so they can walk in my ways. A husband should never be harsh or abusive, but loving and kind to his wife and children. Correct your children in love not anger, because I correct you in love and I have mercy upon you, because I know you live in exile in a dark dry land.

89

You should make confession before YHUH of any sin that you have committed.

Num 5:6 When a man or woman commits any of the sins of mankind, acting unfaithfully against YHUH, and that person is guilty, 7 then he shall confess his sins which he has committed, and he shall make restitution in full for his wrong and add to it one-fifth, and give it to him whom he has wronged. 8 But if the man has no kinsman to whom restitution may be made for the wrong, the restitution for wrong shall go to YHUH for the priest, in addition to the ram of atonement with which atonement is made for him.

My beloved, you are to confess your sins to Me and make restitution to all you harm. If you steal from someone, then ask forgiveness and then go to the person and give him back what you have stolen plus add a gift in cash of twenty percent of the value of the item you stole and take it to the person. If you have robbed a person and not been caught, then if you do not repent and make restitution, I will punish you for your sin and take the value of what you stole plus twenty percent. You will have disasters come on you until the amount of the money is taken from you and the scales are balanced. If you kill someone, then there is no restitution. If you kill an animal, you can make restitution by buying another animal of equal value or paying the value of the animal plus twenty percent more. If the animal is a pet, you still use the same system even though the loss of the pet may be greater than the monetary value to the person. If you borrow a car and you misuse the car and do not care for it as a responsible person would and you damage the car, then you must have the car repaired and add twenty percent of the value of the car to be given to the person you borrowed the car from. Always treat the property of others with respect no matter if it is their house, car, children, or wife. Do not hurt others and make restitution to those you have wronged.

90

You should bring the unfaithful wife before YHUH for judgment.

Num 5:12 If a man's wife goes astray and is unfaithful to him 13 by sleeping with another man, and this is hidden from her husband and her impurity is undetected (since there is no witness against her and she has not been caught in the act), 14 and if feelings of jealousy come over her husband and he suspects his wife and she is impure, or if he is jealous and suspects her even though she is not impure 15 then he is to take his wife to the priest. 16 The priest shall bring her and have her stand before YHUH. 27 If she has defiled herself and been unfaithful to her husband, then when she is made to drink the water that brings a curse, it will go into her and cause bitter suffering; her abdomen will swell and her private areas waste away, and she will become accursed among her people. 28 If, however, the woman has not defiled herself and is free from impurity, she will be cleared of guilt and will be able to have children.

My beloved, sometimes a wife may be unfaithful and if a man suspects his wife of being unfaithful, he should ask to talk to his wife about his suspicion. If she denies the charges against her yet the man continues not to trust his wife, then he must go with his wife to a man who teaches Torah and have the man pray over his wife. I will expose her sin and it will not be in secret any longer, so she can repent and turn aside from her sin. If a wife is unfaithful to her husband, and the husband seeks Me about his wife, I will expose the wife's sins or I will give the man peace and calm his spirit of jealously, so he can trust his wife. If a woman is in sin, then she should repent and do not go that sinful way again. The woman has made a covenant with the man and should not beak the covenant. If you say, "My husband does not love Me anymore" or "My husband does not treat Me well any more," these things do not matter. You made the covenant with Me not only your husband, whether he treats you well every day or not. Only if the husband has committed adultery are you free from the covenant. Now if your husband is abusive and beats you, then go to a Torah teacher and let him pray for your husband, so I can rebuke your husband and correct his ways. I will send on him conviction, so he can repent and turn aside from his sins. If you are loving and kind to your husband or wife, then your marriage will reflect your loving ways towards each other, and you will prosper and live in peace.

91

You should not drink wine or strong drink, eat fresh grapes, raisins or grape skins during a Nazirite vow. You should not enter a house with a corpse, allow your hair to grow long, or touch anything dead during a Nazirite vow.

Num 6:1 If a man or woman wants to make a special vow, a vow of separation to YHUH as a Nazirite, 3 he must abstain from wine and other fermented drink and must not drink vinegar made from wine or from other fermented drink. He must not drink grape juice or eat grapes or raisins. 4 As long as he is a Nazirite, he must not eat anything that comes from the grapevine, not even the seeds or skins. 5 During the entire period of his vow of separation no razor may be used on his head. He must be sacred until the period of his separation to YHUH is over; he must let the hair of his head grow long. 6 Throughout the period of his separation to YHUH he must not go near a dead body.

My beloved, if you and your husband or wife want to make a vow to Me to have a time of separation for Me, you can take a Nazirite vow to set apart for a certain time to draw closer to Me. You must fast strong drink, wine, grapes, and remain clean before Me, then I will honor this time of separation and the vow you have made together. If a single person wants to make the vow of separation, then he can do so, if he has permission from the parent he lives with. If the person lives without a parent, then the person must realize the seriousness of the vow and must decide wisely whether to enter the vow or not. If the parent approves the vow, then the parent must explain to the child the seriousness of the vow, and how I honor a vow. You do not ever have to make a Nazirite vow, but if I call you to such a vow, then listen to My call because I want you to separate you to show you some important things. If you decide to take a vow, then be careful to fulfill it and do what you have spoken. I will give you the strength to do it. There is no temple, so you cannot go to a temple to end your vow. You can submit the end of the vow to Me, and I will bless your time of separation. Cut your hair, wash yourself, and submit unto My directions, because I will speak to you and show you what you want to know and need to know. Listen carefully to My voice.

92

You should recite the priestly blessing and bless Israel.

Num 6:22 YHUH said to Moses, 23 "Tell Aaron and his sons, This is how you are to bless the Israelites. Say to them: 24 May YHUH bless you and keep you; 25 may YHUH make His face shine upon you and be gracious to you; 26 May YHUH turn His face toward you and give you peace. 27 So they will put my name on the Israelites, and I will bless them."

My beloved, learn this blessing and speak it over the members of your house and all visitors who come to your house. This is the blessing I gave to the priests, but the priest of your home can also say the blessing over others, and I will bless them. If the priest of the home lives righteously, then I will hear his prayers, and I will bless who he blesses and curse who he curses. I will bless his lips and give him a message of peace for those of his house and those who come to visit you. You do not realize the power in your words if you walk in righteousness. I will speak through you and bring blessings, curses, healing, and words of wisdom, messages of strength and encouragement, messages that enlighten and show direction, messages that break darkness and bring hope. Your words can be powerful weapons, if you are walking in righteousness. How do you walk in righteousness? Stay away from the world, and do not desire anything from the world. Stay sexually pure. Obey your parents. Love others, and do not harm them. Work hard and earn your wages. Don't shame others, but rebuke a brother who is in sin quietly. Rebuke those believers in sin, because it is your responsibility. Guard over your mouth, and say only kind words to others. Let your anger not overcome you, but control it and do no one evil. Be pleasing in My sight by listening to My words and obeying Me, then you are righteous and your words will be powerful weapons.

93

You should celebrate Passover the next month, if you did not celebrate Passover in the first month.

Num 9:9 YHUH told Moses 10 to say to the people of Israel, "When any of you or your descendants are unclean from touching a corpse or are far away on a journey, but still want to keep the Passover, 11 you are permitted to observe it one month later instead, on the evening of the fourteenth day of the second month."

My beloved, if you know you are to celebrate Passover yet you are called away from your family for business or another reason, then you can celebrate Passover the next month in the same matter as you normally celebrate it. If you touched a corpse or went to a funeral during this time because of a death in your family, then wait until the next month. I want you to be clean for Passover and I want you to celebrate with your family. This is a family celebration that your family should celebrate in your home with lamb roasted on the fire, bitter herbs, and unleavened bread. You may add vegetables and fruits if you like, but the time you celebrate is set by Me. It is My celebration, so you can remember how I passed over your ancestors and did not kill them in Egypt. I spared you and made you My own, so you must tell your children about Me and how I delivered your ancestors from the bondage of slavery. All children must know how mighty and powerful I AM. I can do all things, because I created all things. Enjoy your Passover Meal in your home, and teach your children about this day long ago. Be brave, because others will not understand why you keep the Passover. Tell them I want My children to always keep Passover no matter where they live, because it is a lasting ordinance and blessing to all who keep it.

94

You should blow the shofar on all feasts and new moons.

Num 10:1 At your times of rejoicing-your appointed feasts and New Moon festivals-you are to sound the trumpets over your burnt offerings and fellowship offerings, and they will be a memorial for you before your Elohim. I am YHUH your Elohim.

My beloved, I asked My people to make two silver trumpets to blow to call the people to an assembly, to let the people know they were ready to travel, to sound an alarm for war or to prepare for battle, or a festival time-a time of rejoicing. You should have a trumpet or ram's horn in your house to sound on My feast days. You are calling for My attention to come be in the midst of you. My people called Me to walk in the midst of them in an assembly, while traveling, during war, and in their time of celebration. You should blow the trumpet or shofar at the beginning of your Sabbath and your new moon festivals and all the appointed feasts and anytime your family assembles to come together to seek Me for guidance or advice. I will come be in the midst of you. The trumpet is a symbol to come be in your midst of you, and I will come. Those who look on will notice how you call for Me and how I come to you. I send My Spirit to guide you, to show you the way to go, heal you, to bring you peace-the peace of My Presence. This is a lasting ordinance to be used for all time, and those who are obedient will receive the blessing. Call upon My Name, and I will be in the midst of you. Those around you may not understand you, but I know you are obedient, and I will bless you. When you call I will come, and I will give you good things.

95

You should not cause your children to suffer for your sins.

Num 14:18   I, YHUH, am not easily angered, and I show great love and faithfulness and forgive sin and rebellion. Yet I will not fail to punish children and grandchildren to the third and fourth generation for the sins of their parents.

My beloved, I love My children, but I correct my children because I do love them. I want them to be faithful to Me, so I cut off all peoples who are not faithful to Me. Only those called by My name will be able to live with Me eternally. Therefore I must punish all who sin against Me, because I AM sacred. All those who are not faithful and do not trust in Me are not allowed in My sacred place. If you think you can sin and violate My laws, then think again because I will punish those who break My laws. If you sin, then you will pay the penalty and all your family will suffer for your sins. If I punish you by sickness, then your family must care for you and pay the medical bills. If I punish you by crushing you financially, then your family must also pay for this burden. If I send you to jail or you have to go to court, then your family suffers your loss or has to suffer under high attorney fees. Every time you sin, your punishment of sin falls back on your children. If you commit adultery or get a divorce, your children suffer. If you live a righteous life and obey My laws, then you will be blessed and the blessings will pour over onto your children. Not only will your covering be strong for them, but they will be taught how to walk in righteousness. I will break the darkness from them and they will see the Light. Rejoice that I love you so much and want to bless you and your children.

96

You should not sin defiantly against YHUH.

Num 15:30 But anyone who sins defiantly, whether native-born or alien, blasphemes YHUH, and that person must be cut off from his people. 31 Because he has despised YHUH's word and broken his commands, that person must surely be cut off; his guilt remains on him.

My beloved, do not blaspheme My sacred name by rejecting and despising My sacred words. I gave you My laws for a reason-to give you a good life—protected and cared for-so all men can love each other and all men would have his needs met with no poor living among you. If you choose not to obey Me, then curses will fall upon you. You must love Me with all your heart knowing that I love you and all that I give you is good. I will give only good gifts to those of My children who love Me. If you love Me, you will obey Me. If you know My laws and choose not to obey Me, then you choose My hand of correction. I will not allow My children to sin and go unpunished. If I correct you, then you will seek My face and repent and come back to Me. If you want to please Me, you will obey Me. If you have a bible, then you have My commandments. Learn all of them and keep them, so you will not blaspheme My sacred Name by rejecting My laws. I gave Moses My laws to write down for My people, yet some of My children despise those laws saying they are not for today. You apparently have not read them if you think this way. The message is the same today-to treat others fairly and not to harm someone and love others giving freely to those in need. If you love Me, you will search for the Truth in My words.

97

You should put tassels (tzitzit) on the corners of your clothing.

Num 15:37 Then YHUH said to Moses, 38 "Speak to the Israelites and say to them: 'Throughout the generations to come you are to make tassels on the corners of your garments, with a blue cord on each tassel.'"

My beloved, do not look to the things of the world, but look upon Me and love Me with all your heart, so you can be blessed and prosper. I have given you My commandments so you can follow closely after Me. If you will meditate on My commandments and not do whatever you please, then your life will be good. If you want to have an abundant life, then you must search for Truth in My commandments and hold onto them. That is why I told My people to wear tassels on their clothing to remember My laws and think about them every day. I have sent you My Sprit to convict you of your sins, so you will repent quickly or not sin at all. If you will be in tune with My Spirit, then you can receive the best gifts. If you follow Me, you will be led by My Spirit. If you will remember My laws and study them in the morning and at night, then your life will be blessed. My face will shine on you, and I will give you favor with men so you can prosper. If you do not know all My commands, then search My words for them and ask Me to reveal them to you, so you cannot sin against Me. You are held responsible for the laws whether you know them or not, so know them so you can prosper and be in good health. Guard over your thoughts and be careful what you see. If you turn away from wickedness and focus on Me, you will be blessed and have success.

98

You should not indulge in evil thoughts.

Num 15:39 You will have these tassels to look at and so you will remember all the commands of YHUH, that you may obey them and not prostitute yourselves by going after the lusts of your own hearts and eyes. 40 Then you will remember to obey all my commands and will be sacred to your Elohim. Col 3:2 Set your minds on things above, not on earthly things. (Phil 4:8)

My beloved, I told My Children to wear tassels on their clothing to help them remember to keep My Commandments, so they would not sin against Me. If you are meditating on My Commandments, then you will not be thinking about anything evil. You will be focusing on Me and My Ways. If your heart is clean, then you will not have evil thoughts. You live in a fleshly body, so you are inclined to have evil thoughts because Adam and Eve ate from the tree of good and evil. If My Spirit lives within you, then you will be ruled by My Spirit and not your flesh. My Spirit will convict you of your evil thoughts and tell you to repent. You should not wish evil on anyone. You should want all men to prosper and be blessed. If a man is wicked, then I will judge him and he will pay for his sins. You are not his judge. You will not pass punishment on him. You should pray for him and put him in My Hands, and let Me take care of what punishment should be rendered against him. I know what judgment he needs that will humble him and turn him to Me. If you hold grudges against others, then you harm yourself and keep yourself from drawing closer to Me. If you are angry and mad and want to hurt someone who has hurt you, then you have put a wall between you and Me. Let go of your anger and forgive the person, so you can walk hand in hand with Me. If you really want to have a life filled with many blessings, then you must turn away from your bitterness and hardheartedness. You must trust Me to bring the person to judgment. Do not dwell on evil thoughts, but pray and trust Me to deliver you from all evil men. I will take you to a new place-a safe place-a guarded place, and you will not have to suffer under the hand of this evil person anymore. Just call on Me to deliver you, and I will.

99

You should not touch a dead body.

Num 19:11 Whoever touches the dead body of anyone will be unclean for seven days. 12 He must purify himself with the water on the third day and on the seventh day; then he will be clean. But if he does not purify himself on the third and seventh days, he will not be clean.

My beloved, I told My people that after they touch someone who has died, they must cleanse themselves with water and remove any germs that may be on them from the dead person. No matter how the person died whether by a weapon or natural causes, the person must cleanse himself. Any open containers in the room must be washed just in case the disease is airborne. I gave My people these rules even though they did not understand germs and disease like you do today. I have a reason for all the laws I give-to protect you- to keep you safe. I love you and I want the best for you even though you do not understand why I ask you to do some of the things that I ask you to do. You must obey, because what I ask you to do is best for you. What I say to you is because I love you. Listen. Open your ears. In the last days I will give instructions to those who will listen. I will guide you away from danger and show you where to walk. If you listen, I will guide you and hold you close to Me. Many will come against you, but no one will harm you. You will have to be isolated-a part from the peoples of the world. You must be self-sufficient, but I will show you how. I will bring good things to you just as I provided for My people in the desert. I will provide for you and care for you, because I love My children. I will hold you in My hands.

100

You should pass down your inheritance according to YHUH's laws.

Num 27:8 "Say to the Israelites, 'If a man dies and leaves no son, turn his inheritance over to his daughter. 9 If he has no daughter, give his inheritance to his brothers. 10 If he has no brothers, give his inheritance to his father's brothers. 11 If his father had no brothers, give his inheritance to the nearest relative in his clan, that he may possess it. This is to be a legal requirement for the Israelites, as YHUH commanded Moses.'"

My beloved, I have given My people laws about leaving an inheritance to their children. If you will follow My laws, all will go well with you. I have asked you to leave property to all your children even your daughters, so all your children can be blessed. Do not try to avoid these laws by giving your money to a church or an organization or another person that is not your child, because this is not My way. If you do not have children, then you can give as you please, but it is best to leave your assets to a member of your family if the person is serving Me and walking in righteousness. If you do not have an inheritance to give your children, this is shameful. You should not allow yourself to get into debt, but instead save your money and be able to give your children a good start on their life, so they can also be free from debt. All of your family must be free from the banking system who robs from others by charging high interest rates so you cannot even pay your debts. You must never take out a loan. Call on My name for advice, and I will help you. I will show you the way to go, so you will not fall into deeper debt. You must listen to My voice, and I will give you the ability to be released from all debt so you can be free.

101

You should lay hands on a man to appoint him for service.

Num 27:22 Moses did as YHUH commanded him. He took Joshua and had him stand before Eleazar the priest and the whole assembly. 23 Then he laid his hands on him and commissioned him, as YHUH instructed through Moses. (Deut 34:9, 1 Tim 5:22, 2 Tim 1:6)

My beloved, before you ever commission someone to service Me, pray and fast for several days and see clearly concerning this person before you quickly lay hands on someone. You must ask Me about him and I will show you what you need to see. It is very important that the man who leads the others is chosen by Me. Just as Joshua was chosen by Me to follow after Moses and lead My people, you will know I have chosen the man before you anoint him for service. Laying your hands on a man gives you the ability to transfer the anointing from you to him. This pleases Me, if the man has been chosen by Me. That is why you should not lay your hands on others too hastily, but seek My face concerning the man. You should also make the commission a public one, so all My people will know who the man is and what he has been chosen to do, so those around him can support him in his service to Me. All men are not leaders. Not all men have the same gifts and talents. You have to use the gift I have given you the best you can. You should not look at others and say, "I wish I was like him." No, I want you to serve Me with the gifts I have given you, and then you will be happy and have success and be satisfied in your life. If you long to be different, then you will never be satisfied or serve Me in the way I created you. Rejoice and serve Me with the gifts I have given you.

102

You should not put to death a murderer without a trial.

Num 35:9 Then YHUH said to Moses: 10 "Speak to the Israelites and say to them: 'When you cross the Jordan into Canaan, 11 select some towns to be your cities of refuge, to which a person who has killed someone accidentally may flee. 12 They will be places of refuge from the avenger, so that a person accused of murder may not die before he stands trial before the assembly.'"

My beloved, I set aside six cities of refuge for those to flee who had accidentally killed someone. The person would be sheltered by the men of the city until the man would go to trial for his sin. Even though he did not kill the man intentionally, he did take a life so he must stay in the city and not leave until the high priest died. Now you are also sheltered until you have a trial and all the evidence is compiled and presented. Sometimes the case is easy to solve, and sometimes it is not. At those times you should call on My name, and I will guide you. A man who killed a man because he hated him or had vengeance in this heart against him must be killed. Many wicked men kill men, women, and children every day and defile your land. The land stinks with sin and not one comes to Me repenting of his sin, but instead he blames others for his sins. If a man sins, he should repent or he will go into outer darkness and return no more. This is a man who does not know Me. If he knows Me, he would forgive others and love others. A man who hates does not love Me. A man who plots to kill does not know Me. A man who drinks alcohol or takes drugs to numb himself to sin, does not know Me. Wake up and realize that you must draw close to Me to overcome the powers of darkness and be saved from the evil one.

103

You should not redeem a murderer from the death penalty. You should not accept a bribe from a murderer.

Num 35:31 Do not accept a ransom for the life of a murderer, who deserves to die. He must surely be put to death. **32** Do not accept a ransom for anyone who has fled to a city of refuge and so allow him to go back and live on his own land before the death of the high priest. **33** Do not pollute the land where you are. Bloodshed pollutes the land, and atonement cannot be made for the land on which blood has been shed, except by the blood of the one who shed it.

My beloved, if a man has intentionally killed another man, then he must be put to death. If he killed once, he will kill again. He is a killer and the blood he shed has polluted the land. If his blood is not shed and atones for the blood he shed, then the land becomes defiled. If a man is sentenced to death, do not try to have him released unless he has not had a fair trial and has not had two of more witnesses to his crime. If you release a man who has killed, then his blood is on your hands. If you are a lawyer, do not defend a man you know is guilty of murdering someone. Let him receive his sentence and carry out the penalty. Many men go to death row and sit for years, but the death of the killer should be quick, so the land can be free of the stain of his blood. If you live in a nation where abortion is legal, then the land is polluted and judgment is coming, so the stench of the land can be taken away. Listen to My voice and I will tell you where to go to escape the judgment, if it is coming to the place where you live. You must always be listening to My voice, so you can know which direction to take. If you love Me, you will obey Me and want to do what is right. Do not think evil thoughts about others, but quickly forgive them, so no evil ideas to punish them yourself arise. Let Me punish those who have wronged you. I AM YHUH.

104

You should be fair and not show fear in judgment. You should not pervert the judgment of strangers, orphans, or sinners.

Deut 1:16 And I charged your judges at that time: Hear the disputes between your brothers and judge fairly, whether the case is between brother Israelites or between one of them and an alien. 17 Do not show partiality in judging; hear both small and great alike. Do not be afraid of any man, for judgment belongs to Elohim. Bring Me any case too hard for you, and I will hear it. (Deut 16:18-20, Deut 24:17-18, Ex 23:6)

My beloved, you must judge others fairly and not show prejudice against your neighbor. You must not judge a man by his wealth or where he lives or the color of his skin or by the language he speaks or the customs he keeps, but look at the man's heart. If he loves Me and wants to obey Me, then he is your brother and you must treat him with love and compassion. You will find My people in all colors and all varieties all over the world. You will know them, because they love Me and want to serve Me. Some still are serving other gods and they are blinded, but they will awake when Truth comes to their door. What you must show others is the Truth and if they are of Me, they will receive the Truth gladly. They will be hungry to hear more about Me. If you are intimidated by men, do not be afraid of them. What can they do to you? I will protect you. Judge them fairly and do only good things for others no matter what men may say. Some men in power may try to press you to say and do wrong things, but resist these men and stay far away from them. If you give into a man and do as he says once, then he will come back again and again and ask from you until you are drained of all the good things I have given you. Do not give into evil men, but stand up and be strong and courageous, and I will bless you and care for you.

105

You should not add or take away from YHUH's words.

Deut 4:1 Now, Israel, hear the decrees and laws I am about to teach you. Follow them so that you may live and may go in and take possession of the land YHUH, the Elohim of your ancestors, is giving you. 2 Do not add to what I command you and do not subtract from it, but keep the commands of YHUH your Elohim that I give you.

My beloved, I gave My People commandments to help them live a life that would help them know Me and walk in harmony with My People who love Me. I wanted all men to treat each other fairly with loving kindness and tender mercy. Man is not perfect, and we have to make allowances for him and be merciful to him. I gave you My Laws, so that all men can see a vivid picture of how to live their lives and walk with Me. If you take any of My Commandments away and say that this is not for today, then you have violated My Laws. My Laws are perfect, and no one should change them. You may not understand how to carry out some of My Laws, because there is not a temple anymore. You are not a priest ordained to service My Temple, so you should not be concerned about these laws at the present time. Walk in the laws that are for you. You may not understand how the laws relate to you, then what is the spirit of the laws? My Laws promote kindness towards your neighbor and forgiving others. My Laws promote a fair court system without prejudice or bribes. My Laws provide for a man who has wronged another man to make restitution, so the man can forgive him and they can live in harmony. You must seek Me and I will guide you how to keep all of My Laws. Do not add to My Laws and put a burden on others. Who are you to add to My perfect laws? Man may say that My Laws have passed away, but My Words never pass away. They are written in stone and are a permanent structure in My Kingdom. If you want to draw closer to Me, then you will study My Laws and obey them as I guide you. Just call on My Name to find wisdom from My Words, and I will bring Light to your house and uncover the Truth to be found within them.

106

You should pray to YHUH.

Deut 4:7 What other nation is so great as to have their gods near them the way YHUH our Elohim is near us whenever we pray to Him? 8 And what other nation is so great as to have such righteous decrees and laws as this body of laws I am setting before you today? Ps 32:6 Therefore let everyone who is righteous pray to you while you may be found.

My beloved, pray to Me-call on My Name- and you will find Me. Look to Me all the day and submit your requests for your needs to Me, and I will hear you and I will give you what you need. I will not allow you to be lacking or without, but I will bring to you food, water, shelter, clothes, and safety. The days are growing dark and you will see sights like you have not known before. Men will die from fear, but if you pray and call on My name as your Elohim to save you, I will cover you with My hands and save you. I will tell you what to do in advance, so you can be prepared. If you prepare, you and your family cannot be harmed, but can be safe through perilous times. The evil one will arise and he will want to overtake you, but I will seal you so not one of you is lost. I will keep you from his evil devices. He is wicked and plans to destroy the earth's inhabitants, so he can rule-he and all his evil ones. He wants complete control, but I will help you to become wise servants. You look ahead and see clearly and want to walk in righteousness. Your faith will be a shield to you, so darkness cannot over take you. Others will fail in their efforts to survive, but you will be strong and resistant, because I keep you in the palm of My hands. So pray and find Me.

107

You should search for YHUH with all your heart.

Deut 4:26 I call heaven and earth as witnesses against you today that, if you disobey Me, you will soon disappear from the land. You will not live very long in the land across the Jordan that you are about to occupy. You will be completely destroyed. 27 YHUH will scatter you among other nations, where only a few of you will survive. 28 There you will serve gods made by human hands, gods of wood and stone, gods that cannot see or hear, eat or smell. 29 There you will look for YHUH your Elohim, and if you search for him with all your heart, you will find Him.

My beloved, I scattered you among the nations and drove you out of Israel, because your ancestors forgot Me and all I had done for them. They served other gods, because they wanted a god they could see-a god made of human hands-ruled by demons and demon gods. Your ancestors lost the privilege of living peacefully in My Land. They did not want to follow My laws, so I scattered them all over the world. If you search for Me with all your heart, then you will find Me and I will bring Truth to your house and drive out all the lies your ancestors told you. Your ancestors told you to serve other gods and forget about My feast days and My laws. If you search for Me with all your heart, you will find that all you inherited was lies from your ancestors and no Truth. You must continue to cry out to Me for Truth and follow in the Truth I bring you. I will bring more Truth to you, so you will not walk in darkness and be deceived like the rest of the world. You are My set apart people, and you should walk in Light and know the way to walk in righteousness. Take the weak kneed by the hand and help them up, so they also can serve Me and receive the blessings that come through obedience. You must love Me with all your heart to serve Me faithfully. You must know My laws and walk in My ways, and then you can overturn the curses left on you by your ancestors and receive the blessings of My covenant.

108

You should work for six days.

Deut 5: 12 Observe the Sabbath day by keeping it set apart, as YHUH your Elohim has commanded you. Six days you shall labor and do all your work. (Gen 2:15, Prov 14:23, Col 3:17, 23. 1 Cor 10:31, 1 Thess 4:11-12, 2 Thess 3:10-22)

My beloved, I want you to work hard, because a man who works hard is satisfied with the work of his hands. He has no regrets. He knows that he has done his best, and he has done all that he knows how to do. If you want to be lazy and let others provide for you, then you will suffer loss. I will not bless a person that does not want to work and provide for himself and his family. Everyone in the family should work hard and do what is best for the family. If a man is sick, then help him out and do the job that he was supposed to do until he is well and can return to work. If you think of others and not yourself, then you will be blessed by My Hand. I want you to work for only six days, and rest on the seventh day. This day is My Sabbath of rest and all men should rest and draw close to Me on this day. During the week you are working very hard and have little time to rest, so on the Sabbath day you can put aside all your work and focus on Me and listen to what I say to you. I will tell you what to do, so you can prosper and remain in good health. When you rest My Spirit is on you communing with you and telling you secret things that you need to know for the future. I will tell you things that will help you get along better with the people around you. There are people who have been placed in your path that you will be judged by how you treat them. Be careful when you work with others to treat them fairly. Do not take away some of their profit. I will judge you harshly for this. Many are watching you, so be an example to them and always walk in fairness. Always work hard at your job like I am your master. I am watching and I will bless you according to the labors of your hands.

109

You should love YHUH with all your heart, strength, and might.

Deut 6:5 And you shall love YHUH your Elohim with all your heart and with all your soul and with all your strength. Matt 22: 35 One of them, an expert in the law, tested Him with this question: 36 "Teacher, which is the greatest commandment in the Law?" 37 Yahshua replied: "Love YHUH your Elohim with all your heart and with all your soul and with all your mind. 38 This is the first and greatest commandment. 39 And the second is like it: Love your neighbor as yourself. 40 All the Law and the Prophets hang on these two commandments." (Matt 22:34-38)

My beloved, I have told you to love Me above all other things. If your family decides to go serve other gods, then I have asked you to be separate from them and remain clean so you can prosper and be in good health. I want you to love Me above all earthly possessions. Do not allow anything to keep you from serving Me. What is it that hinders you from walking uprightly? What are your sins? What keeps you sinning? If you can put a finger on it and point to it, then remove that person or thing from your life. Make a sacrifice and remove all sin from your life, and I will bless you. Look around you and open your eyes and see clearly. Are there people who influence you to sin? Are there material things that you desire like money, power, wealth, affluence, the right to rule over others? What is it? It may be something as small as a TV, games, music, dance, or songs. It may be your thoughts are impure and you need to forgive others or stop your sexual lust. Whatever it is, examine yourself and take that far from you. If you have struggled with a sin for years-then call on My name to release you. Fast and pray until you have broken the addiction or the familiar spirit. If you will continue to call out to Me, I will release you from all bondage so you can serve only Me.

110

You should talk about the Commandments in the Morning and at Night.

Deut 6:4 Hear, O Israel: YHUH your Elohim, YHUH is one. 5 Love YHUH your Elohim with all your heart and with all your soul and with all your strength. 6 These commandments that I give you today are to be upon your hearts. 7 Impress them on your children. Talk about them when you sit at home and when you walk along the road, when you lie down and when you get up. (Deut 11:18-19)

My beloved, love My words and treasure them in your heart that you may not sin against Me. Open up your heart and allow Me to fill you up with My words, so you can teach your children My words from the time they are born until they leave your house. Talk about My ways with them all day long, so they can learn the wisdom that I have already given you. You should pray over them in the morning and pray over them at night. Lay your hands on your little ones, and pray a blessing over them and teach them My words in the morning and at night. In the temple My priests would make a morning sacrifice and an evening sacrifice as the sun was setting. You should think of reading to your children in the morning and at night as your daily sacrifice to Me. You will see how I bless your children, because they know My laws and My ways. If you will do this your children will not depart from My ways. They will be in their heart. You may say, "My children are older and they have not been taught the Torah." As long as they are in your house, it is not too late to begin. Start today. They may resist you at first, but soon they will love My words as much as you do. Do not be afraid to make a sacrifice to Me today, and I will bless you.

111

You should fear YHUH.

Deut 6:24 YHUH commanded us to obey all these decrees and to fear YHUH our Elohim, so that we might always prosper and be kept alive, as is the case today.

My beloved, I give you My Laws to show you how to give your life, so you can have life abundantly. I gave you My Laws, so you will be fair and just with all men and treat all men equally with love and kindness. I gave you My Laws, so you could honor and respect those around you and continue in My Ways. I gave you My laws, so you would rid yourself of the evil among you and treat those who rebel against Me in a way that they would understand and repent form their sins. I gave you My laws, so you would know who I AM and serve only Me. I gave you My judgments also, so you would know how to punish a rebellious man and keep him from inflecting others who want to do what is right. If you must punish a man, then you do this for his own good. If he repents and turns aside from his sins, then you have saved the man. If he continues to be hard hearted, then you must rid yourself of the man for the sake of all. Now you live in exile, but you must continue to fear Me and walk in My laws even though no one else around you is following My Laws. If you fear Me knowing that I will punish you for not obeying Me, then you will be greatly blessed. I will prosper you and your family. You will have My angels around you to guide you and direct you. If you do not know the way to walk, then call on My Name and I will guide you. I will tell you the way to go. If you walk in My ways, then you will live in peace and harmony with those around you. If you are forced to leave the country where you live, rejoice that I love you so much. Count this as a blessing and be obedient to My Voice. I will show you where to go and what to do. Trust in Me.

112

You should not become unequally yoked to an unbeliever.

Deut 7:3 Do not intermarry with them. Do not give your daughters to their sons or take their daughters for your sons. 2 Cor 6:14 Do not be yoked together with unbelievers. For what do righteousness and wickedness have in common? Or what fellowship can light have with darkness? Ex 34:16 And when you choose some of their daughters as wives for your sons and those daughters prostitute themselves to their gods, they will lead your sons to do the same. (Gen 24:3, Ezra 9:2)

My beloved, I told My People not to intermarry with people who did not worship Me. If they would have listened to My Command, then they would not have entered into pagan worship. They turned against Me, because they allowed their children to marry people who worshipped other gods. The people they married would introduce their children into pagan worship and the children would begin to serve the pagan gods and not Me. My people were disobedient, and they paid the price for it. They were driven out of the Land and into exile, because they did not want to worship only Me. They looked at what the pagans did, and they desired to worship as they did. They wanted to go to their feasts and enter into their sin. They wanted a different god, and they turned against Me. Do not make the same mistake that your forefathers made. Watch carefully over your children, and talk to them about the importance of marrying believers. If your child marries an unbeliever, it will cause him many problems. If the person will listen to your voice and repent of his sins and turn to Me, then the marriage will be saved. Do not think that you can change a person after you marry him. If the person does not want to serve Me before you are married, then he will not want to serve Me after you are married. Think carefully about your life. Do you want to live with an unbeliever? Do you want an unbeliever to raise your children? Come to Me for guidance concerning your marriage. I will show you the way to go. I will keep you from entering into an unlawful covenant with an unbeliever.

113

You should burn and not use the ornament of any object of idolatrous worship.

Deut 7:25 The images of their gods you are to burn in the fire. Do not covet the silver and gold on them, and do not take it for yourselves, or you will be ensnared by it, for it is detestable to YHUH your Elohim. 26 Do not bring a detestable thing into your house or you, like it, will share in the curse that is on it. Utterly abhor and detest it, for it is set apart for destruction. (Deut 4:15-20)

My beloved, I AM Elohim-the invisible Elohim. Do not try to find a form or statue to worship, but worship Me in spirit and truth. Do not hold onto charms or beads or crosses or any such things, but hold onto Me and love Me. Do not set up for yourself any form to worship. Do not take any souvenirs from other places- any of their gods or any statues; because the curse is on it and if it is in your house, then the curse will hinder your blessings. Remove from your house and burn all statues, forms, charms, beads, crosses, symbols or any such things, so you can be free from all pagan signs and symbols. Research for the origins of all these signs and symbols. Look at their pagan roots and how these symbols and signs have been brought into your religion as a blessed symbol, but you have been lied to by the evil one. He wants you to worship him, so he has perverted all his pagan signs and made them "sanctified." Do not be deceived. Be wise and see what he is doing and walk away from all these curses, so you can be blessed. He wants you to be able to be cursed and receive none of your blessings. I call out to you, "Clean your house. Remove all foreign objects from it. Cleanse your house and keep only My words in your house." If you will do this, you will see blessings come into your house and you will be free of all things that will hinder your walk with Me. Your eyes will be opened, and you will be free to know the path of Light before you.

114

You should remember how your ancestors were humbled, tested, and disciplined by YHUH.

Deut 8:1 Be careful to follow every command I am giving you to- day, so that you may live and increase and may enter and possess the land that YHUH promised on oath to your forefathers. 2 Remember how YHUH your Elohim led you all the way in the desert these forty years, to humble you and to test you in order to know what was in your heart, whether or not you would keep His commands.

My beloved, I took My people-a group of very different varieties-into the desert. Some were Egyptians and some were Hebrew slaves, and I took them away from all the luxuries of Egypt to a deserted arid land with no water or food and numerous obstacles. I wanted My people who call on My name to trust Me and have faith in Me. I made them become hungry and thirsty, and they cursed Moses for bringing them away from the curses of Egypt. I provided for them and made them totally dependent on Me to learn how to trust Me and have faith in Me. I tested them to see what was in their heart, but too much of Egypt was in their heart, so those twenty years and older died in the desert. I took the rest to the Promised Land and they marched into the Land trusting in Me to save them from their enemies. Is there Egypt in your heart? Do you have too much of the world in your heart to trust in Me to care for you and provide for you? In the last days I will care for all the needs of My people-even food and water- like I did in the desert. My people will be forced into isolation, because the wrath of the evil one will be against them. I will take you to a safe place where the evil one will not touch you. You must be ready to trust in only Me. If you are humbled and disci- plined by Me, count it as a gift from Me, so you can be tested and found worthy to enter My kingdom. If you trust Me through the difficult days of your life, you will trust Me when you have abundance and joy.

115

You should teach your children My Commandments.

Deut 11:19 Teach them to your children, talking about them when you sit at home and when you walk along the road, when you lie down and when you get up.

My beloved, I want you to teach your children from My Scriptures. Teach them My Words every day as you talk with them. Tell them now to live their life based on My Words. Teach them My Laws and help them memorize them, so they can be in their hearts at an early age. If you do this, then My Words will build a firm foundation. Your children will be able to stand on it and remain firm when the trials of an adolescent come upon them. They will be able to fight the lusts of their flesh knowing what is right and wrong. I will lift you up and show you the words to tell them. If you call on My Name, I will give you wisdom how to discipline each child and the words you must speak for each child. Each child is different. I have made each one unique. You cannot compare children. You must realize that each one has been made for a different task and should be viewed in a different way. Always keep the same house rules for each child and have the same punishment, but you may need to adjust how you discipline as led by My Spirit. Some children require more attention than others, and you must teach those children how to love others and not be demanding. They should be taught to reach out and love others in a way that blesses them and does not draw from them. You do not want to raise selfish self-seeking children. Teach them how to give to others. Instead of giving to them so much, teach them to give away and bless others. Teach your children to honor you and obey you. If you teach them to honor you and obey you, then you teach them to honor Me and obey Me. This world is very difficult and trying. Give your children a firm foundation. Teach them to stand on My Words.

116

You should have no regard for fortune telling, superstition, casting spells, astrology, spiritualism, conjuring up the dead, palm reading, magic, or witchcraft.

Deut 18:9 When you enter the land YHUH your Elohim is giving you, do not learn to imitate the detestable ways of the nations there. 10 Let no one be found among you who sacrifice his son or daughter in the fire, who practices divination or sorcery, interprets omens, engages in witchcraft, 11 or casts spells, or who is a medium or wizard or who consults the dead. 12 Anyone who does these things is detestable to YHUH, and because of these detestable practices YHUH your Elohim will drive out those nations before you. 13 You must be blameless before YHUH your Elohim. 14 The nations you will dispossess listen to those who practice sorcery or divination. But as for you, YHUH your Elohim has not permitted you to do so.

My beloved, do not go seeking after magic, but seek after Me. There is no magic-only demon worship. If you enter the realm of the supernatural, then you enter the kingdom of darkness. Do not try to find out your future or the answers to any questions by looking to magic charms or astrology or any other such darkness. If you want to know the future or the answers to your questions, then cry out to Me and I will guide you day by day. I will not tell you the future all at once. No man needs to know all his future, because it may crush his spirit and he may become hopeless. If he trusts in Me, then I will guide him day by day and keep him within My boundaries for him, so he makes the right decisions and does what is right. Then I can bless him and he can have abundance. If you become involved in the occult, then call on Me to set you free. Call on Me to release you from darkness. I will break the darkness from you, but you must only serve Me and walk in My ways or the darkness will encompass you again. The darkness will be even more than before, because you have rejected Me and My ways. If you associate with people who like to experiment with the occult, rebuke them for their sins, and if they don't listen, then do not associate with them anymore. Stay far away from them, and do not go their way again. Keep yourself pure and far from darkness, and I will bless you greatly

117

You should not cross seeds to make hybrids. You should not eat the produce of diverse seeds sown in a vineyard.

Deut 22:9 Do not plant two kinds of seed in your vineyard; if you do, not only the crops you plant but also the fruit of the vineyard will be defiled. Lev 19:19 Keep my decrees. Do not mate different kinds of animals. Do not plant your field with two kinds of seed. Do not wear clothing woven of two kinds of material.

My beloved, I want you to be very careful that you plant seeds that not hybrid or mixed seeds. Today many farmers use seeds that have been genetically modified to produce a larger crop. This seed will defile your body and cause you to be sick. You must make sure that all the food you eat is pure and clean. There are many unclean foods in this world. Watch carefully over the food you eat that it has not been contaminated by chemicals. These chemicals will break down your body and affect your immune system. You must keep a healthy immune system, because the days are dark and the enemy wants to kill you. The evil one will use all sorts of food that is unclean to bring disease on your body. You must guard over what you eat and what your family eats. You have been given food laws, but you must look deeper than this. Manufactures add preservatives and additives to the food so, it will store for a long time. These chemicals destroy the value of the food. You must have proper nutrients for your body to stay healthy. Be wise and look at all the food labels, and determine if this is fit for your body or not. Stay close to the land and eat what comes from the land. Do not desire processed food filled with unclean products. You must be strong to stand against the food of the world. I will guide you to eat what is right in My eyes. If you call on My Name. I will show you how to stay well and prosper. I do not desire for you to be sick, but stay in good health.

118

You should not wear clothes woven with two kinds of materials.

Deut 22:11 You shall not wear a garment of different sorts, as of woolen and linen together. Lev 19:19 Keep my decrees. Do not mate different kinds of animals. Do not plant your field with two kinds of seed. Do not wear clothing woven of two kinds of material.

My beloved, I told My Children not to mix the fabrics that they wear. I told them not to mix wool and linen. At this time they had natural fabrics, but now you have synthetic fabrics that have no value. If you wear linen the fabric has a high energy level and will bring healing to your body. If you wear polyester fabric, there is not value to this fabric. It will not promote healing to your body. When you combine linen and wool or cotton, it cuts the energy level and does not promote healing. I told all My priests to wear linen tunics and underwear. They were covered with a high energy fabric that produced healing. They understood how important it was to keep energy flowing through your body. Synthetic fabrics cut the energy level and drain you. You must look at all the fabrics that you wear. You may not be able to afford a new wardrobe, but you can start to take the synthetic fabrics out of your wardrobe. Start to buy cotton, linen, wool, and silk. Depend on natural fabrics to clothe you and your family. If you are unable to change your wardrobe at this time, then draw close to My presence and allow My Healing power to surround you and uphold you. I will show you the best way to go.

119

You should not make a loan to an Israelite with interest. You should not charge the poor and needy interest on loans.

Deut 23: 19 Do not charge your brother interest, whether on money or food or anything else that may earn interest. Lev 25:35-37 If one of your countrymen becomes poor and is unable to support himself among you, help him as you would an alien or a temporary resident, so he can continue to live among you. 36 Do not take interest of any kind from him, but fear YHUH, so that your countryman may continue to live among you.

My beloved, do not charge interest on a loan. This is not My way. Do not take advantage of a man who needs money for his family and charge him interest. Only those who are lacking take out loans, so to charge them interest is an abomination to Me. in your country most everyone is in debt except for the very wealthy, but I say to you release yourself from debt. Be free from all those who charge you interest on your loans. Stay clear of taking out loans. It is better to take an extra job, then to take out a loan. Those in the lending institution will rob you with their high interest rates. The people who own the banks also help run the world, because they have control of the money. If you do not want anyone to control you or have power over you, then pay off your debt. You ask Me how you can pay off your mortgage and I say that it better to live in a smaller house and have no mortgage then live in a large house with a large mortgage. If you are drowning in debt, then concentrate on paying one bill at a time and do not charge any more or take out any more loans. Live on what you make until you have paid off all your debts. If your expenses are medical, then the company will work with you to help meet your budget. If you talk to your lenders you can work out a payment schedule, but you must get free from all debts as soon as possible. The days grow dark and men will use your loans against you to trap you and take away what little you have.

120

You should meditate on the laws of Moses day and night.

Josh 1:7 Only be strong and very courageous, being careful to do according to all the law which Moses my servant commanded you; turn not from it to the right hand or to the left, that you may have good success wherever you go. 8 Keep this book of the law on your lips, and meditate on it day and night, that you may be careful to do according to all that is written in it; for then you shall make your way prosperous, and then you shall have good success. (Deut 11:8)

My beloved, I raised Joshua up to lead My People into the Promised Land. I told him to read the laws I gave Moses and meditate on them day and night, so he would be a strong leader. He stayed righteous before Me and led the people well, but after his death My People did not follow My Laws and gradually they fell into sin. I want you to listen to the advice I gave Joshua and meditate on My Laws day and night. Take one law where you know that you are weak, and focus on it all day and pray. Ask Me to help you keep this law, so you can eventually keep all the laws and they will burn within your heart. My Children who love Me want to obey all My Laws. You may not understand all My Ways, but ask Me to show you the way to walk, so you will please Me. You may not have a teacher of the law in your neighborhood, but there are many teachers available to you through books and videos so take advantage of these sources. They may not know all the Truth, but you can reap some of the Truth from what they have received. No man has all the Truth, so as you search for Truth realize that no man is perfect in all his beliefs. Be careful not to fall into error by trusting one man. I will guide you into all Truth. I love you and want you to cling to Me. I will teach you My Ways. Just focus on My Laws all the day.

121

You should not restore the ruins of a wicked city.

Josh 6:26 At that time Joshua pronounced this solemn oath: "Cursed before YHUH is the man who undertakes to rebuild this city, Jericho: At the cost of his firstborn son will he lay its foundations; at the cost of his youngest will he set up its gates." (1 Kings 16:34, Num 5:21)

My beloved, I told Joshua to take My People to the Promised Land and drive out all the people who live there. I told him to go to Jericho-a well-fortified city filled with mighty warriors-and attack the city. My people were fearless, because they knew that I went ahead of them and fought for them. They followed My Instructions and when the trumpets blasted seven times the walls of Jericho fell on top of the people inside the city. The walls fell inward, so My People could walk in and take over the city and not lose a man. The city was proud and haughty and laughed at My People as they walked around the city. They thought they were invincible, but they were crushed by My Hand because of their wickedness. It was a stench in My Nostrils, so I destroyed all of them. They would never be talked about again. Joshua put a curse on the land if anyone were to try to rebuild the city. I do not want any of the wicked cities of long ago to be rebuilt and any glories go to their name. Do not go to ruins searching for remains of wicked cites, but look for remains of My People and My Words. Search for Truth and not pagan ruins filled with demon spirits and perversion. Do not search for the dead, but look for the living. Look for those who need to hear the Truth about Me and My ways, so they can be delivered from the bondage of sin and be delivered into My Kingdom of Light.

122

You should inquire of YHUH before you make a decision.

Josh 9:14 The men of Israel sampled their provisions but did not inquire of YHUH. 15 Then Joshua made a treaty of peace with them to let them live, and the leaders of the assembly ratified it by oath. 16 Three days later they made the treaty with the Gibeonites, the Israelites heard that they were neighbors, living near them. 2 Sam 2:1 In the course of time, David inquired of YHUH. "Shall I go up to one of the towns of Judah?" he asked. YHUH said, "Go up." David asked, "Where shall I go?" "To Hebron," YHUH answered. (Num 27:21)

My beloved, before you make any decision you need to ask Me for My advice, so you will not be deceived. Do not go the way of the pagans who do whatever they like, and then they are blinded and covered in deception, yet they think they are wise and making sound decisions. They are building hay and stubble, and they will end up in destruction. Those who call on My Name and ask Me to guide them will not be deceived by the evil one, but will be wise and aware of what is happening today and what will happen in the future. If My People would constantly seek My face for guidance, then they will be always going in the right direction and they would not suffer loss. If you see a brother who wants to go his own way, rebuke him quietly and tell him only the pagans do as they want. Many of My people are fleshy and seek after fleshy desires. They will be tested with fire in the last days. Many will lost their lives, because their ears are dull and they cannot hear and did not follow My Voice. I tell you this day to take My Advice and get out of Babylon-away from the world system. Release yourself from debt. Do not crave worldly possessions, but crave Me. Do not think of all the things you can buy, but think of all the things you can give up that are of the world, so you can sacrifice your flesh and walk in My Spirit. Have self-control and discipline and cut off your fleshly cravings for perversion, and rejoice that you are a consecrated people set aside to do My Work and walk in My Ways.

123

You should choose whom you will serve and serve only Him and do not waiver.

Josh 24:14 "Now therefore, fear YHUH, serve Him in sincerity and in truth, and put away the gods which your fathers served on the other side of the River and in Egypt. Serve YHUH! 15 And if it seems evil to you to serve YHUH, choose for yourselves this day whom you will serve, whether the gods which your fathers served that were on the other side of the River, or the gods of the Amorites, in whose land you dwell. But as for me and my house, we will serve YHUH." 1 Kings 18:21 Elijah went up to the people and said, "How much longer will it take you to make up your minds? If YHUH is Elohim, worship him; but if Baal is God, worship him!" (Deut 10:12)

My beloved, serve Me and only Me. Do not waiver in whom you love and want to serve. You are an abomination to Me unless you love Me with your whole heart. Do not long for the world or foreign religions. If you serve only Me, then why do you keep pagan holidays and worship other gods? I AM a jealous Elohim and I know you are in exile, but look only to Me. Do not do as the pagans do and worship statues. Take all statues and pagan symbols out of your house. Do not look to the heavens for guidance. Throw out your astrology charts and horoscopes. You should ask Me for direction. If you are going to any man or group of people for direction, wisdom, guidance, healing, or seeking the future, then you are in error. I want you to pray together with other believers and seek Me. I want you to celebrate our feast days together and study the scriptures together, but if you want to know whether to sell your house, buy a car, move to another place, start a business, or any other family decision, you should come to Me as a family and ask Me what you should do, because I have a different purpose for each family. Do not go to the people of the world, but come only to Me. What wisdom can others give you? Only I can give wisdom. Only I can show you the right path, so serve only Me and do not seek other gods or sources.

124

You should destroy the gods that your father worshipped.

Judges 6:25 Now on the same night YHUH said to him, "Take your father's bull and a second bull seven years old, and pull down the altar of Baal which belongs to your father, and cut down the Asherah that is beside it; 26 and build an altar to YHUH your Elohim on the top of this stronghold in an orderly manner, and take a second bull and offer a burnt offering with the wood of the Asherah which you shall cut down." 27 Then Gideon took ten men of his servants and did as YHUH had spoken to him; and because he was too afraid of his father's household and the men of the city to do it by day, he did it by night. (Ex 34:13)

My beloved, have you ever asked, "Why has all this happened to Me? What have I done to deserve all this?" If you have asked yourself these questions, then you should ask Me because I will tell you the answer. I AM the one who brings judgment on the land and if a land is in sin, then I will bring judgment to punish them for their sins. I will send disasters, famine, and financial ruin. I will send enemies to fight against them until they are destroyed. I will crush the land who does not serve Me. If you are in a sinful nation and judgment comes on the land, then this is why all these things have come upon you. Listen to My voice to guide you to a safe place. I will tell you in advance, so you can prepare to leave. I may tell you years in advance or I may tell you to flee at the last moment. It all depends on where you live. You may not be walking in righteousness and if you are in sin, then your own personal judgment will fall on you. If you will repent and not go back to the sinful state again, I will release you from all punishments and I will bless you for your faithfulness. Continue to stand strong and do not sin. If all sorts of trouble are on your family, then repent as a family and turn from your wickedness. Keep My Laws and do your best to serve Me even though you are living in exile and have no one around you that keep My Laws. Be faithful and I will bless you greatly.

Which Commandments Should I Obey?

125

***You should not honor your children above YHUH.
You should not allow your children to break the
commandments of YHUH.***

1 Sam 2:29 'Why do you kick at My Sacrifice and at My Offering which
I have commanded in My Dwelling, and honor your sons above Me, by
making yourselves fat with the choicest of every offering of My
People Israel?' 30 "Therefore YHUH Elohim of Israel declares, 'I did
indeed say that your house and the house of your father should
walk before Me forever'; but now YHUH declares, 'Far be it from
Me- for those who honor Me I will honor, and those who despise Me
will be lightly esteemed.'" (Matt 10:37)

My beloved, you should honor Me above all things. You should show Me respect
by obeying all My Commandments and making your children respect Me. You
should push your children to do what is right, and if they disobey you, then you
should punish them. Do not close your eyes to their sin, but see your children for
who they are. If they are rebellious, then punish them for their rebellion. It does
not matter how old your children are. You must make sure they respect you and
obey you. If they do not respect you today, they will not respect you tomorrow.
You will be paid back in your old age for your lack of discipline. They will forget
about you and caring for you. If you make your children respect Me and you
(you are an extension of My Hand), then they will obey My Laws and walk in
righteousness. You must love your children enough to punish them. Do not give
up on your children, but love them and correct them. If you do not correct them,
then your sins will come back to you through the sins of your children and their
grief will be spilled over onto you. Teach your children to honor My Sabbath Day
and set it apart and rest. This is the beginning of My days. Teach them to honor
all My feast days, and then you will be blessed by your children and by Me.

126

You should not seek for a man to guide you.

1 Sam 12:16 "Now then, stand still and see this great thing YHUH is about to do before your eyes! 17 Is it not wheat harvest now? I will call upon YHUH to send thunder and rain. And you will realize what an evil thing you did in the eyes of YHUH when you asked for a king." 18 Then Samuel called upon YHUH, and that same day YHUH sent thunder and rain. So all the people stood in awe of YHUH and of Samuel. 19 The people all said to Samuel, "Pray to YHUH your Elohim for your servants so that we will not die, for we have added to all our other sins the evil of asking for a king." (Num 21:7)

My beloved, do not seek after a man to guide you, but seek only after Me. My people said, "Give us a king to guide us. We want to be like the other nations and have a man lead us. We want someone we can see." My people sinned against Me, because I wanted them to trust only Me and allow Me to guide them. Look what happened to them. Saul brought them all sorts of troubles. He made many mistakes and took their young men into battle and gathered taxes from My People. If they had only had Me as their leader, I would have defeated all their enemies. I do not want large amounts of gold and silver, so My People would not have paid large amounts of money to a king so he could live in wealth. My children, look to Me and not a man for guidance. You should not have a king set up over yourself. You should not have one church or man to make all your decisions, because men make errors. You may be grieved because you live in exile and the leadership of your country is corrupt and you do not have a righteous man to lead your country. I see your grief and I grieve with you. I will bring My Children back home soon, and you will come My Land singing knowing I have done many miracles for you, and blessed you greatly.

127

You should look at the heart of a man, not his appearance.

1 Sam 16:6 When they arrived, Samuel saw Eliab and thought, "Surely YHUH's anointed stands here before YHUH." 7 But YHUH said to Samuel, "Do not consider his appearance or his height, for I have rejected him. YHUH does not look at the things man looks at. Man looks at the outward appearance, but YHUH looks at the heart." (Luke 16:15, John 8:15)

My beloved, do not look at the outside of man, but look at his heart and help him to overcome. If you see a man who loves Me and wants to be faithful to Me, then this is a man who is beautiful before Me no matter what he looks like in appearance. If a man has a very handsome exterior but does not serve Me, then he is an abomination to Me. If a man is handsome, he may love the appearance of this flesh and worship his appearance and want it to stay beautiful, so he spends all this money on staying beautiful and being well dressed. This man loves to serve himself and does not want to serve Me. This man is not beautiful before Me, but a stench in My nostrils. Do not judge outward appearances. Instead watch what they say and do and how they treat others. You should be loving and kind to others, and always seek to do what pleases Me. How can you be beautiful before Me if you do not want to please Me? How can you please Me? You should keep My commandments. Do as I tell you to do and not as man tells you to do. Look in My words and find Truth. Men will deceive you, but I will bring you Truth. Man may appear to be rich and good looking and progressing, but if his heart is not bent towards Me, then he is dying and will end up in the lake of fire. Beware of outward appearances.

128

You should allow YHUH to judge between you and the one who has wronged you and not harm that person.

1 Sam 24:12 May YHUH judge between you and me. And may YHUH avenge the wrongs you have done to me, but my hand will not touch you. 15 May YHUH be our judge and decide between us. May He take my side; may He rescue me from your power. (Gen 16:5, Gen 31:53)

My beloved, if someone has wronged you, then put that person in My Hands and ask Me to judge between you who is right. I will judge fairly between you and I will move on behalf of the one who has been wronged. I will chastise the one who has wronged you, and I will bless you and deliver you from their oppression. Those who call on My Name for help in times of trouble, I will help and deliver them from those who are causing him troubles. I AM your Father and I will not allow anyone to harm My Children, but I wait until you call on My Name for help. I want you to look to Me for help–to always cling to Me and I will deliver you from the evil ones. No one knows the things I know. No one has such great wisdom to solve all problems. I can make the tangled mess you have made untangled once again. It will take time, but I can repair all wounds and broken bridges. I can repair and heal, restore, build up, support, cleanse all those who come to Me and have been hurt by others. Those who steal from you will be paid back for their sins. Those who mock you or discredit you will be brought low. You will be lifted up, and they will be humiliated. If you will call on My Name, I will make right those who have wronged you.

129

You should pray for a discerning heart to distinguish between right and wrong.

1 Kings 3:7 "Now, O YHUH my Elohim, you have made your servant king in place of my father David. But I am only a little child and do not know how to lead your people. 8 Your servant is here among the people you have chosen, a great people, too numerous to count or number. 9 So give your servant a discerning heart to govern your people and to distinguish between right and wrong. For who is able to govern this great people of yours?" 10 YHUH was pleased that Solomon had asked for this. (Prov 2:3-5)

My beloved, if you ask Me to tell you the difference in right and wrong, I will give you a spirit of righteousness so your spirit will always tell you the way to go. If you start to commit a sin, your spirit will let you know the way to go. My spirit is placed in you to show you the way you must go. You will make a decision whether to want to obey Me or not. A righteous servant will obey Me and a rebellious servant will not obey Me. If the servant who is rebellious continues to disobey and not repent, then he will no longer be My Servant. You must be obedient to Me and if you discern right and wrong, then an obedient servant will always obey Me. You may not know every way of Mine, but if your heart is bent towards Me, then I will teach you all My ways and My laws. My laws reign supreme and the laws I gave you here on earth are the same laws in My Kingdom. You have been blessed to be given such superior laws that are just and fair and make all men equal in My eyes. If you are just and fair to others, then you will be blessed. If you are greedy and not fair, then you will be punished and humbled until you are obedient to Me and fair to others. My Children will be punished for their sins until they repent and are no longer rebellious, so rise up and do what is right in My eyes.

130

You should pray towards Jerusalem.

1 Kings 8:48 and if they turn back to you with all their heart and soul in the land of their enemies who took them captive, and pray to you toward the land you gave their fathers, toward the city you have chosen and the temple I have built for your Name; 49 then from heaven, your dwelling place, hear their prayer and their plea, and uphold their cause. (1 Kings 9:3, Deut 4:29)

My beloved, turn your face towards Me and pray towards My Land-the Land I gave you-in reverence for the Land from which you were thrown out of because of your sin. Even though you are in exile and you are far from your Land and your home, you should pray towards the Land I gave your forefathers recognizing that this is your permanent place of rest and nowhere else on earth can you rest. You are in a temporary residence, and your home is far away. When I bring you back to the land I gave your fathers, you will have peace that you have never known, because My presence dwells on My land and My eyes rest on My people who live there. You must be brave and strong. Listen to My voice and when you hear Me calling, then come and bring your family–all of them. If your family is reluctant to come, plea with them to come and guide them to their home. If they refuse to come, they will suffer loss. You must continue to pray for those who refused to come, because their days will be difficult. You see My Land now under warfare and political scheming to divide the land for peace. Soon this will end, and they will need new people to come fill the Land to work and till the soil and bring produce to market. You say you have never farmed, but you will. You will help restore the Land after the war, and I will give you wisdom how to care for the Land. It will blossom and bloom and the Land will be fertile and produce abundance.

131

You should look for YHUH in the quiet places.

1 Kings 19:11 Then a great and powerful wind tore the mountains apart and shattered the rocks before YHUH, but YHUH was not in the wind. After the wind there was an earthquake, but YHUH was not in the earthquake. 12 After the earthquake came a fire, but YHUH was not in the fire. And after the fire came a gentle whisper. 13 When Elijah heard it, he pulled his cloak over his face and went out and stood at the mouth of the cave. Then a voice said to him, "What are you doing here, Elijah?" (Mark 6:31, Luke 4:1)

My beloved, you may look for Me in various places, but if there is not stillness and quiet, you will not hear My Voice. If you want to hear Me, then quiet the world around you. Turn off the TV, radio, computer, games, music, and let there be quiet, then you will hear Me in the stillness. Many of My Children say they cannot hear My Voice, but they are not still and quiet before Me. Take time to rest in My Presence. Turn off all outside activities and noise. This may mean that you rise earlier or stay up later, so you can have this quiet time. If you carve out a time for Me every day, I will meet you there. I will come to you and speak with you. You should quiet yourself so your mind is not filled with thoughts, and direct all your thoughts towards Me in prayer. Use My words as tools to focus on Me. Read My words and focus on the meaning and praise Me from your heart and do not question Me, but humbly lift up your praise towards Me, then ask what you will and I will answer you. If you are in sin repent, because sin keeps you from hearing My Voice. If you want to hear My voice better, cut away the world and only focus on Me and My ways. Know that any sacrifices you make to draw closer to Me, I will honor and see your good works. I will reward you when you come to a quiet place and find Me.

132

You should seek YHUH for your healing.

2 Kings 1:2 Now Ahaziah had fallen through the lattice of his upper room in Samaria and injured himself. So he sent messengers, saying to them, "Go and consult Baal-Zebub, the god of Ekron, to see if I will recover from this injury." 3 But the angel of YHUH said to Elijah the Tishbite, "Go up and meet the messengers of the king of Samaria and ask them, 'Is it because there is no Elohim in Israel that you are going off to consult Baal-Zebub, the god of Ekron?' 4 Therefore this is what YHUH says: 'You will not leave the bed you are lying on. You will certainly die!'" So Elijah went. (1 Peter 2:24, Ps 103:1-5)

My beloved, seek Me first in all things. Do not run after men for your healing. I have given you medicine and I have given you doctors, but you must remember that doctors are men and they do not have all understanding and wisdom that I have. If you trust only in men to heal you, then you will fall into error. If you become ill, call on My name and ask Me to heal you or show you what path to take to receive your healing. You must cling to Me for advice and healing. I AM jealous and I do not want you to search after pagan practices to heal you or think that a doctor is your only authority and you should believe everything he says to do. If you do, you will fall into a trap. If a man is good at his skill of healing, then he can save many lives and he will be rewarded for his sacrifices. I see many people crushed under medical bills and they have never come to Me to help them, or either they come to me and ask My advice but never take it. They say, "The doctor says," and he has the only authority in their life. Do not set up a doctor as "god," so you do all he says. You should come to Me first for healing and seek natural healing not synthetic healing, which makes your body suffer. A natural healer will give you medicine to benefit your body. Seek me to heal you, and I will show you the way.

133

You should not disrespect YHUH's servants.

2 Kings 2:23 From there Elisha went up to Bethel. As he was walking along the road, some youths came out of the town and jeered at him. "Go on up, you baldhead!" they said. "Go on up, you baldhead!" 24 He turned around, looked at them and called down a curse on them in the name of YHUH. Then two bears came out of the woods and mauled forty-two of the youths. 25 And he went on to Mount Carmel and from there returned to Samaria. (2 Sam 6:20-23, Lev 13:40, Ps 31:18)

My beloved, do not mock any of My children. Do not say mean things or call them mean names, because what you say to them-you say to Me because I AM their father. If someone was mean to one of your children, you would feel as if someone insulted you also. That is how I feel when someone hurts one of My children. You will pay for your mean words you say to one of My children. You should be loving and kind to all men, but especially My children. If you will look for Me inside of them, then you will do well. If you look for their faults, then you will find some faults, because no man is perfect and all men have their faults. If someone sins against you, forgive him and go on your way not remembering the offense any longer, because the sin will be accounted for and he will have to pay in full for his offense against you. You must look at My children as an extension of Me and love them as you would love Me. When you are angry, control yourself before you speak, so you will not spew venomous words out without thinking of the harm it will do to someone. Once the words are out, you cannot take them back and the words will cut deep. You will wound those who if you had self-control would not be wounded. Think before you speak and show no disrespect for My children.

134

You should be ready to leave your home if YHUH tells you to leave.

2 Kings 8:1 Now Elisha had said to the woman whose son he had restored to life, "Go away with your family and stay for a while wherever you can, because YHUH has decreed a famine in the land that will last seven years." **2** The woman proceeded to do as the man of Elohim said. She and her family went away and stayed in the land of the Philistines seven years. (Jer 42:3-4, Ruth 1:1)

My beloved, if you listen, I will guide you and keep you from disaster. If you listen, I will guide you to safety. Your eyes should always be on Me and your ears should always be open. You should be able to hear My voice, so you can follow Me. Many say they are My children, but they do not hear My voice. How can they be My children if they do not hear My voice? Don't you know your Fathers' voice? Don't you think I will deliver you from upcoming judgment? Why should My children who serve Me and walk in righteousness have to go through judgment on a sinful people? Judgment is coming to many nations, but if you call on Me, then I will release you from the place where you live, so you can be free from the disasters that are coming to your land. You must be free to be able to go when I call you to come. You may have to sell your house and business. You may have to leave family and friends. You may have to leave your possessions or some of your possessions behind. Walking with Me means not being attached to earthy possessions, but clinging only to Me and trusting only Me to care for you and guide you to a safe haven. I AM setting up safe havens for My people around the world to protect them from the troubled days coming ahead, so listen for Me to guide your to safety.

135

You should humble yourself (fast) and seek YHUH's face.

2 Chron 7:14 If my people, who are called by my name, will humble themselves and pray and seek my face and turn from their wicked ways, then will I hear from heaven and will forgive their sin and will heal their land. James 4:10 Humble yourselves before YHUH, and he will lift you up. (Deut 28:10)

My beloved, if you are My chosen child and you live in Israel-your land-and you unite with other believers and humble yourself by fasting and praying, I will hear your prayers and heal the land that I have given you. If you live in exile and judgment is about to be cast on the country where you live, then go to a new country and I will show you where to live. I will be calling all My children back to My Land soon and together you will unite and prepare for the last days. You will know that I have gone before you, because I will open a wide door for My children to come to My Land. Now many want to harm My Land, but soon I will remove all My enemies and they will be no more than empty wastelands. I will take back all My Land for Me and My people. No longer will My Land be in the hands of pagans who worship false gods. My Land will be filled with My people who love Me and I will heal the land and restore all the treasures to the Land and bring up hidden treasure for My children. You must listen to My voice and go where I say go and wait when I say wait. If you are waiting for Me to open a door for you, then I will. You must trust Me to bring you back to the Land of your forefathers. I will bless you and allow you to live on the Land I have given to you.

136

You should not buy, sell, or trade on Sabbath.

Neh 10:31 When the neighboring peoples bring merchandise or grain to sell on the Sabbath, we will not buy from them on the Sabbath or on any holy day. (Neh 13:15-17, Ex 20:8-11, John 2:13-16)

My beloved, do not conduct any business on My Sabbaths. Do not exchange any money. Do not buy any item whether with cash or credit card. Do not sell or negotiate a sale of an item on Sabbath. Do not make a trade of an item whether no money is involved or not. You should not be thinking of how you can make a profit on My Sabbath. You should be thinking of how you can draw closer to Me on My day. You should long to have Sabbaths come, so you can put aside all those things of the world and just rest and spend time with Me. Draw closer to Me by reaching out to Me and hearing My voce for guidance. If you are grieved on My Sabbath when you cannot do as you wish, then do not even keep My Sabbaths. That is why I took the Sabbath away from My people, because they were an abomination to Me. They took My Sabbath and worshipped other gods on it and they dreaded when it would come, because they had to stop work and not make a profit. Many of My children act the same way today. Either they do not keep seventh day Sabbath or either they dread when Sabbath comes, because it is such an inconvenience to them. If you love Me, you will love My Sabbaths and want to spend the day with Me enjoying My Company. I will bless you for your diligence to serve Me.

137

You should trust YHUH to protect you.

Ps 91:9 If you make the Most High your dwelling-even YHUH, who is my refuge-10 then no harm will befall you, no disaster will come near your tent. Ps 27:5 For in the day of trouble He will keep me safe in His dwelling. Ps 121:7 YHUH will keep you from all harm- He will watch over your life; Prov 12:21 No harm overtakes the righteous, but the wicked have their fill of trouble. (1 Sam 17:41-45)

My beloved, you don't realize that angels are around you protecting you from the evil ones. As long as you call on My Name for protection and cling to Me and My Name, then you will always be covered by My Hand and be protected. Perilous times are approaching for the children of men. If you are My child, I will protect you even during the darkest of days. Economies may crash and nations fall. Wars may tear at the world and destroy land, people, and property. The earth may rock and shift. Strange things may appear in the heavens-things you have never seen before. Even though all these things come upon the earth, you will be protected from all of them. I will guide you to safe places and instruct you how to avoid the dangers. You will listen and obey, and you will be safe. If you see dangers and horrors, you must look at it for what it is-the evil ones-a delusion-judgment on the wicked. David saw the giant, but he knew I would protect him. He was not afraid. You must look at horrors and not be afraid. You must call on Me to protect you. Men will lose their minds over the dangers and horrors that will come upon them, but you will trust in Me to protect you. You must know that legions of angels surround you and fight for you on My behalf, so be brave and strong and trust Me to protect you.

138

You should trust YHUH to protect your children.

Ps 102:28 The children of your servants shall dwell secure; their offspring shall be established before you. Job 1:8 Then YHUH said to Satan, "Have you considered my servant Job? There is no one on earth like him; he is blameless and upright, a man who fears YHUH and shuns evil." 9 "Does Job fear YHUH for nothing?" Satan replied. 10 "Have you not put a hedge around him and his household and everything he has? You have blessed the work of his hands, so that his flocks and herds are spread throughout the land." (Ps 89:4, Ps 69:36)

My beloved, if you trust in Me to care for you, I will protect you and your children. I will lift you up above the circumstances. I will put a hedge of protection around you and your children. I will cover you with My hand. I will keep you and your family close to My side. My servants will minister to you and hold you close, so no harm comes to you. If you do not trust Me and you are fearful and think that danger is around every corner, then you open a door for the enemy to come in and defeat you. Fear is not a product of trust. In Me there is no fear. If you trust in Me, you will be at peace and no fear will overtake you. If you walk in Me, you walk in peace. Rejoice and be glad that you have a Father who loves you so much and protects you day and night, so you can prosper and be in good health. You should always trust Me even when things happen that you do not understand—even when your plans are not successful. I have a purpose for you and My plan for you will stand. You will be used greatly for My kingdom, if only you trust Me and allow Me to guide you. Trust Me with your whole heart and I will protect you and your children.

139

You should make a covenant with your eyes not to lust after anyone.

Job 31:1 "I made a covenant with my eyes not to look lustfully at a girl." 1 John 2:16 For everything in the world-the cravings of sinful man, the lust of his eyes, and the boasting of what he has and does-comes not from the Father but from the world. 17 The world and its desires pass away, but the man who does the will of Elohim lives forever. Matt 5:28 But I tell you that anyone who looks at a woman lustfully has already committed adultery with her in his heart. (Matt 6:22)

My beloved, guard carefully over your eyes. Do not lust after others. Do not look with desire on others and want to commit adultery or fornication. Do not desire to sin against your body and pollute yourself, but carefully guard over your eyes and do not allow them to wander. Keep your eyes on what is clean and pure. Keep your eyes focused on the things that are loving and kind. If you are tempted, turn your eyes away quickly so you do not fall into sin. There are many who love to sin and will try to make you sin. Beware. You must be on guard all the time, and do not allow the enemy to catch you off guard. When you look for a mate, look for someone who has kept himself pure and has carefully tried not to fall into sin. This is a person who loves Me and wants to do only what is right. This is a person who will continue to be faithful in marriage and will not sin against you by committing adultery. If you seek carefully and ask Me to help you find a mate, then I will guide you and you will find the one I have chosen for you. If you are careful with your eyes and guard them from sin, then I will bless you and you will have success.

140

You should not become impatient with YHUH.

Is 5:18 You are doomed! You are unable to break free from your sins. 19 You say, "We want YHUH to speed up His work, to hurry it along, so we can see it! We want the YHUH of Israel's plan to come true right now, so we can be sure if it!" Is 7:13 Then Isaiah said, "Hear now, you house of David! Is it not enough to try the patience of men? Will you try the patience of my Elohim also?" Is 25:1 YHUH, you are my Elohim; I will exalt you and praise your name, for in perfect faithfulness you have done wonderful things, things planned long ago. (Jer 17:15, Num 16:9)

My beloved, who are you to question Me? Who are you to say, "Why can't it happen today? Hurry up. I cannot wait any longer." You can wait and you must be patient to wait, because My timing is always perfect and My plan for you is perfect. You must trust Me to bring it all together for you. If I have spoken to you a word of what I will do in the future, then I will do it. I AM faithful, but I AM steadfast. Time in not a hindrance to Me. I do not look at time and say, "Time is running out." I have planned precisely and each element will follow in line one after another. You have been given warnings about the last days and what will happen. You know what to expect, but you cannot hurry these events. You must know that I will help you and protect you every day-through good and bad. You must trust Me and know that all things will come in due time just as I have spoken. Your flesh wants to have it happen today, so quiet your flesh. Fast and pray and get your flesh under control. If you humble yourself, then you will not cry out what you want, but you will cry out, "Your will be done." You will trust Me to complete all those things I have promised and do it in a way that will give victory to all of My children, so be patient with Me and trust Me.

141

You should stand firm in your faith.

Is 7:9 If you do not stand firm in your faith, you will not stand at all. Is 26:2 Open the gates that the righteous nation may enter, the nation that keeps faith. 3 You will keep in perfect peace him whose mind is steadfast, because he trusts in you. Hab 2:4 See, he is puffed up; his desires are not upright- but the righteous will live by his faith. (Heb 10:38, Rom 1:17, Gal 3:11)

My beloved, you must live by faith. You must trust Me to take care of you and protect you. You are My child. Why would I desert you? You must believe in Me that I will meet all your needs. I hear you cry out to Me with all your troubles and I will deliver you from all of them. You must have faith to believe that I AM faithful and I do not speak lies, but all My promises will come to pass. The problem with My children comes when they are disobedient and they do not repent when they sin, and then they are punished for their disobedience. Do not think that I will not punish My child for his sin. I must teach My child the correct way to go, and if he wants to rebel against My ways, then I will not spare the rod. You know yourself that a child left unpunished becomes rebellious and disrespectful to all authority and wants to have his own way. None of My children will be allowed to rebel and not be punished. You must obey Me and serve Me in all you do, and then you will prosper and be able to walk in My promises. I will not bless rebellious children who will not listen to My words. If you are not prospering today, look at your life and repent and do what is right in My sight. You will then walk in faith, because you know that you can receive all the promises I have given you. Do not be afraid when men persecute you for keeping My laws. I AM your Rock. When you stand on Me, you cannot be moved. You must continue to stand firm in the faith no matter if all others around you disobey Me. Stand in your faith, and I will deliver you in times of troubles.

142

You should not carry out plans that are not YHUH's plans. You should not form an alliance without YHUH's guidance.

Is 30:1-2 "Woe to the obstinate children," declares YHUH, "to those who carry out plans that are not mine, forming an alliance, but not by my Spirit, heaping sin upon sin; 2 who go down to Egypt without consulting me; who look for help to Pharaoh's protection, to Egypt's shade for refuge." Prov 19:21 Many are the plans in a man's heart, but it is YHUH's purpose that prevails. Ps 33:11 But the plans of YHUH stand firm forever, the purposes of his heart through all generations. (Ps 33:10, Prov 16:1, Prov 16:9)

My beloved, do not make your own plans without asking Me for counsel. Call upon Me to give you wisdom, so all your plans can be secure. Should you go to other sources to plan your future? No, you should come to Me first, and I will guide you. I may send you to another person to help you or I many bring another person to you to help you, but if you do not seek Me, then how can I help you with your problems? So many people go to someone to help them plan their retirement or their financial portfolio. You should come to Me to help you make all your plans for the future. If you come to Me first in all matters, I will bless you with wisdom and your path will be successful. If you do not want to follow My plan for you, then I will spoil all your plans until you submit yourself to Me and stop your rebellious ways. I can shake an economy or destroy it in a day, and if your faith is in currency, then you will fall. If your faith is in Me, then I can lead you past all the problems and disasters and you will not be touched by the world system. Armies may invade, but I will shelter you. You may have the enemy all around you, but I will cover you. Have no fear, but trust Me in all you do and I will care for you.

143

You should not look at anything evil.

Is 33:15 He who walks righteously and speaks what is right, who rejects gain from extortion and keeps his hand from accepting bribes, who stops his ears against plots of murder and shuts his eyes against looking at evil- 16 this is the man who will dwell on the heights, whose refuge will be the mountain fortress. His bread will be supplied, and water will not fail him. Ps 119:37 Turn my eyes away from worthless things; preserve my life according to your word. Num 15:39 You will have these tassels to look at and so you will remember all the commands of YHUH, that you may obey them and not prostitute yourselves by chasing after the lusts of your own hearts and eyes.

My beloved, who is righteous? Who may come before Me? Who may stand in My sacred place and speak his requests? Who may be at one with Me? Who will be free from the lake of fire? Only My servants-those who love Me-who want to do what is right will be at one with Me. Their heart is bent towards Me and they try to keep all My laws. It grieves them not to keep My laws. They want to escape those who are evil-those who want to drag them into their lies and deceit. My child will want to be far from them. My child runs from evil and shuts his eyes to the evil of this world and will not allow evil to come into his house. He will stand strong at the gates of his house and protect it like a mighty giant, so no evil can come in. He will do what is right towards others. He will treat others fairly. He will want to be just. He will not speak lies or take money to change the truth to benefit others. He will be true to Me and not be swayed by money or the power that it brings. My child loves the poor and needy and wants to benefit them. He will extend his hand to those in need. He will reach out and help them up. He will search My words for truth and meditate on My words looking for all the treasure he can find in My words knowing that all riches come from Me. This man will always have food and water and will be greatly blessed.

144

You should not be afraid.

Is 43:1 But now, this is what YHUH says-He who created you, O Jacob, He who formed you, O Israel: Fear not, for I have redeemed you; I have summoned you by name; you are mine. 5 Do not be afraid, for I am with you; I will bring your children from the east and gather you from the west. 6 I will say to the north, 'Give them up!' and to the south, 'Do not hold them back.' Bring my sons from afar and my daughters from the ends of the earth- 7 everyone who is called by my name, whom I created for my glory, whom I formed and made." Luke 12:6 Are not five sparrows sold for two pennies? Yet not one of them is forgotten by Elohim. 7 Indeed, the very hairs of your head are all numbered. Don't be afraid; you are worth more than many sparrows. (Mark 5:35-42)

My beloved, you should not fear anything as long as you trust in Me. You should not be afraid of people-governments who press you with laws to devour your faith in Me. You should not fear disaster, because all judgment is brought upon a place by Me because of their wickedness. I will tell you to move away from that place because judgment is coming or I will protect you in the midst of the judgment. No matter what befalls the land, I will protect you because you are Mine. If you are not keeping My commandments, then you should be afraid, because My judgment-My wrath-will be poured out on you until you repent and keep My commandments. Do you know what My commandments are? Do you know if you are subject to My judgments? What laws did I give Moses? Are these laws forever? If they were given to My people as life instructions, then aren't you My people? Aren't you supposed to keep My laws? What punishments will come upon you, if you don't' keep My commandments? You should never be afraid, but you should fear Me and tremble if you are not obeying My laws. You must love Me enough to obey Me. You must love Me with all your heart, so you keep all My laws. They are your life-your protection-My hands wrapped around you-a barrier against all evil.

Which Commandments Should I Obey?

145

You should not question YHUH and His plans for you.

Is 45:6 So that from the rising of the sun to the place of its setting men may know there is none besides Me. I am YHUH, and there is no other. 7 I form the light and create darkness, I bring prosperity and create disaster; I, YHUH, do all these things. 9 "Woe to him who argues with his Maker, to him who is but a clay pot among the clay pots on the ground. Does the clay say to the potter, 'What are you making?' Does your work say, 'He has no hands'? 10 Woe to him who says to his father, 'What have you begotten?' or to his mother, 'What have you brought to birth?' 11 This is what YHUH says-the Holy One of Israel, and its Maker: Concerning things to come, do you question Me about my children, or give Me orders about the work of my hands? 12 It is I who made the earth and created mankind upon it." (Rom 9:20-21)

My beloved, I have created you for a purpose. I have made you like no other human beings. You are unique-special-set apart to do a good work. You are what I want you to be. Do not question why I have created you as such. You have a unique plan that only I know and I have proclaimed don't question Me and say, "Why did you form me in such a way? or Why do you want me to do such a thing?" instead say, "What is it that you want me to do? I am your servant and I will do all you ask. I know whatever you ask of me will be what is best for me and my family." If you will try to please Me in all you do and say, then you will prosper and you will have success. Many say day after day, "Why are you letting this happen to me?" If there is sin in your life, then you will have bad things happen to you. If you want Me to bless you, then repent and do what is good in My sight. Who are you to question Me? You know nothing. I know all things. Your fleshly body has kept you from understanding the spiritual things of My kingdom, because you cannot comprehend them. Only if I reveal it to you and take the hidden and make it real to you do you understand anything about Me. Call on Me to make Myself real to you. Call on Me to make My plans for you real to you, so you can walk in all I have for you while you are here on earth.

146

You should not fear the insults of men.

Is 51:7 "Hear me, you who know what is right, you people who have my law in your hearts: Do not fear the reproach of men or be terrified by their insults. 8 For the moth will eat them up like a garment; the worm will devour them like wool. But my righteousness will last forever, my salvation through all generations." (Is 50:7-9, Matt 5:11)

My beloved, many men will insult you and mock you because you love Me and My ways, but do not fear them. I will blow away the thrash around you and leave only what is of value. I will keep My people close to Me. I will cover them by My Hand and keep them from their enemies. If men hate you, then love them. They will admire you for your steadfast love towards others, and they will know that only a loving Elohim could fill you with so much love. You should not look at men and tremble, but boast of what I have done for you. You should be bold and strong and tell others the truth about My ways. If you share My love with others and do not condemn others, then My truth can speak though you and men will hear and believe. Not all men will receive Me. Only My children will receive the truth about Me gladly. The Evil One has children mixed among My children, so on the last day I will send My angels to take up My little ones who are sealed by My spirit and they will be caught up with Me in the air and become part of My army who totally destroys all our enemies and takes back all the Land for us. You will then live in a Land of peace and no man will insult you or mock you, but you will live with all men in peace. Do not fear men, but fear Me who sends My laws to purge your heart.

147

You should fast. You should not do as you wish when you fast. You should give to the needy when you fast.

Is 58:3 "Why have we fasted," they say, "and you have not seen it? Why have we humbled ourselves, and you have not noticed?" Yet on the day of your fasting, you do as you please and exploit all your workers. 5 Is this the kind of fast I have chosen, only a day for a man to humble himself? Is it only for bowing one's head like a reed and for lying on sackcloth and ashes? Is that what you call a fast, a day acceptable to YHUH? 6 Is not this the kind of fasting I have chosen: to loosen the chains of injustice and untie the cords of the yoke, to set the oppressed free and break every yoke? 7 Is it not to share your food with the hungry and to provide the poor wanderer with shelter-when you see the naked, to clothe him, and not to turn away from your own flesh and blood? 8 Then your light will break forth like the dawn, and your healing will quickly appear; then your righteousness will go before you, and the glory of YHUH will be your rear guard. 9 Then you will call, and YHUH will answer; you will cry for help, and He will say, "Here am I." (Neh 1:4, Dan 10:12, Mark 2:18-20)

My beloved, if you fast and humble yourself, then do not do as you please, but be loving and kind to others. Do not be hard on those around you, because your stomach is hungry. Submit your flesh to My spirit and do as I desire for you to do. Give to the poor and needy the food you would have eaten for the day. If you know of a brother in need, go to him and help him. If you come to one who needs help, help him. If you know of those who are sick, go to them and comfort them and pray for them. These are the ways to make you fasts heard in My sacred place. If you force others to labor while you fast, what kind of fast is this? Fast on a day when your laborers rest and you don't have to oversee them, so you can go about doing good things for others. If you know of elderly who are lonely, go visit them. If there are children who live in a shelter, care for them and give them love for that day. If you know of agencies that need volunteers, then go help them for that day. You say when you fast you cannot do any of these things because your flesh is in so much pain, then do what you can do but do not oppress others around you with unkind words and your complaints of hunger. I would rather you not fast. If you do fast and promote loving kindness, I will hear your prayers and come to you and help you.

148

You should stop false accusation and slander.

Is 58:9 If you will remove the yoke from among you, stop false accusation and slander, 10 generously offer food to the hungry and meet the needs of the person in trouble; then your light will rise in the darkness and your gloom become like noon. 11 YHUH will always guide you; He will satisfy your needs in the desert, He will renew the strength in your limbs; so that you will be like a watered garden, like a spring whose water never fails. (Prov 10:10, 18, Ex 23:1)

My beloved, do not falsely accuse your brother or speak wickedness about anyone. Do not point your finger and say they have done something when they have not. Take responsibility for your own actions. If you have done wrong, then do not blame others. Admit your sins and repent. Do not falsely accuse someone of something you have done to cover up your own sins. This grieves Me. You must not lie. I hate liars and I hate falsehood. Satan is a liar and the author of all lies. He takes truth and twists it and deceives all who will listen. He wants no one to have truth, but all people to go to the lake of fire so none of My children will survive. Only My children who are called by My name-My seed of righteousness- will not fall into his trap. They will cling to Me and lies will not be in their mouths. They will not slander others or gossip about others, but they will build up others and encourage others with their words. They will use the power of their tongue to strengthen and not destroy. They will want to take others by the hand and guide them into righteousness and not bring them into darkness. You must be strong in these last days not to bend to evil, but to stand firm and not move. You must be strong enough to help the weak along the way. Use your words to help others. Stand beside them in prayer and the light within you will arise like the dawn and be a shining light for those around you. Be strong. Be brave. The days are dark. You must be on guard. Allow no lies to come forth from your mouth. Allow only My words to be spoken, and you will shield those around you and be a mighty tower for those in trouble.

149

You should not seek your own pleasure on Sabbath.

Is 58:13 "If you keep your feet from breaking the Sabbath and from doing as you please on my holy day, if you call the Sabbath a delight and YHUH's holy day honorable, and if you honor it by not going your own way and not doing as you please or speaking idle words, 14 then you will find your joy in YHUH, and I will cause you to ride on the heights of the land and to feast on the inheritance of your father Jacob." The mouth of YHUH has spoken. (Is 56:1-2, Ex 31:16- 17, Ex 35:2, Jer 17:21-22)

My beloved, you should delight in My Sabbaths and long for Sabbath to come, so you can rest in My presence. If you delight in Sabbath, then you will not be doing as you please, but you will be at one with Me. Do not pursue your own interests or do what you do on a usual day, but rest and be at peace. Allow your body to rest and let peace fill your heart. In such a stressful world, you need time to rest and be at peace. Do not seek after your own pleasure or do not even speak about your own pleasures, but think about Me. Sabbath is a good day to hear My voice and find direction-to gather with family-and bring unity between your family. If you have trouble between family members, then start the family members praying together and your problems will stop. Your children will learn to seek My face, and not turn aside from My ways. They will flourish in Me and become wise. If you teach your children My words on Sabbath, they will learn from Me and grow. Be kind and loving to your children and teach them how to walk in love. You must not teach your children the ways of the world. Close all portals on Sabbath-no TV, no computer, no worldly books or magazines, but only read My words and enjoy your family. This is a good time to draw closer together as a family. Seal out all unbelievers and devote this time only to praise Me and learn of Me, and then you will prosper and have success.

150

You should pray for the peace of Jerusalem.

Is 62:6 I have posted watchmen on your walls, O Jerusalem; they will never be silent day or night. You who call on YHUH, give yourselves no rest, 7 and give him no rest till he establishes Jerusalem and makes her the praise of the earth. Ps 122:6 Pray for the peace of Jerusalem: May those who love you be secure. (Is 66:10, Gen 12:3)

My beloved, pray for the peace of Jerusalem, the land of My children. This is My land that I have chosen. I have placed My mark there saying this is the land of My children. No one can touch My land unless I allow it. If you go to My land you will see war and destruction and you will wonder why this is happening. My children have sinned and they are paying the price for their sins. If you sin, you are punished. If the peoples of a land shed innocent blood, the land cries out to Me for vengeance and I hear and I extend My Hand to destroy those who are killers-murderers. If you live in such a wicked place, I will show you where to go until it is time for you to stay with Me. If you love Jerusalem and dwell within her gates, you know the dangers and your prayers are fervent. If you live far away and have never seen your land, you should still pray because one day soon I will call you to come to Me and dwell with Me in My city- the one I have chosen. My city has great treasures that are hidden, but will be revealed in the last days. The evil one knows it has value to Me, but he is not aware of how much value-only I know these hidden things. So pray for peace for all My people. Many of My children are in Jerusalem and the surrounding areas. Many are in exile and are suffering, because they have lifted up My name and the evil one wants them to die. Pray for their protection and peace for all of My children.

151

You should not do whatever you want to do.

Jer 3:4 "Have you not just called to Me: 'My Father, my friend from my youth, 5 will you always be angry? Will your wrath continue forever?' This is how you talk, but you do whatever you want to do." (Jer 3:12-15, Hos 2:15)

My beloved, I have given you my laws and I have given you My ways of having a good life. Why would you want to disobey Me when I only want to bring you good things? I want to teach you the way of love and compassion for others and how to walk in righteousness. I want you to walk in wisdom and be on a higher plane than those of the earth. You should see with eyes of gold and trust in Me with all your heart. You should want to please Me, because you love Me. You should not do as you please breaking all My commandments. You should want to serve Me with your whole heart. Do not be rebellious, but put aside all your worldly ways and cling to Me. You may live in exile, but you can still walk in righteousness. You may have no one around you who wants to serve Me, but you can still be an obedient child and your rewards will be great. You may only be a witness where you are placed for a short time–a light in a dark place, but if you allow your love to be a light to others, you will make a difference when you are there only for a short time. Do not be afraid of the future, but trust Me to guide you. The pathway I chose for you is right for you, but no one else can follow along behind you. You must do as I say, and you will be protected in the last days. Listen to My voice, and do not do as you please.

152

You should accept correction from YHUH.

Jer 6:8 Accept correction, O Jerusalem, or I will turn away from you and make your land desolate so no one can live in it. Job 5:17 Blessed is the man whom YHUH corrects; so do not despise the discipline of the Almighty. 18 For He wounds, but He also binds up; He injures, but His hands also heal. Ps 94:12 Blessed is the one you discipline, YHUH, the one you teach from your law. (Job 36:10, Deut 5:29)

My beloved, do not refuse My correction, but listen to My voice and when you disobey Me, repent quickly. Do not allow your heart to become hard and push Me away from you. You will suffer the consequences. You will pay for every one of your sins. You will not be able to prosper, and disaster will follow you. Be brave and strong, and do not be influenced by the world. All those who love the world will die and they will be no more, but My children who walk in righteousness I will give them the gift of eternal life and the ability to live at one with Me forever. No longer will you wear a suit of flesh, but you will be clothed with power from Me. You will have authority to speak and it will be done, because you are a child of the King of the Universe. You will be an extension of My hand. You will reach out the scepter and you will be able to have authority over all those under your care. You must learn to obey all My laws and walk in My ways, so you learn the ways of life and you can teach others around you how to walk in love just like your Father has shown you. If you do stumble, repent quickly and accept how I correct you. The pain of My lash is only for a moment. Be humble under your correction and do not sin again, so you can receive blessings from My hand.

Which Commandments Should I Obey?

153

You should not reject the laws of YHUH.

Jer 6:19 Hear, O earth: I am bringing disaster on this people, the fruit of their schemes, because they have not listened to my words and have rejected my law. (Jer 8:8, Is 5:24, Deut 8:19)

My beloved, do not reject My laws. Do not reject My words. Do not set your face against Me, but turn to Me and accept all My laws and receive all My promises. Many men of religion have said that My laws are for other generations-not today, but My laws are everlasting-perfect laws that do not need to be revised. You can apply the laws that I gave to Moses to your life today, because they were written for My people so you would be able to live a good life based on love, compassion, fairness, and justice. No man should be given greater elevation than the other man. All of My children are equal in My eyes, and you should judge all men fairly. You should love your brother and even your enemies that hate Me. You should be a light to all those around you. You should rejoice over My loving-kindness that I have poured over you, so that you are greatly blessed if you keep My laws. You are not wise unless you can submit yourself to Me and follow My laws. All wisdom is found in My words. No man can give you wisdom. Wisdom only comes from Me. Guard over yourself and do not accept instruction from men unless they follow My laws. If you do all that My laws say to do, you will not carry a heavy burden, but you will have life and you will be complete in Me, and then you will understand WISDOM.

170

154

You should not trust a person who slanders or deceives others.

Jer 9:3-9 YHUH says, "My people do one evil thing after another and do not acknowledge Me as their Elohim. 4 Everyone must be on guard against his friend, and no one can trust his brother; for every brother is as deceitful as Jacob, and everyone slanders his friends. 5 They all mislead their friends, and no one tells the truth; they have taught their tongues to lie and will not give up their sinning." Prov 10:18 He who conceals his hatred has lying lips, and whoever spreads slander is a fool. (Lev 19:16)

My beloved, do not trust anyone who delights in talking about others and tears down their character. If you see a brother in sin, go to him secretly and confront him about his sin. Do not tell his sin in public, but talk to him in love so he can repent and not be rebellious in his heart. If you love your brother and show him compassion, then he will be supported and will be strengthened and able to turn from his sin. A man who slanders others is a man who will slander you when given a chance, so do not trust him or be his friend. Anyone that delights in hurting others or tearing down their character in one form or other is a person who does not have love and have compassion for others in his heart. He is prideful, arrogant, haughty, and full of deceit. They are not one of My children, but they are sons of the wicked one. You must be careful, because the sons of the wicked ones are always filled with deceit and lies and want to hurt others at every turn. Their heart is dark and spiteful-full of hate. Be careful. Judge those around you. Do not take anyone into your confidence unless you can trust them. Judge others by the light they shine forth to others. Do you see their love and compassion for others? Then you can trust them.

155

You should only boast that you know YHUH.

Jer 9:23 This is what YHUH says: "Let the wise man not boast of his wisdom or the strong man boast of his strength or the rich man boast of his riches, 24 but let him who boasts boast about this: that he understands and knows Me, that I am YHUH, who exercises kindness, justice and righteousness on earth, for in these I delight," declares YHUH. 2 Cor 10:17 But, "Let the one who boasts boast in YHUH." (1 Cor 1:31)

My beloved, boast of all My wondrous works. Boast that you know the Creator of the Universe and you speak with Me daily-are at one with Me daily. Rejoice that you are My child and boast of your inheritance-the things I have given you-My Land, riches from My kingdom-the gifts of the spirit: love, kindness, joy, and peace. Know that I give only good things to those who love Me-who seek Me with your whole heart. Do you boast of earthly riches? What profit will worldly riches bring you? Those riches will pass away and be no more, but the riches from My kingdom are eternal. Do you boast of power and control? Who gave you power and control? Power and control come from Me, because I control all things. I allow men to have power only if it is in My plan and it will benefit Me. Do you boast of strength? Strength will pass away in old age. It is temporary and will not last forever. The things of the flesh—beauty and strength last only for a season and then they are gone, but the gifts I give are eternal. Boast only of the gift I give-salvation-and tell men how I came to earth and died, so they could be saved. I shed My blood so you could live making you My child and having eternal life to reign with Me. Boast of these things, and then you will be blessed.

156

You should listen to YHUH in times of prosperity.

Jer 22:21 I spoke to you in your prosperity, But you said, 'I will not hear.' This has been your manner from your youth, that you did not obey My voice. 22 The wind shall eat up all your rulers, and your lovers shall go into captivity; surely then you will be ashamed and humiliated for all your wickedness. Prov 30:8 Keep deception and lies far from me. Give me neither poverty nor riches. Feed me with the food that is my portion, that I not be full and deny You and say, "Who is YHUH?" or that I not be in want and steal, and profane the name of my Elohim. (Jer 3:25)

My beloved, if you listen to Me in your time of prosperity, you will not have to be concerned about the famine or the sword, because it will not come near to you. I will speak to you and say, "Get up. Leave this place and do not return. Take all your possessions and leave." You will get up and prepare you and your family to leave. You will put your house in order so you can leave. You will not have to flee by night or through dangerous areas. If you listen to Me, I will tell you in advance and you will see the path to travel long before you go. You will have time to put all your affairs in order before you leave. You will walk not run, because danger will not be coming upon your heels as you leave. You will be able to safety do as I say. Those who do not listen in time of prosperity will say, "I like it here and My family is here. This is the land where I was raised. My job or my business is here." They will feel secure and remain in a false happiness, but they were not listening and their future grows dim. They say they are praying and do-ing good deeds for others, but their heart is far from Me. You must wake up and listen. The days grow dark, and only those who love Me will walk in My ways.

157

You should pray for the city in which you live to prosper.

Jer 29:7 Also, seek the peace and prosperity of the city to which I have carried you into exile. Pray to YHUH for it, because if it prospers, you too will prosper. 1 Tim 2:1 First of all, then, I urge that entreaties and prayers, petitions and thanksgivings, be made on behalf of all men, for kings and all who are in authority, so that we may lead a tranquil and quiet life in all godliness and dignity. (Eph 6:18)

My beloved, seek My face and pray humbly towards Me for the prosperity of the city where you live, and that the city may live in peace. Even though you live in exile if you cry out to Me, I will bless you where you are planted. In a short time I will call you back to My Land, and you will build a place there and prosper. I will keep you safe from your enemies, and I will prosper your family and make you stable and unmovable. I will help you with your trip back to My Land. I will open doors for you, so you can come. I will lay it upon the leaders of the country to open its gates, and allow all My People to enter. Now this is not the time. The land is at siege. Its neighbors on all sizes want to destroy My Land and divide it. If you think you can divide My Land among its enemies and not see Me come forward to pronounce judgment on the Land, then think again. I will come forth with a mighty force and cast My Hand against everyone who tries to divide My Land. My Wrath will be cast on these nations who take from My Land. If you live in any of these nations, you better leave quickly. The time is ripe for its punishment. Flee to another land, and establish yourself there. Pray for yourself and your family and your city, and I will hear and prosper your city. Do not place yourself in a nation who is an enemy to Israel.

158

You should flee from Babylon (a land who worships pagan gods).

Jer 51:6, "Flee from Babylon! Run for your lives! Do not be destroyed because of her sins. It is time for YHUH's vengeance; He will pay her what she deserves." 24 "Before your eyes I will repay Babylon and all who live in Babylonia for all the wrong they have done in Zion," declares YHUH. Zech 2:7 "Come, O Zion! Escape, you who live in the Daughter of Babylon!" Rev 18:4 Then I heard another voice from heaven say: "Come out of her, my people, so that you will not share in her sins, so that you will not receive any of her plagues." (Num 16:26, Deut 30:4, Is 48:20)

My beloved, flee from the land who worships other gods day and night, because judgment is coming and you will be covered by it if you do not escape. You say, "All the countries of the earth worship other gods. Where can I go to escape judgment?" Call on Me and I will guide you. Call on My Name, and I will open a door for you to escape. I will show you the place to go. Judgment falls on a country only when it is ripe-when its sins have mounted up against it and the people have done more evil then good-when the people have turned their hearts against Me and do as they want to do. They care only about themselves. They put themselves up as gods. You will see them be torn down and scattered, destroyed, taken captive by their enemies-the people they trusted in to save them. If you will listen and follow My instructions, I will show you a way out, and you will escape the coming judgment. I have been looking for those who love Me, and I have found them. I have spoken that I will send a call out for My Children who serve Me, and they will leave before destruction comes. Listen, the watchmen are on the wall calling, "Flee Babylon. Flee Babylon. Her destruction is at hand!"

159

You should delight in the Sabbath and not be grieved by having to keep Sabbath.

Amos 8:2 Then YHUH said to me, "The time is ripe for my people Israel; I will spare them no longer. In that day," declares the Sovereign YHUH, "the songs in the temple will turn to wailing. Many, many bodies-flung everywhere! Silence!" 4 Hear this, you who trample the needy and do away with the poor of the land, 5 saying, "When will the New Moon be over that we may sell grain, and the Sabbath be ended that we may market wheat?"skimping the measure, boosting the price and cheating with dishonest scales, 6 buying the poor with silver and the needy for a pair of sandals, selling even the sweepings with the wheat. (Ex 31:13)

My beloved, if you love Me, you will love My feast days. You will look forward to My days of celebration, so you can bring Me gifts and dance and sing with Me. You say, "I live in exile. I have hung my harp on the willow tree. I am grieved over all the people around me who do not love YHUH and do not want to celebrate His feast days. I long to sing, dance, and rejoice." I know your grief, but lift up your voice and rejoice over the many blessings I have given you. Rejoice. Sing. Dance. You have been given a gift of seeing how to please Me and enjoy My special days. You should not be sad that you are not in My Land, but be glad that I have brought Truth to your house in the midst of a land in famine-the famine of My Words-not knowing how to find Truth in My Words, but clinging to man-made laws. I will help you learn how to celebrate each feast day and be glad. I know you long to leave your place of exile, but the time for My People to be called back to their land is soon. Rejoice that you have a land to escape to in the last days, so I can cover you with My Hands. If you delight in My Sabbaths and feast days, I will delight in you. I will bless you and your family and bring you many gifts.

160

You should live only on the word of YHUH.

Matt 4:1 Then Yahshua was led by the Spirit into the desert to be tempted by the devil. 2 After fasting forty days and forty nights, He was hungry. 3 The tempter came to Him and said, "If you are the Son of YHUH, tell these stones to become bread." 4 Yahshua answered, "It is written: 'Man does not live on bread alone, but on every word that comes from the mouth of YHUH.'" (Deut 8:3)

My beloved, the Evil One came to tempt Me when I walked in the flesh, and My flesh was hungry. He wanted Me to demonstrate that I AM the Elohim of the universe. He underestimated Me in flesh and he wanted to make Me sin, but I refused. I had control over My flesh at all times. I lived a perfect life, because My nature is perfect so I can't deny Myself. I could have easily turned the stones into bread, but I wanted to be an example of faith. Whatever I did, I wanted My flesh to bring glory to the Father who rules all things. I wanted to show the evil one that I had submitted Myself to walk humbly in the flesh and not just do as I please. I came to save My Children from eternal darkness and to teach them My laws. I would not teach them as the religious teachers of the day were teaching them, but My Law was given to them to provide life. You can eat and be filled by digesting My Words. My Words are life and if you eat of My Words every day, you will find life more abundantly. Do not be deceived by the evil one when he tempts you. He will come trying to lead you away from Me, but speak My words of life and he will flee from you. To resist him you must know My Words or he will use My Words against you and deceive you. You must feel My Presence on you as you feed on My Words. My Spirit will guide you into all Truth and the evil one will not be able to turn you from Me.

161

You should not put YHUH to the test.

Matt 4:5 Then the devil took him to YHUH's city and had Him stand on the highest point of the temple. 6 "If you are the Son of YHUH," he said, "throw yourself down. For it is written: "'He will command his angels concerning you, and they will lift you up in their hands, so that you will not strike your foot against a stone.'" 7 Yahshua answered him, "It is also written: 'Do not put YHUH your Elohim to the test.'" Ex 17:7 And he called the place Massah and Meribah because the Israelites quarreled and because they tested YHUH saying, "Is YHUH among us or not?" (Deut 6:16)

My beloved, do not put Me to the test like My Children did in the desert when I took them out of the bondage of Egypt. They tested Me ten times. They complained against Me and tested Me with their disobedience and their lack of trust. They wanted to go back to Egypt and all the food they had in Egypt. They wanted to satisfy the desires of their flesh. They wanted to do as they pleased to keep their Egyptian gods and feasts to their gods. I took them to the desert to cleanse them from the land of Egypt. I killed all those who did not trust Me and took their children to the Promised Land. You must be careful not to test Me by complaining to Me about not having the things of the world or disobeying Me- knowing you are doing wrong. Do you think I will not see your outright disobedience? You must love Me. If you love Me with all your heart, mind, and strength, then you will be given the gift of eternal life and you will reign with Me forever. I will test you to see if you are faithful, but you do not test Me by questioning My will for you or complaining against Me or by rebelling against Me like My People did when they made a golden calf and worshipped it. You must love Me and obey Me, and then you will see how much I will bless you because you are obedient.

162

You should follow Yahshua.

Matt 4:18 As Yahshua was walking beside the Sea of Galilee, He saw two brothers, Simon called Peter and his brother Andrew. They were casting a net into the lake, for they were fishermen. 19 "Come, follow Me," Yahshua said, "and I will make you fishers of men." 20 At once they left their nets and followed Him. Matt 11:28 "Come to Me, all you who are weary and burdened, and I will give you rest. 29 Take my yoke upon you and learn from Me, for I am gentle and humble in heart, and you will find rest for your souls. 30 For my yoke is easy and my burden is light." (Ezek 47:10)

My beloved, do not grow weary under the weight of the world, but come to Me and I will lift your burden. I will make your burden easy to bear, because you call on My Name and you follow close to Me. If you allow Me to guide you as the yoke guides the oxen, then you will always go in the right direction. You will not suffer loss, but you will reap a bountiful harvest. If you come quickly and do not delay, then you can receive the most blessings. My timing is perfect. Do not question my timing, but do as I tell you to do. When I called My disciples, they recognized Me, and they dropped everything they were doing and came to Me. They followed Me and obeyed Me. Recognize My Voice and listen to Me, and you will do well. If you hear My Voice, then get up quickly! Do not delay and follow Me. Those who are obedient, I will bless. Those who ignore My call will suffer for their disobedience. I only call My Children- those who have My righteous seed-only those who will recognize My Voice-who know My Name, because I created them for a unique purpose-to be my sacred people-a nation of priests-to rule over nations. You say, "How can this be?" When I pull back the heavens for this earth and create it anew, I will scatter you among the nations and you will be My newly called disciples.

163

You should know you are spiritually poor.

Matt 5:3 Blessed are those who know they are spiritually poor; the kingdom of heaven belongs to them! James 2:5 Listen, my dear brothers and sisters: Has not YHUH chosen those who are poor in the eyes of the world to be rich in faith and to inherit the kingdom He promised those who love Him? Is 66:2 "Has not my hand made all these things, and so they came into being?" declares YHUH. "These are the ones I look on with favor: those who are humble and contrite in spirit, and who tremble at my word."

My beloved, blessed are you when you know you are lacking in the things of the Spirit and you long for Me, because I will give you the ability to enter My Kingdom. If you know you are dead in your sins without Me and you call out to Me to fill you and make you alive with My Spirit, then you have entered My Spiritual Kingdom. Do not be afraid to cry out to Me and ask Me to fill you, because great men have fallen because they did not call on Me to help them and fill them. If you know your own spiritual state and how you are lacking, then you have discernment. You are not lacking, but you know your own deficiencies, and you are not too prideful to call on Me for help. My Faithful call on Me all day long. When I hear their cries, I lean My ear close to them so I hear their every sigh. If you want to be close to Me, you must be intimate with Me. You must be at one with Me. You must be united with Me, so we work as one with each other and not against each other. If you love Me, you will walk side by side with Me. You will know right from wrong. You will run from darkness and cling to the Light. You will shun those that do not walk in the Light. You will not make excuses for them, but you will see clearly and want no part of them. That is when your Light will shine like the dawn.

164

You should be gentle to others.

Matt 5:5 Blessed are the meek (gentle), for they shall inherit the earth. Ps 37:10 A little while, and the wicked will be no more; though you look for them, they will not be found. 11 But the meek will inherit the land and enjoy great peace. Matt 11:29 Take my yoke upon you and learn from Me, for I am gentle and humble in heart, and you will find rest for your souls.

My beloved, My People are gentle and kind and slow to anger. My People are not aggressive and push people aside, but they bind up wounds and encourage others. These will inherit the Land-My Land that I give to only the faithful. When I return I will drive out the wicked and only the righteous will dwell in My Land. If you are My Child, you will walk in My Ways and be righteous in all you do. Do not think that you can treat others anyway you please and enter My Kingdom. You must be loving and kind, gentle, and caring. You must show My Love to others by your actions. Others will know you are My Children by your love for them. If those around you are filled with hatred and bitterness, do not absorb their hatred and bitterness, but resist those wicked spirits and be loving and kind. Your kindness will burn into those who are filled with hatred, and they will question their anger. Lift up your eyes and focus on Me and not the things of the world. Do not allow worldly things to pull you away from Me. Be on guard and live your life as one who sacrifices for others, then you will feel like you have become alive at last. I will help you, so you can become a person who is kind, loving, merciful, and do good things for others. Guard your tongue. Do not be harsh with others, but be gentle, and I will give you My Land as a reward.

165

You should hunger and thirst after righteousness.

Matt 5:6 Blessed are those who hunger and thirst for righteousness, for they will be filled. Is 49:10 They will neither hunger nor thirst, nor will the desert heat or the sun beat upon them. He who has compassion on them will guide them and lead them beside springs of water. John 7:37 On the last and greatest day of the Feast, Yahshua stood and said in a loud voice, "If anyone is thirsty, let him come to Me and drink. 38 Whoever believes in Me, as the Scripture has said, streams of living water will flow from within him."(John 4:13)

My beloved, do you desire to be righteous? Do you want to only do what is right? Do you read My words and search for the truth, so you know My Ways and always choose the right path? Then you are hungering and thirsting for righteousness, and I will bless you. I will show you the way, if you desire to know what is right. The flesh is strong and you must sacrifice your flesh every day, so you can put aside earthly desires and focus on the works of the spirit. You must always be on guard that you do not allow the world to suck you into its grip. You must be steadfast always doing what is right in My eyes. Only those who desire to find Me will find Me, and I will reward those who diligently seek Me. Be like the woman at the well and go tell all you know about My wondrous love and compassion for all men. Do not be mean to others, even if you have been raised by your parents not to associate with a certain group of people. No man is better than another just because he has a certain group of ancestors-whether Jacob or any man is in his linage. You must love others and have no prejudice. If you love Me and seek after Me, then you will love others and treat all men equally because My love will fill your heart. Keep your eyes open and read My Words for Truth, and you will be filled and be satisfied.

166

You should be pure in heart.

Matt 5:8 Blessed are the pure in heart, for they will see Elohim. Ps 24:4 He who has clean hands and a pure heart, who doesn't make vanities the purpose of his life or swear oaths just to deceive. 5 He shall receive a blessing from YHUH and justice from the Elohim of his salvation. 2 Sam 22:27 To the pure you show yourself pure, but to the devious you show yourself shrewd. Ps 51:10 Create in me a pure heart, O YHUH, and renew a steadfast spirit within me.

My beloved, blessed are those who keep their hearts pure and do not allow themselves to be filled with sin and unforgiveness. Forgive your brother and do not hold onto any wrongs others have done against you. Do not be filled with hatred and bitterness, but forgive those who have wronged you. It is better to forgive than be cast in hell. Forgiveness is a gift of love, and if you cannot forgive someone, then call on My name and I will help you forgive. I will heal the wounds the person inflicted on you, so you can forgive. I know some crimes against you are extremely hurtful, but you must forgive all men. You must remain pure before Me, or you will not see My face, but be cast aside in the lake of fire. Many men have longed to see Elohim, yet they have not kept themselves pure. They allowed hatred and bitterness to overtake them, and they did not want to forgive but to seek revenge. Some even murdered the person who wronged them to silent them, but still the wounds were not healed because they did not ask Me to help them forgive the person. I AM an Elohim of love. To become My heir you must also be full of love and forgiveness. People will hurt you and some will wound you, but forgive all men and remain pure in heart.

167

You should be a peacemaker.

Matt 5:9 Blessed are the peacemakers, for they will be called sons of Elohim. Jam 3:17 But the wisdom that comes from heaven is first of all pure; then peace-loving, considerate, submissive, full of mercy and good fruit, impartial and sincere. 18 Peacemakers who sow in peace raise a harvest of righteousness. (Num 25:10-13)

My beloved, be a person who always tries to make peace and not stir up discord among your brothers. If you desire to serve Me, you will want to make peace with everyone around you. If you create peace and not start arguments, then you will be called sons of the Most High Elohim. You are My Children, if you love others and promote peace and happiness. If you are evil, then you will stir up trouble and want to see others angry with each other and fighting with each other. You will delight in rumors and gossip and any kind of falsehood that will cause others to become angry. If you laugh at others who are hurting, you are not a peacemaker. No, you only want strife and to stir up hatred. You do not want to forgive, but to get revenge on all men who harm you. Open your eyes and see how loving others and forgiving others is far better than seeking revenge. Your body becomes filled with anger, bitterness, and hatred, and you pour out venom on all you talk to about how much you hate a person. You are ready to explode at any moment, because you are so filled with hatred. You are unkind, because your anger has consumed you. Be brave and strong, and turn aside from all un-forgiveness, so you can be saved and have eternal life with Me. Only if you love others can you be called a peacemaker.

168

You should rejoice when you are persecuted because of righteousness.

Matt 5:10 Blessed are those who are persecuted because of righteousness, for theirs is the kingdom of heaven. 11 Blessed are you when people insult you, persecute you and falsely say all kinds of evil against you because of Me. 12 Rejoice and be glad, because great is your reward in heaven, for in the same way they persecuted the prophets who were before you. 1 Peter 4:13 But rejoice that you participate in the sufferings of Yahshua, so that you may be overjoyed when His glory is revealed.

James 5:11 As you know, we count as blessed those who have persevered. You have heard of Job's perseverance and have seen what YHUH finally brought about. YHUH is full of compassion and mercy. 1 Peter 3:14 But even if you should suffer for what is right, you are blessed. "Do not fear their threats; do not be frightened."

My beloved, be brave because the days are growing dark, and the Evil One will try to rid the earth of all My little ones, so at last he can rule without their hindrance. He thinks he can succeed in this plan, but if he reads the words I gave My Prophets he would know I will protect all My Children. Some of My Children will die by the sword, because of their resistance. Some will be imprisoned, because they disagree with what is happening and call it injustice. Some of My People who listen will escape to the wilderness, and I will care for them. Where is this wilderness? I will call all My People to Israel, and when the Evil One sets himself up as an abomination to rule over all with his power and authority, you will flee from Jerusalem and all the surrounding areas to the wilderness. I will care for you there. You say, "I do not live in Israel," but I will call all My People to Israel, so I can care for them in the last days on My Land. I will come back to My Land and secure My Kingship, and the Evil One will be locked up for 1000 years. I will teach My Children My loving kind ways, and they will rejoice in it. You may be fearful when you hear this, but I cared for My People after I took them out of Egypt, so I can care for you and bring you bread from heaven also. It will be a glorious time for you. I will not feed you for 40 years like My Children who were rebellious in the Wilderness, but I will feed you only a few years because you will be obedient. So rejoice when others hate you, because you will be counted as faithful.

169

You should be the salt of the earth.

Matt 5:13 You are the salt of the earth. But if the salt loses its salt-iness, how can it be made salty again? It is no longer good for any-thing, except to be thrown out and trampled by men. Mark 9:50 "Salt is good, but if it loses its saltiness, how can you make it salty again? Have salt in yourselves, and be at peace with each other." Col 4:6 Let your speech always be with grace, as though seasoned with salt, so that you will know how you should respond to each person. (Lev 2:13)

My beloved you are the salt-what cleanses the earth of unrighteousness. You are the salt that heals the earth. You are the ones that open up the flood gates and bring cleansing to the land. If you lose your ability to cleanse and heal because of your unrighteousness, then what good are you? Are you fulfilling the plan I have for you? Are you being My Hands and Feet? You are My servants, and you are to walk upon this earth and change the places where you walk by spreading your love and compassion upon others. You are the one who can bring change to a lost and dying world. There are many who need your touch today. Open your eyes and see how you can help others around you. If you raise the standard of righteousness around you, then others will see your good works and they will want to change their lives, then you will be successful in walking in My ways. Be strong and brave, My little one. Be strong and brave and overcome the world. I will help you to stand firmly even in the darkest of days. Wash your hands and make them clean, so you can be salt to the world around you.

170

You should be a light to this world.

Matt 5:14 You are the light of the world. A city on a hill cannot be hidden. 15 Neither do people light a lamp and put it under a bowl. Instead they put it on its stand, and it gives light to everyone in the house. Prov 4:18 The path of the righteous is like the morning sun, shining ever brighter till the full light of day. 1 Thess 5:5 You are all children of the light and children of the day. We do not belong to the night or to the darkness. (Phil 2:15)

My beloved, you are supposed to be an example of love to others every day. Your good deeds and your loving kindness should set you apart from the others around you. The world should look at you and give praise to Me, because I have created you. You should be different from those around you-not wanting to pollute yourself, but to keep yourself clean pure and righteous. You are My Chosen Ones, and I scattered you to the nations and sent you into exile for your sin. Now you are returning to Me, and your light is a witness in the last days to all the nations so that all will see the love you have for Me. The earth will rock and quake and men will die of fear, but you will trust in Me and I will shelter you from the darkness and the tremors of the earth. I will put My Hand over you, and you will be safe. No other people will I cover with My Hand, so it will be an example to those in fear of My loving kindness for you. Many will have their eyes open and see because of the protection and mercy I give to you. You must be kind and loving to all those around you. You must be an example to others, so they can see your kind deeds and want to be kind like you are. If you are evil like those around you, where is the salt? Where is your light? Look up my little ones. Look to Me and know that if you serve Me, you serve a loving Father who wants you only to show love to others. Arise! Be pure and righteous before Me.

171

You should live such a righteous life that people seeing you do good deeds will have respect for your Father who is in heaven.

Matt 5:16 In the same way, let your light shine before men, that they may see your good deeds and praise your Father in heaven. 1 Peter 2:11 Dear friends, I urge you, as aliens and strangers in the world, to abstain from sinful desires, which war against your soul. 12 Live such good lives among the pagans that, though they accuse you of doing wrong, they may see your good deeds and glorify Elohim on the day He visits us.

My beloved, let the light of My Presence within you shine brightly for those around you by showing love for others. If you love others, those around you will notice and praise Me for your good works. The world is dark and the Evil One wants to destroy all those who are loving and kind, so the world will have no light to awaken the seed of righteousness. I protect My Children and guard over them, so they can continue to give to others and show compassion and mercy on others. If you love Me, you will want to show your love for others. You will think less of yourself and more of others. You will give generously to those in need around you. This can be done by giving a kind word to someone, spending time with someone to encourage him, running an errand for someone who is unable to do it himself, visiting the sick, praying for those in bondage or need healing, giving to the poor, needy, orphans or widows. The list is long and varied how you can show love to others. The world is watching to see what loving kind things you can do for others. The world takes note when you give from your heart. Those who love Me praise My Name and thank Me for you, because you give so freely the love you have received from Me. Give love to those who love Me, but also to those who do not know Me, so they can see love and a picture of loving kindness.

172

You should teach YHUH's laws. You should practice YHUH's laws.

Matt 5:17 Do not think that I have come to abolish the Law (given to Moses) or the (Old Testament) Prophets; I have not come to abolish them but to ulfill them. 18 I tell you the truth, until heaven and earth disappear, not the smallest letter, not the least stroke of a pen, will by any means disappear from the Law (given to Moses) until everything is accomplished. 19 Anyone who breaks one of the least of these commandments and teaches others to do the same will be called least in the kingdom of heaven, but whoever practices and teaches these commands will be called great in the kingdom of heaven. Rom 3:31 Do we, then, nullify the law by this faith? Not at all! Rather, we uphold the law. (Deut 8:11)

My beloved, anyone who teaches My Laws will be great in My Kingdom and will have great favor in My Eyes. Where are My Laws? They are the laws I gave Moses for My People. Moses taught My People My Laws in the desert, and they learned My instructions for life. They were not burdened with man-made laws, but they followed only My Ways. If you only teach My Laws to others, then you give them the gift of life and you will receive great rewards. Some men are confused by what laws they should teach and what I was referring to when I said, "I did not come to abolish the law or prophets but to fulfill them." My coming was prophesied in the laws and through the prophets-once to come as a Servant and lay down My life for My Children and again to come as a King and reign over all My Children and destroy all their enemies. I fulfilled the prophecies about coming as a Servant to die for you, and I will come soon to fulfill My reign over you. Beware because I am coming soon. I will not abolish any of the laws given to Moses, but I will correct them and put them into effect. Some take My laws and twist them to suit their own pleasure, but when I reign the laws will be pure and exact. I will teach My Children the laws exactly how they were meant to be kept, and all men will live in peace and harmony. I AM just and fair, and all men will look to Me as the shining star for generations and generations to come.

173

You should not murder.

Matt 5:21 You have heard that it was said to the people long ago, 'Do not murder, and anyone who murders will be subject to judgment.' 22 But I tell you that anyone who nurses anger against his brother will be subject to judgment. Gen 9:6 Whoever sheds human blood, by humans shall their blood be shed; for in the image of Elohim has Elohim made mankind. (Ex 20:13, Matt 19:18)

My beloved, I have told you not to murder-to kill an innocent person. If you are in war and your enemies are trying to take away your freedom and invade your land, then you should kill those who endanger your family. If you are in a war where your nation goes into another nation and tries to take away their freedom, then your nation is in error and will be punished. If the nation that you are invading is very wicked and your nation wants to stop the wickedness of that nation, then your nation will be rewarded. The invasion of your nation is used as judgment on the wicked nation for a season until they repent. Once the nation has been humbled, then it is time for restoration. If a man comes to your house to harm your family, you must protect your family from danger. If you do harm the person and he dies, then he has been judged for his sin. If a person enters your house and you tell him to leave and he does, then you should not punish him. If you are angry with someone and the anger becomes hatred and you want to kill the person, then you are in sin. Go to the person you hate and work out a time to sit down and talk about the problem. This may be very difficult for you to do, but I command you to resolve all your hatred against anyone so you can be free from sin. You cannot love others, if you have hatred in your heart for someone. Be brave and humble yourself, and go to them and resolve your differences. If the person has wronged you, then forgive him and then you will know true love.

174

You should not belittle your brother.

Matt 5:22 Again, anyone who says to his brother, 'Raca,' (you good for nothing) is answerable to the Sanhedrin. But anyone who says, 'You fool!' will be in danger of the fire of hell. Rom 14:10 Why do you criticize and pass judgment on your brother? Or you, why do you look down upon or despise your brother? For we shall all stand before the judgment seat of YHUH. Ecc 12:14 For YHUH will bring every deed into judgment, including every hidden thing, whether it is good or evil. (Rom 2:16)

My beloved, be careful of what you say to your brother. Do not judge him harshly with your words. If he is in sin, then rebuke him in secret and stay with him until he can overcome his sin. Do not belittle your brother in front of others and humiliate him in front of unbelievers, because he is My Seed-My Child. You are belittling Me and My Creation. Do not even consider this. This is an abomination to Me. If you have something against your brother, then go to him and resolve your differences so you will not say angry words against him. Be patient with your brother and love him and do good things for him. Help your brother become successful and prosperous, so he will have a good life. Then My Face will shine on you, and you will be blessed. Watch carefully over all the words you say for you will have to give an account of your life on Judgment Day. You will be judged according to your love towards others and how you love Me and trust in Me. Yes, you will stand before a multitude and be judged on your faithfulness to Me. You will be judged as to whether you are worthy to be redeemed and live with Me eternally. Many will think they are worthy, but they are not. Do not deceive yourself, but hold onto Me and be led by My Spirit, and then you will prosper and have success.

175

You should end disputes quickly. You should practice instant reconciliation.

Matt 5:23 Therefore, if you are offering your gift at the altar and there remember that your brother has something against you, 24 leave your gift there in front of the altar. First go and be reconciled to your brother; then come and offer your gift. Num 5:7 And must confess the sin they have committed. They must make full restitution for the wrong they have done, add a fifth of the value to it and give it all to the person they have wronged.

My beloved, if you come to Me and you know someone has something against you, then go to the person and work out your differences with him, so you can come before Me clean and righteous. Do to come to Me with dirty hands, but come to Me with forgiveness in your heart and humility, so you can go to your brother humbly and ask for forgiveness. You must not sleep until you have asked forgiveness for your sin towards another. Did someone sue you and want to take you to court? Go to the person and try to solve this reasonable. Come to a compromise, so you will not have to enter the courtroom of men and their perverted court system of lawyers and judges who manipulate cases to fit their agenda. Work out your differences as brothers. If one who is not a believer is taking you to court, then I will be your advocate-your lawyer-your judge. If you are guilty, then you will pay the price. If you are innocent, then I will release you from the court system. You must listen to Me, and I will help you. I will show you how to deal with those who will rise up against you in the last days. You must listen, and not be deceived. All who say they are your friend is not your friend. Judge the person by their actions and how they love others and how they want to serve Me. There may be enemies among you. Beware!

176

You should not commit adultery.

Matt 5:27 "You have heard that our fathers were told, 'Do not commit adultery.' 28 But I tell you that anyone who looks at a woman
lustfully has already committed adultery with her in his heart." (Matt
19:3, Ex 20:14, Gen 1:27, Gen 2:24)

My beloved, do not commit adultery, because this separates marriages and causes the deepest kinds of wounds in the family. If you see someone who is not your
spouse and you lust after him and begin to imagine what having intercourse with
his person would be like, then you dishonor your spouse and you should repent. If
you go to your mate and love him and hold him and have intercourse with him,
then all these sexual fantasies will pass. You must love your mate and daily satisfy
your mate, so your sexual desires will not lead you astray and make you fall into
temptation and sin. If you are not married and you have sexual desires and no
one to fulfill them, then submit yourself to Me as a living sacrifice so you can abstain from all evil. It is an abomination to Me for you to enter into sexual pleasure
with someone who is not your spouse and you are not in covenant with him. You
must wait until you are married, and then you must please your mate and honor
your mate. Both of you should keep yourself pure and separate from the world. If
your mate leaves you and commits adultery and wants to divorce you, give him
the divorce he wants but keep yourself pure until I bring you another mate. The
person who left the marriage and committed adultery will be judged harshly for
bringing pain to the family that I gave him, so beware of adultery.

177

You should get rid of whatever causes you to sin.

Matt 5:29 If your right eye causes you to sin, gouge it out and throw it away. It is better for you to lose one part of your body than for your whole body to be thrown into hell. 30 And if your right hand causes you to sin, cut it off and throw it away. It is better or you to lose one part of your body than for your whole body to go into hell. Heb 12:1-2 Therefore, since we are surrounded by such a great cloud of witnesses, let us throw off everything that hinders and the sin that so easily entangles, and let us run with perseverance the race marked out for us. (Rom 13:12)

My beloved, look at yourself. What causes you to sin? Is someone influencing you to do the wrong things? Get rid of the people in your life who do not want to follow Me and go your separate way. Go down the narrow road of righteousness. It is much better to lose friends than to follow along with your friends into sin that leads to eternal destruction. What is it that causes you to sin? Is it TV? Does it make you lust or destroy your moral character? Do you let crude remarks and wicked scenes seen on TV not bother you and you never turn off the TV? Have you become numb to sin? Throw out your TV. Rid yourself of the temptation to watch sinful images? Is it your job? Does it keep you from spending time with Me and your family? Call out to Me and I will help you get another job that will allow you family time. Is it the books you read? Do they cause you to lust? Do you read worldly material and never read My Words? Throw out your books and focus on My Words. Is it your computer? Do you spend endless hours on the computer enjoying the things of the world? Your computer can be a tool to help you learn more about Me, but the best way to know Me is to read My Words, and listen for My Voice. Talk to Me about your needs and any questions you have or decisions you must make. I AM your Elohim. If you want to please Me, rid yourself of all that causes you to sin.

178

You should not divorce except for marital unfaithfulness.

Matt 5:31 "It has been said, 'Anyone who divorces his wife must give her a certificate of divorce.' 32 But I tell you that anyone who divorces his wife, except for marital unfaithfulness, causes her to become an adulteress, and anyone who marries the divorced woman commits adultery." Deut 24:1 Suppose a man marries a woman but she does not please him. Having discovered something wrong with her (she is sinful), he writes her a letter of divorce, hands it to her, and sends her away from his house. Lev 20:10 If a man commits adultery with another man's wife-with the wife of his neighbor-both the adulterer and the adulteress must be put to death. (Num 5:11-31)

My beloved, I told Moses to tell you not to divorce your wife unless she had committed adultery. If the woman was caught in the act of adultery, then she and the man who committed the sin was stoned. If the woman was not caught in the sin, then she was taken to the priest and had to drink the water of purification. This water would make her sterile if she had been unfaithful to her husband or fertile if she had been faithful to her husband. If a man committed adultery, then he was put to death if there were two or more witnesses. The husband is supposed to be the example to his wife and children, because he is the priest of the home. The husband is judged harsher and the sin of his adultery is passed onto his sons in the form of a curse-one that can only be broken through prayer and fasting. Open your eyes and see how harmful adultery is to the family. It breaks the bond of commitment to each other-the vow you made to each other that is based on trust. It always brings death to the family in some kind of way. I would never divorce you as My bride unless you committed adultery by going after other gods, so I expect you not to divorce. You must love each other and try to be a peacemaker and not to allow hatred or anger to develop between you. Let there be love, kindness, and forgiveness in your marriage. You should try very hard to make your marriage a good one built on trust. I will help you. Call on My name, and I will bring healing to your marriage.

179

You should not break your oath to YHUH.

Matt 5:33 "Again, you have heard that it was said to the people long ago, 'Do not break your oath, but keep the oaths you have made to YHUH.'"
Num 30:2 When a man makes a vow to YHUH or takes an oath to obligate himself by a pledge, he must not break his word but must do everything he said.

My beloved, if you make a vow to Me and say I promise that I will do a certain thing for Me, then you must do what you have promised Me that you will do. So many in crises will call out to Me and say, "If only you will help Me this one time, I will always serve you." If you have prayed this prayer, then you better be fulfilling your promise to Me. If you ask Me to help you and promise to do something in return, then you must do as you have said. I AM looking for an honest man and a man who does not lie. I AM looking for a man who is faithful and true-who whatever he utters he will accomplish. Some men do not even give notice to the words they speak, but My Children are very careful when they speak. They are quick to guard their tongue, so they do not sin against Me or their brother or make vain promises that they will not keep. When you search your heart, you will find words you have spoken carelessly-with no thought of what you have said. These careless words that you have not fulfilled-spoken but never accomplished-said but never put into action-you will have to give an account at the Last Day. You will have to face your unfulfilled promises. You will have to correct your wrongs. You will have to be without sin to enter My Kingdom, so guard over what you speak.

180

***You should not make promises, because you may not
live to keep them. Simply state your intentions.***

Matt 5:34 But I tell you, Do not swear at all: either by heaven, for it is Elohim's throne; 35 or by the earth, for it is His footstool; or by Jerusalem, or it is the city of the Great King. 36 And do not swear by your head, for you cannot make even one hair white or black. 37 Simply let your 'Yes' be 'Yes,' and your 'No,' 'No'; anything beyond this comes from the Evil One. Deut 23:22 But if you refrain from making a vow, you will not be guilty.

My beloved, guard carefully over your mouth, so that you will only speak truth. My Children should only speak truth, because I AM Truth and the evil one is the author of lies and walks only in deception. He deceives others, so they will follow him. He can offer them nothing but lies, and he promises them whatever they want to follow him. The deception is a strong delusion, and many fall into that trap. Beware that you do not listen to lies and do not speak lies. Let only truth come forth from your mouth. Let truth reign in your heart, so when you speak you will do as you say you will do. If you tell someone you will do something, then do what you say you will do. Be careful to think through your obligation before you speak. Do not hastily say, "Yes I will," because I will require you to keep what you have spoken. You are to be an example of My love and truth. How can you be an example to others if you cannot be trusted-that whatever you say you may not do? This should not be so, My little one. Do not take others for granted and say, "Oh, I will make it up to them later." This is not My Way, and it is evil in My sight. Do not make excuses why you cannot do as you have spoken, but instead find a way to keep your promises, and then I will bless you greatly.

181

***You should not stand up against (seek revenge against)
someone who does you wrong.***

Matt 5:38 "You have heard that it was said, 'Eye for eye, and tooth
for tooth.' 39 But I tell you not to stand up against someone who does
you wrong. If someone strikes you on the right cheek, turn to him the
other also." Deut 19:16 If a malicious witness takes the stand to
accuse a man of a crime, 21 Show no pity: life for life, eye for eye,
tooth for tooth, hand for hand, foot for foot.

My beloved, do not stand against someone who wants to do wrong to you. Do
not try to get back at him, but put him in My Hands. I will deliver you from the
person and punish him for his sins against you. You need only love your brother
and do not try to become even with him, because I will make sure he has paid
the full penalty for his sins. If you try to even out the score between you, then
judgment will also fall on you. Only I know what the person needs to humble
him and bring him to repentance. Do not be afraid of a man who is mean to you,
but call on My name and I will deliver you from him. If someone asks you to do
something for him and he is asking it to be mean to you, then pour your love
out on him and do more than he expected you to do. Tell him about My Love
for him-a precious gift that only I can give. You must love others and be kind to
them. There will be times when you do not want to do what the person wants
you to do because of their intentions, but pouring love upon them will make them
look at you in a different way and think more about My love for them. My People
were under Roman rule during My time on Earth, and these soldiers treated
them harshly. They asked My People to carry their heavy war packs for a mile
and this angered My People, but I said to love them and go the extra mile. This is
what you should do to show others you have My love inside of you. Give to others
more than they expect you to do.

182

You should give more than is required of you.

Matt 5:40 And if someone wants to sue you and take your tunic, let him have your cloak as well. If anyone forces you to go one mile, go with them two miles. Deut 15:11 There will always be poor people in the land. Therefore I command you to be open-handed toward your brothers and toward the poor and needy in your land.

My beloved, if someone is oppressing you, treat him with love. If he tries to take from you, give more then what he asks. Let your kindness burn him to the heart. Always give to others more than is required of you. When you are employed by someone, do all that is required of you and then do more. Favor will come to you and your employer will bless you. If your employer is a mean person filled with greed, then I will bless you and care for you. If you give to others whether they are against you or not, then I will bless you. It is better to give to others than receive from others. If you give, then you will teach the others around you to give. If you give to others, you are stacking up treasure for yourself in My Kingdom of Light. If you give, your children will see you giving and their hearts will not be selfish, but will open their hands to others. You must not hold onto earthly possessions, because they will all pass away. If you have things in your house you are not using, then give them to the poor and do not collect so many things that have no value except to sit out and be admired by all. This is vanity! Cleanse your house of all unneeded items and you will do well. Take your money that you do not need and give to others. Give more than is required of you, and I well bless you by My right hand.

183

You should allow others to borrow from you.

Matt 5:42 Give to the one who asks you, and do not turn away from the one who wants to borrow from you. Luke 6:30 Give to everyone who asks you, and if anyone takes what belongs to you, do not demand it back. 31 Do to others as you would have them do to you. Deut 15:8 Rather, be open-handed and freely lend them whatever they need.

My beloved, give generously to others, and I will give back to you. I will send blessings to you in the form of good health, children, prosperity, peace, friends, family who supports you, and the knowledge of knowing your Creator in an intimate way-which is the greatest gift I can give to you. I AM Love and I want all My children to be like Me and love others. If you love others you will give to others and not think about yourself. You may say, "I have little money to give," but you can always give your time and your love to others. If someone needs a friend- a shoulder to cry on- a friend to listen to him, go to him and give him support and pray with him-rejoice with him-mourn with him-whatever the occasion may bring-go to your friend. If your child needs you, be there for your child. If you neighbor needs you, go to him and help him. Visit the sick in the hospital and visit those in jail who want to repent and serve Me. Think of the lonely, the dying, and the grieving person who needs you to comfort them and pray for them. You say, "This is a full time job and you can't devote all your time to this," but I say be led by My Spirit, and I will show you where you need to be for that moment. Depend on Me to guide you, so you can give freely. I will bless you on earth and store up riches for you in heaven, so when you come to My Kingdom I will give you a house adorned in jewels and costly metals. You will be rewarded for your acts of love as you give to others when you reach My Kingdom of Light.

184

You should love your enemies and those who work against you.

Matt 5:43 "You have heard that it was said, 'Love your neighbor and hate your enemy.' 44 But I tell you: Love your enemies and pray for those who persecute you, 45 that you may be sons of your Father in heaven." Prov 25:21 If your enemy is hungry, give him food to eat; if he is thirsty, give him water to drink. 22 In doing this, you will heap burning coals on his head, and YHUH will reward you. Lev 19:18 "Do not seek revenge or bear a grudge against anyone among your people, but love your neighbor as yourself. I am YHUH."

My beloved, love those who hate you. Love those who curse you for My sake. Love those who are sinful, but hate the sin they are in and rebuke them in love. Do not cast them aside because they are in sin, but try to help them turn towards Me and have a righteous life. If they continue to reject Me, continue to love them. Do not hate them, but separate yourself from them so they do not cause you to sin. Are there people who really annoy you? Ask yourself why the person really annoys you? Ask Me to give you love for that person so you can show My love to them. Soon love will fill your heart for the person, and then you can tell them about My wondrous love. If you work with others that are worldly and not like you, instead of shunning them, love them and be a light to them. Are you strong enough to live a life without sin and show them the love I have given you? If you are weak and struggling, then wait until you are firmly planted, and then show them My love for them. You must love others, because this is what My purpose is for you. I do not want you to hate any one even your enemies. If someone is mean to you every day, pray for the person that his heart will be softened towards you. Continue to forgive him and show love towards him and eventually he will not hate you anymore. My love through you will cover the darkness in him, and he will see the light.

185

You should quietly give to the needy to please YHUH,
not to gain approval from other people.

Matt 6:1 "Be careful not to do your 'acts of righteousness' before men, to be seen by them. If you do, you will have no reward from your Father in heaven. 2 So when you give to the needy, do not announce it with trumpets, as the hypocrites do in the synagogues and on the streets, to be honored by men. I tell you the truth, they have received their reward in full. 3 But when you give to the needy, do not let your left hand know what your right hand is doing, 4 so that your giving may be in secret. Then your Father, who sees what is done in secret, will reward you." (Jer 17:10, Heb 4:13, Ps 44:21)

My beloved, do not do good deeds just so men will be impressed. If this is your motive, then you are as a stench in My nostrils. If you do good things for others because you love others, then you are pleasing in My sight. Give to the poor, but do not tell others about it. Give and be generous, and I will bless you. If you give a large sum of money to a charity and your name is announced for all to hear, then this is all the reward you will get. If you tell the charity to keep your name hidden, then this will please Me. I will give you a reward for your humility. I do not want you to do good so men will reward you, because I cannot reward you. You have already received your reward. I want men to love others and do good things for others. Their only reward will be the joy they see in others as a result of their help. If you look for ways to help others so their day will be better, then you do well and you follow after love and not serving your own self. If you try to make love your motive, then you do well. Men who are humble and want to serve others in love are the men who I lift up and prosper. Be humble before Me and men. Do not tell men the good things you do. Instead let others see your good works and thank Me for your kindness to others. Be loving and kind, and others will notice your good works. You do not have to announce your good works to others. I see all things.

186

You should pray privately and simply, not to impress other people.

Matt 6:5 "And when you pray, do not be like the hypocrites, for they love to pray standing in the synagogues and on the street corners to be seen by men. I tell you the truth, they have received their reward in full. 6 But when you pray, go into your room, close the door and pray to your Father, who is unseen. Then your Father, who sees what is done in secret, will reward you." Luke 5:15 Yet the news about Him spread all the more, so that crowds of people came to hear Him and to be healed of their sicknesses. 16 But Yahshua often withdrew to lonely places and prayed. (2 Kings 4:33, Acts 9:40, Ps 34:15)

My beloved, look to Me for all the things you need. Pray at all times-for strength to stand and not sin-for direction–for guidance-for deliverance. Pray to Me and I will hear you. Pray to Me in secret, so we can be as one-intimate together-as husband and wife-pure love for each other. Pray to Me and talk with Me, and you will know Me and I will know you. If you pray only with others, then how can you really know Me? Pray in secret, so we can be as one. Praying is like a constant communication with Me-an ongoing conversation all the day. How can you make it through a day without My Presence loving you and guiding you? Do you fast? If you do, you will be heard. Fast and pray, so you can know My will or to be released from darkness or bondage from sin. Fast for others if they need strength to overcome. I see your sacrifice and will consider your request. If someone is ill or in sin, fast and pray for their recovery while you still have hope. Do not delay-their soul is at stake. A fast that I honor is when you give up something you enjoy to spend time with Me. Turn off your TV or your favorite books or games and spend time studying My word. Do not think that I will not see. If you do it unto Me, then I will bless you. Fast one day a week from sundown to sundown, and you will be able to control your flesh and keep yourself in line. If you say that you are too weak, then try hard to make yourself strong. Fast and pray for I AM near to you.

187

You should not use vain repetitions when praying.

Matt 6:7 And when you pray, do not keep on babbling like pagans, for they think they will be heard because of their many words. 8 Do not be like them, for your Father knows what you need before you ask Him. Mark 12:38 As He taught, Yahshua said, "Watch out for the teachers of the law. They like to walk around in flowing robes and be greeted in the marketplaces, 39 and have the most important seats in the synagogues and the places of honor at banquets. 40 They devour widows' houses and for a show make lengthy prayers. Such men will be punished most severely." (Ecc 5:2)

My beloved, when you pray to Me just talk to Me. Do not use prayers that are written down in a book. Do not memorize prayers to pray to Me. I do not want to hear these prayers, but I want to hear your heart being poured out to Me. Allow your true words to pour out to Me. Let us be at one and talk as one. You can ask Me anything, but do not question Me concerning events that happen in your life. Know that I do what is best for you. If you are asking Me to do something for you and it never happens, then do not question Me why I will not allow it to happen. Do not become angry because I do not give you everything you ask for, because I will give you good gifts. Only I know what the future holds, and I know what to give you at a certain time. I will open doors for you. Just walk through them. If I close a door, know I will open another one for you. Do not be sad or discouraged because I will give you only the best. Do not pray in front of others to impress them, but you can pray as a group- as one to be heard before My throne- as a strong voice. I hear all the prayers of My children-every sigh for help and every time you praise Me for My gifts. Do not stop praying with your whole heart. Do not memorize prayers, but let us be as one and then I will guide you by My Spirit.

188

You should ask your Father for what you need.

Matt 6:9 This, then, is how you should pray: Our Father in heaven. John 16:23 I tell you the truth, my Father will give you whatever you ask in my name. 24 Until now you have not asked for anything in my name. Ask and you will receive, and your joy will be complete. (Prov 30:7-8)

My beloved, pray to your Father in heaven. Come to Me for help. Do not look to man. He cannot help you. Ask Me so you can have good gifts. It is not selfish to ask Me to help you. I want My children to cry out to Me for help and trust Me to help them. I will send you help. My messengers will come to you and I will send you messages through My Spirit. I will not leave you alone without help. I can do all things. Ask and receive so your joy will be full, but do not ask anything of Me if you have not forgiven those who wronged you. Don't wrong others, but if you do, then go to them and make restitution and ask forgiveness. Repent and do not wrong others. If others wrong you, forgive them quickly. Do not hold a grudge. You must be at peace inside not nursing anger or being upset. If you put all these things aside, you can be at peace with Me, and I will bless you with food and water and clothes and shelter. I will give you and your children good things. I will bring good gifts to your door to your very house, so you do not have to go search for it. I will bring it to you, because I love you. I will prosper your business if you call on My name. I will build up your profit and give you wisdom how to run your business. I will help you if you only ask Me. Keep asking and we will be as one.

189

You should ask YHUH to help you do His will for your life.

Matt 6:10 May your kingdom come, your will be done on earth as it is in heaven. Luke 22:41 He withdrew about a stone's throw beyond them, knelt down and prayed, 42 "Father, if you are willing, take this cup from Me; yet not my will, but yours be done." (Acts 21:14, Ps 40:8)

My beloved, do not seek your own will, but seek My will for your life and then you will be fulfilled. My will is what is best for you. I will give you only good things and allow good things to come to you. I want you to have the best gifts. I want you to have the gifts that will produce fruits of the Spirit and help you walk in righteousness. You want your own way, but if you trust Me to do what is best for you, then you can subdue your flesh and be able to listen to My will for you. I never tell you all at once what you will do in your life, because I want you to come to Me day after day and seek Me so you can walk in My perfect timing. My time is the best time, because every detail will fall together at once and you can praise Me for the miracle that happens to you. I want you to see My Hand moving in your life. Sometimes you are waiting and waiting for what I have spoken to come to pass, but you must be patient because I will fulfill My words. Take this time to prepare yourself so you can be consecrated and at one with Me. Do not be deceived by your flesh, but be at one with Me so you can hear My voice and know My will for you. Do not tell others what My will is for their life, because I will show them only if they seek Me to find it. Rejoice and be glad that I love you so much to reveal to you My will for you.

190

You should ask YHUH for your daily food.

Matt 6:11 Give us the food we need today. Ps 111:4 YHUH is gracious and compassionate. 5 He provides food for those who fear him; He remembers His covenant forever. Ps 145:13 YHUH is faithful to all his promises and loving toward all He has made. 14 YHUH upholds all those who fall and lifts up all who are bowed down. 15 The eyes of all look to you, and you give them their food at the proper time. 16 You open your hand and satisfy the desires of every living thing.

My beloved, I give food to all the nations. I bring rain at the right time to pros-per the crops. When too much rain comes it floods. When no rain comes to the land, the ground cracks and does not produce a crop. I open the heavens and I close the heavens. No man can do that even though he tries his hand at weather. I just laugh from My Throne Room. Man is but a breath-a mere dot-as nothing, and yet his pride overweighs him and he thinks he is magnificent and forgets Me. I can take all away from him, and then he has nothing. Lift up your eyes and know Me and where your life comes from. I breathe into you and give you life. I take it away when your days are done and you are at last out of the flesh that tries you daily. You hunger. You thirst. You weep. You laugh. You rejoice in My Presence. You are in My Hand. Acknowledge who I AM. Praise Me for all my gifts that I give you-life, rain, sun, clouds for shade, trees for oxygen, food, clothes, shelter, children, good health, family, friends, employment, and money. Praise Me for all things, and I will receive your praise and smile. I bring abundant food to My children, because I love you. If you are lacking food, call on My name. In the last days I will provide for you just as I provide for you today. Do not be afraid, but be glad that I care for all my children no matter where they are- in exile or not. I care for My beloved ones.

191

You should ask YHUH to forgive you for what you have done wrong.

Matt 6:12 Forgive us for what we have done wrong, as we also have forgiven those who have wronged us. 1 John 1:9 If we confess our sins, He is faithful and just and will forgive us our sins and purify us from all unrighteousness. 10 If we claim we have not sinned, we make Him out to be a liar and His Word is not in us. (Ex 34:7, Ps 32:1, Ps 130:4)

My beloved, forgive others and do not seek revenge. Forgive others, so you can also be forgiven. If you hold on to your anger and bitterness and it festers and becomes hatred and revengeful, then you do not have love for this person. You are in sin and you must confess your sin and forgive this person. No matter what the person has done, you must forgive him and I will punish him for your sin against you. I can punish in a way that brings repentance, because I know what the person needs and what will break the person and humble the person and allow him to seek repentance. If you punish the person, then this is his punishment and it may not lead to righteousness. If I punish the person for their wrongs, then I will punish him in a way that is best for him. You must realize that you do not have to punish him, but I can pay him back for his wrongdoings and I AM faithful to do so no matter how horrible the crime against you. Even if the person has killed one of your loved ones, I can issue an equal judgment against him. You must trust Me to do this. You must forgive the person and put the person in My hands for judgment, and I will punish him according to his crimes. You can also be forgiven, because you have decided to love and not hate the person. Forgiveness is the greatest gift you can give a person, because My punishment can lead the person to eternal life.

192

You should ask YHUH to help you not fall into temptation.

Matt 6:13 And lead us not into temptation. 2 Thess 3:3 But YHUH is faithful, and He will strengthen you and protect you from the evil one. 2 Tim 4:18 YHUH will rescue me from every evil attack and will bring me safely to his heavenly kingdom. To Him be glory forever and ever. Amen. (Ps 22:28, Luke 22:39-46, Matt 26:40-41)

My beloved, pray that you will be strong and if testing comes that you will endure and overcome. Pray that you will not fall into temptation. The world is full of all sorts of glittering mirages, but only through My wisdom that I give you will you be able to see the truth and know they are only traps. If you continue in Me, you will not fall into sin and fall when the temptation comes. You may not view temptation in the same way as I do. Anytime you make a choice to do something that will satisfy your flesh instead of benefiting My spirit within you is a temptation. Of course you can see how drugs, adultery, or loose sexual morals can ruin your life and affect your body, but what about the food you eat and what you drink and the amount of sleep you have? What about what you see or watch? What about what you hear or listen to? What about the people you are friends with? What about the church you go to influencing you to go against My words? What about family members that have led you astray? What about your job and how it hinders your walk with Me? Think about all these temptations to overeat or eat unhealthy, to sleep excessively or not enough, to watch perverted movies or TV, to listen to perverted music, to follow misled people. Trust in Me and do not fall into temptation.

193

You should ask YHUH to be delivered from the Evil One.

Matt 6:13 But deliver us from the evil one. John 17:15 My prayer is not that you take them out of the world but that you protect them from the evil one. 2 Thess 3:2 And pray that we may be delivered from wicked and evil men, for not everyone has faith. 3 But YHUH is faithful, and He will strengthen and protect you from the evil one.

My beloved, I will protect you from the evil one and all of his forces, because you are My child. The evil one hates you, because you are heirs to My throne and you will rule over the nations. Your authority will be above his and he wanted to rule all men, so he hates you and wants to kill you. His hatred has made him grow weak, and he is no longer a beautiful light that brings music to Me through praise. He led others in praise to Me, but he wanted power over all and not to serve Me. He was expelled from his place in My kingdom and he was sent to earth. There he ruled men for a while after the fall of Adam and Eve, but I came and shed My innocent blood for you so you could be released from the evil one and be free to live in oneness with Me. You are My child, My treasure, and I love you deeply. The evil one cannot comprehend My love for you, because he has become evil. He does not know love. He deceives all men. He has many follow him by his lies. He knows how to manipulate men to do his will, but he cannot deceive My children because I reveal his darkness to them. I bring light to his deception. If you call on My name to protect you from evil, I will cover you by My right hand and lead you away from evil. If you trust Me to care for you, I will keep all darkness from you, and I will deliver you from all wickedness.

194

You should forgive others of all their offenses against you.

Matt 6:14 For if you forgive men when they sin against you, your heavenly Father will also forgive you. 15 But if you do not forgive men their sins, your Father will not forgive your sins. Mark 11:25 And when you stand praying, if you hold anything against anyone, forgive him, so that your Father in heaven may forgive you your sins. John 20:23 If you forgive anyone his sins, they are forgiven; if you do not forgive them, they are not forgiven. (Num 14:18)

My beloved, when men wrong you, forgive them quickly and do not allow un-forgiveness to swell within your heart, because it leads to hatred and hatred will destroy your soul. A man who hates cannot love others so his love is tainted, and he can never fully love others. He is a man that is crippled-unhealthily-filled with grief. He must learn to forgive those who have wronged him, so I can punish them for their sins. How can I punish them if you are in sin because you continue to hate others? Yes, you are right in your feelings towards others, but you must release them into My hands and forgive the person, then I can cleanse you from all unrighteousness and you can be at one with Me again. I will punish the person for his sins against you, and he will pay the penalty. He cannot escape the penalty. You will see how he is paid back by Me, but do not rejoice over his suffering because I want you to have compassion and mercy. I want you to love others even those who wrong you, because this is the love I have for you. You must learn to forgive quickly and seek no revenge or carry no grudges. If you will do this, then I will bless you and give you only the best gifts. I will pour blessings into your house. You will teach your children to forgive, and then they will also prosper. If you say "I cannot forgive him," then call on My name and ask Me to bring forgiveness to your heart, and I will help you forgive him.

195

You should fast secretly and not for show.

Matt 6:16 When you fast, do not look somber as the hypocrites do, because they make sour faces to show men they are fasting. I tell you the truth, they have received their reward in full. **17** But when you fast, wash your face and groom yourself, **18** so that it will not be obvious to men that you are fasting, but only to your Father, who is unseen; and your Father, who sees what is done in secret, will reward you. **(Is 58:5-11)**

My beloved, do you have a problem in your life? Do you have a decision that needs to be made? If you are struggling and cannot live a righteous life, if you cannot break the sin from you-the sin continues to return and you cannot stop sinning, then you need to fast and pray. What will fasting do for you? It will break the darkness from you. You are making a sacrifice by not feeding your flesh and making your flesh submit to your will. You are humbling yourself and denying yourself and gaining self-control. This sacrifice of your flesh is a pleasing aroma to Me, and I hear your prayers and break the darkness for you by sending you more of My light. Curses can be broken from you. Light can penetrate and truth can come into you, so you are no longer blinded and deceived. If you are fasting for someone else, then you can break the darkness over that person so he can see clearly. Do you have a spouse, parent, or child in sin? Fast once a week for that person and I will hear you. Do so in secret. You do not have to tell anyone you are fasting. Keep it a secret and I will reward you openly. I will show you that I see your fasts as a sweet fragrance coming up to Me, and I will come near to you and commune with you and hear your groaning. I AM Light, and as I come close to you Light will penetrate you and release you from sin. I reward you for your sacrifices by answering your prayers. No enemy can stop your fasts. Only I can reward you for your sacrifice.

196

You should store your riches in heaven not on earth.
Don't store things that you're not using.

Matt 6:19 Do not store up for yourselves treasures on earth, where moth and rust destroy, and where thieves break in and steal. 20 But store up for yourselves treasures in heaven, where moth and rust do not destroy, and where thieves do not break in and steal. 21 For where your treasure is, there your heart will be also. 33 But seek first His kingdom and His righteousness, and all these things will be given to you as well. (Luke 12:16-26, 1 Tim 6:19, 1 Peter 5:4)

My beloved, do not store up for yourself earthly possessions. Give what you have left over to the poor and needy. Do you collect things? Do you gather up things and store them in boxes or an attic or storehouse? Why do you do this? Take all these things and if they have value give them to the poor and needy. Give generously to others. Do not collect possessions and keep them if you are not using them. Keep for yourself only what you need and give away the rest. Think of how you can help others. Look around you and look at what others need. Maybe you do not know what others need, but I do. Call on My name, and I will tell you how to help and what to give to others. Some people only need your love, understanding, and encouragement. Some people need more-guidance-direction. Some need nursing–caring for their self-inflicted wounds from past sins or even wounds from sins of others towards them. Some people need deliverance and support through fasting and praying to break them from bondage. Some people need to be told the truth. Some people have needs that must be bought like food, clothes, and shelter. Some people have stumbled and want to get back up and need a strong shoulder to lean on. Whatever a person needs, be there for them and you will store up rewards in heaven where no man can take them from you.

197

You should not love money.

Matt 6:24 No one can serve two masters. Either he will hate the one and love the other, or he will be devoted to the one and despise the other. You cannot serve both Elohim and money. Eccl 5:10 Whoever loves money never has money enough; whoever loves wealth is never satisfied with his income. 1 Tim 6:10 For the love of money is a root of all kinds of evil. Some people, eager for money, have wandered from the faith and pierced themselves with much grief.

My beloved, do you love money and all it can bring to you? Do you love to live in luxury? Do you never have enough money no matter how much you make? Do you give to the poor and others? Are you generous? Are you stingy? If you love money, you will love to spend it on yourself and you will not want to give to others. If you love money, you will want to store it up and not give it away. If you love the things of the earth, you will burn up with the things of the earth. The love of money is the Evil One's trap. If he can entice you with the power of money, then he can entice you into other sins. Man is weak and loves to satisfy his flesh, but My children are strong because they call on My Name for help. They want to stay clean and not yield themselves to sin. Those of My children, who are given money, give to the poor and needy and stay righteous before Me. You live in a wealthy land-so wealthy that the people have forgotten their Elohim who blessed them. I AM sending misery to them, so they will call on My name once again and repent of their sins. This is their last chance to repent as a nation or worst things will come upon them. You should fear your Elohim and stay far from evil. Be kind and loving and do not be eager to gain wealth-so eager that you make hasty decisions. Many have lost all they have running after wealth. Be wise and call on My name for help.

198

You should not worry about your material needs.

Matt 6:25-32 Thereore I tell you, do not worry about your life, what you will eat or drink; or about your body, what you will wear. Is not life more important than food, and the body more important than clothes? John 14:1 Do not let your hearts be troubled. Trust in Elohim; trust also in Me. 1 Peter 5:7 Cast all your anxiety on him because he cares for you. (Ps 111:5)

My beloved, do not worry about what tomorrow may bring. You must trust Me to care for you. You must seek after Me and do My will and I will give you all you need. I will give you food, clothes, and shelter. I will fill your pantries, so you will have abundance. I will fill your closet with clothes, so you will not wear torn or worn out clothes. I will give you a house to meet your needs. You must not worry. I will supply you a job- a means of income, so you can support your family and care for them. Do not worry but trust in Me. Ask Me to help you and I will, if you are not in sin and are not going your own way. If you follow My laws and do My will as led by My Spirit, then you are righteous before Me and I will give generously to you. Always do the right things. Do not deceive others or mislead others. Do not break the laws of the land. Don't break your promises to others. Do not wrong your neighbor. Forgive others who wrong you. Quickly repent in your heart, and love others. Remember no one is perfect and all make mistakes. If they sinned against you deliberately, then I will punish them. You don't have to punish them. I will set it right. I AM just and fair. I AM loving and kind and full of mercy. I will bless you as you bless Me. I will give to you as you give to others.

199

You should put YHUH first in your life.

Matt 6:31 So do not worry, saying, 'What shall we eat?' or 'What shall we drink?' or 'What shall we wear?' 32 For the pagans run after all these things, and your heavenly Father knows that you need them. 33 But seek first His kingdom and His righteousness, and all these things will be given to you as well. (1 Kings 3:11-13)

My beloved, if you will seek Me first and look to Me for all your needs, then you will have all the things that you need to live a good life. If you need food, call on My Name and I will provide for you. Did I not send ravens to feed My prophet during famine? Whatever it is that you need, I can get it for you. Nothing is impossible with Me, because I hold the universe together or it would fall apart. I can do all things. You say, "How can we be so important to you on this little planet in such a vast universe?" but I say to you, "How many children have I laid down My life for so you could be released from the bondage of sin?" You are My children. The angels look into you and wonder. I have cast My love upon you and the Evil One knows My love for you and wants to destroy you, because you are valued far more than the others. You are tested by fire and will be counted as righteous. No other beings are tested before they enter My kingdom. I created them for a certain task in My kingdom and placed them there. If you understand how import-ant you are to Me, you will know that I will care for you. Seek Me and know My plan for you, so you can rise up and have faith in Me and My ways. You will reign on High over many in the days to come, if you endure in faith throughout the last days so be strong. Be faithful. Seek Me first in all things and I will bless you.

200

You should not worry about the future.

Matt 6:34 Therefore do not worry about tomorrow, for tomorrow will worry about itself. Each day has enough trouble of its own.
Phil 4:6 Do not be anxious about anything, but in every situation, by prayer and petition, with thanksgiving, present your requests to YHUH. (Ps 89:1, Lam 3:22-24)

My beloved, do not worry about the future, but trust in Me to provide for you. You are My beloved child. Of course, I will give you good things, if you are an obedient child and listen to My voice. Any child that is disobedient you punish to correct his sinful ways. Any of My children who are disobedient are punished, and I withhold blessings and this gets their attention. They wonder why this is happening to them, and then they call on My Name and repent. After they repent I can bless them. I want to bless you with many good things, but I AM just and fair and can only bless those who follow in My ways and keep My commands. If you are in sin, repent for your future grows dark. If you are righteous your future is good, and I will bless you on all sides. What if you are a child and your parents are not living according to My word, then if you trust in Me and cry out to Me, I will hear you and bless you no matter if your parents serve Me or not. Look to Me and do not worry about your future days ahead. If you trust in Me, I will guide you every day to make the right choices. I will show you what to do and where to go. Listen for My voice, because the days grow dark. I must take My people to shelter, so they will not be harmed during the troubles that are coming on the Earth. Days will be turbulent and men will die from fear, but you will be safe in My arms of love.

201

You should not judge others unmercifully.

Matt 7:1 Do not judge, or you too will be judged. 2 For in the same way you judge others, you will be judged, and with the measure you use, it will be measured to you. John 8:7 When they kept on questioning Him, He straightened up and said to them, "If any one of you is without sin, let him be the first to throw a stone at her." Lev 19:15 Do not pervert justice; do not show partiality to the poor or favoritism to the great, but judge your neighbor fairly.

My beloved, do not look at others and criticize them, but look at others and love them and have mercy on them. Do not be harsh to others, but support others. Look at yourself and judge yourself. If you are in sin, then repent and turn away from sin and sin no more. Do not turn to the things of the world, but instead turn to Me for comfort and support. If you see a brother in sin, then go to him secretly and rebuke him in love and tell him you will stand beside him and be there for him until he can turn from his sin. He may have fallen into a sin that is addictive and he needs someone to stand beside him until the addiction has left his body or the spirit has loosened its hold on him. Do not give up on your brother, but instead love your brother and do good to him and I will reward you. I never give up on you, so I expect you to continue to love your brother through the hard times. If your brother rejects Me and says he will no longer serve Me, then let him go and he will fall into outer darkness and his sins will kill him and he will be no more. My little one, do not think that you can criticize My creations, because the amount you criticize others, I will judge you. You must forgive others and love them. Go to them when they are in error and pray with them, but do not harshly judge your brother for every little thing because I will have less mercy on you.

202

You should not try to correct others until your own blinding faults are gone.

Matt 7:3 "Why do you look at the splinter in your brother's eye and pay no attention to the log in your own eye? 4 How can you say to your brother, 'Let Me take the splinter out of your eye,' when all the time there is a log in your own eye? 5 You hypocrite, first take the log out of your own eye, and then you will see clearly to remove the splinter from your brother's eye." Ps 51:10 Create in me a clean heart, O YHUH, and renew a steadfast spirit within me.

My beloved, look at yourself and judge yourself before you judge others. Look for the darkness in your heart before you try to examine the darkness in others. Cleanse yourself and be made whole, so you can be a spiritual leader to others-not to judge them but to walk as an example before them. I AM looking for those of My children who are a righteous example to many. Be brave and strong and resist the enemy and all his temptations. You must be on guard always watching over yourself very carefully, so as not to become unclean by exposing yourself to the things of the world. The world is all that is Babylon, and Babylon will be judged. If you have Babylon in your heart, you will be judged. If you do not value worldly possessions, then you will not be judged. If you desire only to follow Me, then you will be rewarded for drawing closer to Me. I AM looking for those who hate Babylon and all its perversion and do not want to look into the gods of Hollywood and the demons in 'rock-n-roll' or worldly music. If the music does not bring praise and glory to Me, then it brings praise and glory to men and it's an abomination. You must be able to judge that if the thing does not bring goodness and purity, then it is not of Me and must be refused, so you can walk out of the darkness of Babylon. Arise and see clearly, so you can be cleansed.

203

You should not waste time on argumentative people.
Do not argue over doctrine.

Matt 7:6 Do not give dogs what is sacred; do not throw your pearls to pigs. If you do, they may trample them under their feet, and then turn and tear you to pieces. Titus 3:9 But avoid foolish controversies, arguments about genealogies, quarrels, and fights about the Law. These things are useless and worthless. (Job 15:2-4)

My beloved, I have given to you a great treasure- a sacred gift- the knowledge of knowing Me–your Savior, your Father, your beloved one. You know Me because I have chosen you and given to you knowledge that not all men have. It is a precious gift to know Me, because I have placed My seed of righteousness inside of you to make you My child and My beloved one. Do not think that all are marked for salvation, because My children are few. If you talk to others, then some will receive My words gladly and want to know Me. Feed these little ones. Some will not listen to what you say and leave you and not seek for Me anymore. They are only serving themselves, and do not want to serve Me. Others will rebuke you and treat you harshly if you tell them about Me. Go away from these people as soon as possible and do not try to go to them and convince them, because their mind is made up not to love Me. There is no seed of righteousness in them, and they cannot know one who did not create them to be My child. They are gentiles-dogs-who return to their own vomit-their own sins, because they cannot see clearly Do not become entrapped in debates or arguments with them over doctrine. You cannot convince them. They want to live their life of sin like pigs that wallow in garage and enjoy their filth. They are disgusting people desiring to satisfy their sinful nature. Go far away from them and give your pearls only to those who want to love Me.

204

You should treat others as you like to be treated.

Matt 7:12 So in everything, do to others what you would have them do to you, for these sums up the Law (given to Moses) and the (Old Testament) Prophets. Lev 19:18 You shall not take vengeance, nor bear any grudge against the sons of your people, but you shall love your neighbor as yourself; I am YHUH.

My beloved, think of how you would like others to treat you and then live your life according to this. If you do not want others to criticize you harshly or talk about you behind your back or betray you or deceive you or sin against you in any way, then do not do these things to others. Be righteous and guard over your tongue-over every word, because you will be held accountable for every evil word you say and you must pay the price. You will have to pay for your sins-no matter how small or large. All men are treated fairly by Me, and I judge all men according to their deeds. I judge man fairly. I do not have favorites. My measure of judgment is the same for all men. My judgment is weighed according to the measure of your sin. You are given only the amount of judgment you deserve. No judge is fair like I am. No judgment can eliminate the weaknesses of the flesh when men are judges. If he calls on My name, I will give him the way to bring righteous judgment. Love others and do good things for them and bring kind loving words to them. Do not allow mean cruel words or actions to be a part of you, but let love be your guide. Love all men no matter what color they are or how much money they have or where they live or who their parents are. Look into their heart-past all their wounds-and see the good there. Love them for what they will become, because this is how I love you.

205

You should follow the narrow path to life.

Matt 7:13 Enter through the narrow gate. For wide is the gate and broad is the road that leads to destruction, and many enter through it. 14 But small is the gate and narrow the road that leads to life and only a few find it.

Is 35:8 And a highway will be there; it will be called the Way of Holiness; it will be for those who walk on that Way. The unclean will not journey on it; wicked fools will not go about on it.

My beloved, enter through Me–the narrow gate-so you will not face destruction. Only through Me do you find eternal life. I AM the narrow gate that through Me you find life. If you choose the broad gate-the world-you choose death and destruction. Those who enter through Me are few. Few are those who humble themselves and enter My kingdom through the narrow gate of righteousness. Man wants his own way. He wants to do whatever he pleases, but My children do as I ask them to do knowing that whatever I ask them to do will be the best for them and bring good things to them. I want to give good thinks to My children. I want to give you the best gifts, but I can only do this if you enter through the narrow gate-a gate of humility-of submission to Me-making yourself a bond servant to Me, so you put aside your desires and seek only My desires. A beloved servant wants only to please Me and seek My will in his life. Pray over ever decision that you make, so you can be led by Me to make the right choice. You must be always listening and wanting to do My will. Die to your flesh and let your spirit arise and commune with Me. Your fleshy desires interfere with your ability to commune with Me. The more you say "No" to your flesh, the closer you draw to Me and know who you really serve. Rejoice that you know Me.

206

You should beware of false prophets.

Matt 7:15 Watch out for false prophets. They come to you in sheep's clothing, but inwardly they are ferocious wolves. 1 John 4:1 Beloved, do not believe every spirit, but test the spirits, whether they are of YHUH; because many false prophets have gone out into the world. (Jer 23:16, Rev 16:13)

My beloved, beware of false prophets who come to you presenting themselves as men of "God" who follow after Me yet their life does not bear fruits of righteousness. They do not speak truth, but speak what you want to hear. They say, "Do not be concerned about the last days. You do not have to prepare, because you are saved by the blood of the Lamb and you walk in the grace of God who will forgive you for all your sins. All you have to do is ask. You will be safe. He will take you up and deliver you from tribulation. You will suffer no persecution. You will be blessed and have plenty of luxuries. So do not prepare. Relax and take it easy." I say to you that this is an abomination to Me. Some truth is in what they say. I did die to save you from your sins if you repent, but what is repentance? You must turn from following after the desires of your flesh and follow after Me. If you see someone who looks just like the world, **you will know** this person is **not** following Me. You will face persecution and mockery for what you believe. You will have tribulations in the last days. You will have to flee from one city to the next. You must be prepared to leave all you own and follow Me. What is important to you? If you try to save your life you will lose it, but if you give up your life for Me you will gain eternal life.

207

You should recognize other believers by their fruit.

Matt 7:16 By their fruit you will recognize them. Do people pick grapes from thorn bushes, or figs from thistles? 17 Likewise every healthy tree bears good fruit, but a poor tree bears bad fruit. 18 A healthy tree cannot bear bad fruit, and a poor tree cannot bear good fruit. 19 Every tree that does not bear good fruit is cut down and thrown into the fire. 20 Thus, by their fruit you will recognize them. Gal 5:22 But the fruit of the Spirit is love, joy, peace, patience, kindness, goodness, faithfulness, 23 gentleness and self-control. (Prov 20:11)

My beloved, do not look at others and see if they have money or power or fine possessions, but look at others with a close eye and examine if they have the fruits of the spirit. What fruit are you looking for? If a people are grafted into Me-the true vine-then they will be loving and kind, giving and helpful. They will be trustworthy, and no lies will come from their mouth. They will look at all men with compassion-no prejudice will be in their heart. They will want to be able to be a servant to others and be humble having little regard for themselves. Where do you find such people? They are grafted into the vine and they suck from Me, and I give them life-an abundant life. If you go forward in obedience to Me, then My hand of protection is on you and the evil one cannot harm you. If you are not in My will, then you will come into troubles, and you will wish you would have made the righteous choice. My people are few. Look around you to see who bears fruit. Look and see who has My love and compassion within them. Cling to those who love Me and want to go through the narrow gate and walk in the path of righteousness. These will be saved in the last days from all forms of darkness. Rejoice and be glad that I will deliver you from evil. I will give you good fruits to share with those around you.

208

You should call YHUH your Master only if you obey Him.

Matt 7:21 "Not everyone who says to Me, 'Lord, Lord,' will enter the kingdom of heaven, but only he who does the will of my Father who is in heaven. 22 Many will say to Me on that day, 'Lord, Lord, did we not prophesy in your name, and in your name drive out demons and perform many miracles?' 23 Then I will tell them plainly, 'I never knew you. Away from Me, you evildoers!'" Luke 6:46 "Why do you call Me, 'Lord, Lord,' and do not do what I say?" (Rom 2:13, Hos 8:2)

My beloved, do you call Me your Master? Do you serve Me? Do you do My will? Do you follow My laws? Do you love Me? If you love Me, you will want to do My will and keep My laws. You will want to be obedient. A child who loves his parents will obey immediately, but a rebellious child will want to disobey. He will want to turn his face away and not do as he is asked. His pride will make him rebellious. He will want his own way and not want to listen. If you are like a rebellious child today, then repent and turn aside from your sin. Read My Words and study them and know what I desire of you, then you will walk in My will and do good things for others. If you are a teacher of My Words, it is very important to teach My laws, because unless you teach My laws, you will not know Me and what I expect of you. You say you are led by My Spirit, but I say unless you keep My laws you are led by your own spirit of rebellion. No man can serve Me unless he keeps My laws. You could say to Me, "I did miracles in your name," but unless you are walking in righteousness, you will not be part of My kingdom. If you love Me, you will search My laws and have a strong desire not to break one of them. You will crave to know Me, and you will call on Me all the day and I will help you. Do not rely on the traditions of men, but rely on My words to guide you. Men will come against you and say all matter of evil to you, but do not listen to their words. They are as nothing to Me. I AM in the midst of those who serve Me. All others do not know Me.

209

You should be compassionate.

Matt 9:11 And when the Pharisees saw this, they said to His disciples, "Why is your Teacher eating with the tax-gatherers and sinners?" 12 But when He heard this, He said, "It is not those who are healthy who need a physician, but those who are sick. 13 But go and learn what this means, 'I desire compassion, and not sacrifice,' for I did not come to call the righteous, but sinners." Hos 6:6 For I desire mercy, not sacrifice, and acknowledgment of YHUH rather than burnt offerings.

My beloved, I told My people when they turned away from Me, that I desired their love and compassion towards others rather than going through the motions of bringing their offerings to Me only because it was demanded of them. They did not bring their offerings to Me because they loved Me and wanted to serve Me. Their offerings became an abomination to Me, so I destroyed the Temple. I no longer wanted their empty sacrifices and even their resentment that they had to bring their burnt offerings. I was happy to destroy their Temple. I was happy to scatter them across the nations, because no longer did I want them to defile My Land or My Temple. Their sins were disgusting to Me, so I washed the land clean of them. Soon I will call them back again to the land. I will wake them up and show them the truth about Me that they have lost in numerous years of wandering among the pagans. I will even rebuild My Temple and restore the burnt offerings, but My people will come joyfully to My altar and share their meal in My presence. If you think you can go to a church every Sunday and this will save you from destruction, you are wrong. You must know Me and hear My voice and be obedient to My words and My laws because you love Me. You will love others and be compassion towards them. Even if you keep My laws, if you hold the law above loving others you sin, because the law was made to love others and show others compassion and justice.

210

You should have faith in YHUH.

Mark 11:22 "Have faith in YHUH," Yahshua answered. 23 "I tell you the truth, if anyone says to this mountain, 'Go, throw yourself into the sea,' and does not doubt in his heart but believes that what he says will happen, it will be done for him. 24 Therefore I tell you, whatever you ask for in prayer, believe that you have received it, and it will be yours." Ps 62:8 Trust in Him at all times, O people; Pour out your heart before Him. YHUH is a refuge for us (Matt 9:20-30)

My beloved, you must have faith in Me as a child trusts his father to care for him knowing he will provide him food, clothes, and shelter. You must trust Me as a child trusts his father. You must know I will provide you food, clothes, and shelter. I will also give you other blessings as your deeds deserve. Do you help others? Do you love those around you? Do you give to those in need? Do you want to serve Me with your whole heart? Do you give up the things of the world, so you can walk in righteousness? What will you give up for Me? Will you give up friends who hinder your walk with Me? Will you give up family who hinder your walk with Me? Will you walk away from dishonest business opportunities even though you will make much money? Will you walk away from sin that hinders your walk with Me? You must examine yourself and trust Me to care for you. I will never leave you. I AM a good Father who cares for you if you call on My name. I will come quickly to you. I want you to commute with Me all the day. I love to hear your voice and talk with you. I want us to be as one. If you are anxious or you doubt Me, then this grieves Me. I want you to trust Me and not worry. I can do all things. No problem is too big for Me. It may be too big for you, but not for Me. You must trust Me to handle all your problems and keep your life free from all entanglements. You must have faith like a child would trust his father to give him good gifts.

211

You should drive out evil spirits in the name of Yahshua.

Matt 10:1 He called his twelve disciples to him and gave them authority to drive out evil spirits and to heal every disease and sickness. Deut 13:5 You must purge the evil from among you. (Matt 10:5-8, Acts 16:16-18, Acts 19:13-16)

My beloved, I sent out My disciples and I told them to seek out the lost tribes of the House of Israel-those scattered among the nations-not the tribes of Judah and Benjamin who dwell in Israel. Those who dwell in Israel have seen the Light and were too blinded in deception to see Me as their Savior. I told them to go to My people and tell them about Me and deliver them from darkness and bondage by healing their diseases cast on them by the Evil One and to expel all the evil spirits within them. My people will be able to see Me and know Me only after the power of the Evil One has been broken. The only way to break the darkness from them is to take authority over the spirit in My name and command them to leave. You must say, "Leave in the name of Yahshua" and they will flee, because I have given you the authority to drive them out. You should lay hands on the sick and ask Me to heal them, so they can rise up off their bed and begin to serve Me. They must confess their sins and ask forgiveness before anyone can be healed or freed from demons. If they do not repent, then the evil spirits will come back and bring other spirits with them. You must be at peace with all men. Forgive those who wrong you, and then you can be healed. If you seek Me for these things, I will come to you and heal you.

212

You should stay in one house when you are ministering in a city.

Matt 10:11 Whatever town or village you enter, search for some worthy person there and stay at his house until you leave. (Gen 19:1-3)

My beloved, I sent My disciples-those who followed after Me and wanted to obey My teaching-out to the lost tribes of Israel-those scattered to the nations. At that time two of the twelve tribes lived in My land-Judah and Benjamin, but the others were expelled from the land and scattered into every nation because they were sinful and arrogant. I sent them away from the Land, because they followed other gods. They still had the seed of righteousness within them, so when My disciples were sent out they would know them. My disciples would choose a man who had the seed of righteousness within him to stay at his house while he was in the town teaching the people about My words. My children may be scattered to the nations, but they are not forgotten. I want My children to learn truth and truth is arising and truth is coming to the door of the righteous so they can awake and walk in My ways. The days are dark, but the end draws near and you must be ready-prepared to face the days of tribulation. You must walk in My ways and teach those around you about truth and how to walk in truth. Many of My people have only lies from the Evil One, so speak truth to those around you and those who have My righteous seed will realize and see truth and be awakened by your words of truth. Be brave and bold and speak truth to others.

213

You should put your blessing of peace on the house where you visit.

Matt 10:12 As you enter the home, say "Peace be upon you." 13 If the home is deserving, let your peace rest on it; if it is not, let your peace return to you. 1 Sam 25:6 Say to him: Long life to you! Good health to you and your household! And good health to all that is yours! Ps 122:8 For the sake of my family and friends, I will say, "Peace be within you."

My beloved, as you go into another's home, say "Peace rest on this home." If there are those living in the house who want to follow Me and walk in My ways, then peace will remain on them and work in them, so they can overcome the Evil One and have victory. If no one who lives in the house wants to follow Me, then My peace will not remain on the house. If you walk away from a house and your peace returns to you, then the house has lost a great treasure. Do not be angry with those in the house, but be sad that their hearts were too dark to receive, but continue to pray that they will have light come to them so they can receive. If My seed of righteousness is in them, then the light will expose the seed and it will begin to grow. You will know those who have the seed of righteousness within them. You will see their searching and hunger and grief for not finding the truth. Others who do not have the seed of righteousness will be set on doing evil and want to see others suffer and will not respond to peace, but will reject it. Beware as you talk to others about truth and if they are receiving the truth you will know it, because you will feel truth pouring out of you into the person. If not, you will feel a wall in front of you. So go forth and be on guard as you tell others the truth of eternal life.

214

You should leave a town that does not listen to your words of Truth.

Matt 10:14 If anyone will not welcome you or listen to your words, shake the dust off your feet when you leave that home or town. 15 I tell you the truth, it will be more bearable for Sodom and Gomorrah on the day of judgment than for that town. (Acts 13:49-52, Neh 5:13)

My beloved, if you go to a town and tell them the truth about salvation and eternal life and they will not listen to you, then leave the town. You will know if the town wants to receive truth or not. If they want to receive truth, they will listen and want to learn more. If they do not want to listen, they will argue with you or mock you or walk away in disgust. Do not stay in a town like this. Darkness rules over this town and the people want to live in wickedness. This town will be judged harshly on Judgment Day, because Truth came to their town and they rejected it. If a few in the town want to listen, then stay only for them. Teach them truth and tell them where to find My laws and how to walk in My ways. Teach them of My love for them and how I want to bless them. They will be weak, so you will have to continue to come back to minister to them so they can be strengthened. If they live in a town filled with darkness, they should be encouraged to leave and live in a place where there are many others who want to serve Me. If you choose wisely where you live, then your children will grow up with children who love Me and want to walk in My ways. If you are in a city where you are persecuted or mocked or where no believers in Me live, then call on My Name and I will take you to a new place to live.

215

You should be as wise as serpents and harmless as doves.

Matt 10:16 Behold, I send you forth as sheep in the midst of wolves: be wise as serpents, and harmless as doves. Rom 16:19 Everyone has heard about your obedience, so I rejoice because of you; but I want you to be wise about what is good, and innocent about what is evil. (Gen 3:1, Hos 7:11)

My beloved, you walk among men who hate you, because they hate Me and want to destroy all My children. I have told My children to be on guard. Always look out for the enemy. He will try to harm you, so you must be smart and know his deceitful ways. He is not one that ever tells the truth. He is the father of all lies. He is a deceiver and liar and wants to cause harm to My children and bring fear to them. He knows that fear opens portals for the enemy to come in and oppress you or possess you, but if your trust is in Me, there is no fear only faith, and no portal is opened. I have said many times, "Fear not," so you must trust only Me. Be wise to not be deceived by the Evil One. If anything causes you fear, then pray to Me so I can bring peace to you and remove all your fear. You must also be harmless and not harm others. You cannot show love to others, if you try to harm them. You should never harm others, but you should love others and be kind to others. You will be a good example to a wicked world of My love. Men may be shocked at your love and compassion. Be kind even when others are not kind. Be on guard no matter if others around you want to have pleasure and joy in the things of the world. You should separate yourself from the things of the world and be a righteous person-clean and pure always doing what is right in My sight. Be wise, and also be at peace with those around you so I can bless you.

216

You should not worry about what you need to say to others about Yahshua.

Matt 10:17 Be on your guard against men; they will hand you over to the local councils and flog you in their synagogues. 18 On my account you will be brought before governors and kings as witnesses to them and to the Gentiles. 19 But when they arrest you, do not worry about what to say or how to say it. At that time you will be given what to say, 20 for it will not be you speaking, but the Spirit of your Father speaking through you. Ex 4:12 Now go; I will help you speak and will teach you what to say.

My beloved, do not be concerned about what you should say to others about Me. Just be willing to testify on account of Me. Be willing to say that I AM your Elohim and King and serve no other god. Be willing to stand up for Me when others deny Me. There will be a time when all around you will deny Me and reject Me for fear of what will happen to them and their family, but if you stand firm and do not fear I will give you the words to speak inflamed with the fire of My Spirit. Anyone carrying My righteous seed within him will know you speak My Truth. They will hear My words and be glad that Truth has come to their door. Rejoice and be glad that you are the bearer of truth and do not deny anyone from bearing the truth. If you start to tell someone the truth, you can tell if they are receiving it. If they do not receive the truth, then you have given them a special gift and they have rejected it. They have not rejected you, but Me. You are only the servant who brings the message from the Master, "Come to Me. The time is short and the days grow darker." Listen, My people, to all who call Me by Name- to all who call on Me, tell those around you about Me and My wondrous ways. Tell them of My love and compassion. Show them an example of My love by how you live your life. Open your mouth and I will speak through you by My Spirit.

217

You must love YHUH more than your family.

Mark 10:29 Anyone who loves his father or mother more than Me is not worthy of Me; anyone who loves his son or daughter more than Me is not worthy of Me; 38 and anyone who does not take his cross and follow Me is not worthy of Me. 39 Whoever finds his life will lose it, and whoever loses his life for my sake will find it. Gen 12:1 Now YHUH said to Abram, "Go forth from your country, and from your relatives, and from your father's house, to the land which I will show you." (Matt 10:21-36, 19:29-30, Deut 33:9)

My beloved, you will have many hate you because you love Me. You will have men want to kill you, because you are an obedient servant to Me. There will be those who betray you and turn against you, because you believe the Truth. Even your family members may turn against you, because you are righteous and want to follow My ways. Anytime you try to go against the established laws or practices in any religion, people will be angry with you because you are questioning their man-made doctrines. Man does not want to change from his easy life style where he can sin as much as he wants and "repent" and think he has repented but he goes and sins again. How is this repentance? You should turn away from your sins and never sin again. You may have an addiction and you want to stop. Seek Me and I will help you. Seek out help and advice how to quit. Get a faithful friend to stand beside you and encourage you to overcome. The addiction is probably a spirit and must be rebuked from you, so seek someone who knows his authority over the enemy to pray for you. Do not allow a reoccurring sin to keep you from following Me. Be free and clean and follow Me with your whole heart. I will protect you from the Evil One. I will see no harm come to you. You may see men hate you, but I will bring you eternal salvation.

218

You should flee to another city when you are persecuted.

Matt 10:23 When you are persecuted in one place, flee to another. I tell you the truth, you will not finish going through the cities of Israel before the Son of Man comes. (Acts 14:5-7, Jer 6:20-21)

My beloved, the world will hate you, because you love Me and want to live a righteous life. The wicked want to live in darkness, but when one of My children who live in light exposes their sins by the example of their righteousness, then the wicked will hate him and want to get rid of him. You must always be on guard and watch for those who hate you and want to kill you. You must be wise and look ahead. If you live in a place where you are persecuted, then go to another town until you can dwell safely. I do not want My children to endure persecution, if I open a door for them to leave. Pray and ask Me to set you free from the one who torments you, and I will show you a new place to go so you can abide in safety. Your light will be an example to those who have ears to hear and eyes to see. The wicked do not want to change, so go to a place where the people will receive you. If you have been persecuted, then I will reward you for your endurance. I will give you great rewards in My kingdom. The days ahead are dark, so prepare to come in contact with those who hate you. You should always show your love towards others. Do not show hatred towards those who hate you, but show My love. Do not seek revenge. I will pay back those who hate My children-who mock or torment them. You are only to show the world love, and I will bless you.

219

You should teach others what Yahshua has spoken.

Matt 10:24 A student is not above his teacher, nor a servant above his master. 25 It is enough for the student to be like his teacher, and the servant like his master. If the head of the house has been called Beelzebub, how much more the members of his household! 26 So do not be afraid of them. There is nothing concealed that will not be disclosed, or hidden that will not be made known. 27 What I tell you in the dark, speak in the daylight; what is whispered in your ear, proclaim from the roofs. (Acts 5:17-21, Prov 1:20-23)

My beloved, I have given you My words, so teach them to others. Be careful to only teach what I have spoken or judgment will come upon you. You must not teach man-made doctrine, but you must teach My words. If you are not sure what is Truth, then go search for it. Go find the Truth yourself. No man has to teach you, but I can teach you. Read My words and Truth will come to the surface. Truth will be brought to light and you will see it. You must remember that My commandments that I wrote in stone and gave to Moses are in the books of the law- Genesis, Exodus, Leviticus, Numbers, and Deuteronomy. You should study these books for Truth. All My prophets recorded My words that I gave them about coming future events. My prophets were killed, but their words were true and were preserved so you can search them for truth. My disciples gave their account of My life, and then they wrote to the churches concerning Me. These books will profit you greatly, if you search for the whole Truth. Do not pull a verse out and say, "This is what it means." No, read the whole book or chapter and see how the verse was used by the author. Only I bring life to scripture and anointing and only when Truth is found will life come to you. Cry out to Me, and what is kept hidden will come out of the scriptures and bring you Truth. Cry out and you will find Me, and I will speak to you hidden truths.

220

You should welcome those who are righteous.

Matt 10:40 He who receives (welcomes) you receives Me, and he who receives Me receives the One who sent Me. 41 Anyone who receives a prophet because he is a prophet will receive a prophet's reward, and anyone who receives a righteous man because he is a righteous man will receive a righteous man's reward. 42 And if anyone gives even a cup of cold water to one of these little ones because he is my disciple, I tell you the truth, he will certainly not lose his reward. (2 Kings 4:10)

My beloved, welcome all of My little ones who serve Me and walk in righteous. Take them into your house and bless them and I will bless you. Serve them and I will serve you. Feed them and I will feed you. Give them water and I will take care of your thirst. Clothe them and I will clothe you. If you welcome My children into your home and treat them kindly with love and hospitality, then I will bless you for your loving kindness. Do not shun any of the believers, because they are poor or sick or in another social class or ethic group than you. All people are equal. My children are all created in My image in all different colors, sizes, and shapes. They all worship Me in different ways, and they show loving kindness to others in different ways, but they all love Me and love others. You will know My children by their love for others-their giving kind ways. My child loves others and looks pass the flesh into the heart. The flesh is only a wrap around the spirit, but the spirit of light should show through the flesh and light the path of others. If you love to help others and long to please Me, then you are a true child of Mine. You will lend a hand to anyone in need and be an extension of My hand, so all can be blessed by Me.

221

You should learn from Yahshua.

Matt 11:29 Take my yoke upon you and learn from Me, for I am gentle and humble in heart, and you will find rest for your souls. 30 For my yoke is easy and my burden is light. Deut 31:12 Assemble the people-men, women and children, and the aliens living in your towns-so they can listen and learn to fear YHUH your Elohim and follow carefully all the words of this law. Deut 5:1 Hear, O Israel, the decrees and laws I declare in your hearing today. Learn them and be sure to follow them.

My beloved, come to Me and learn from Me and I will guide you. Just as an ox wears a yoke and the farmer guides him down the field, I will guide you. My yoke is not heavy or a burden to wear. The worries and concerns of life are a burden, but if you just allow Me to guide you and trust Me to provide for you, then you will feel free. The world has a very strong pull on you, if you look at all the things that could happen to you like chains around you pulling you tighter and tighter. You must know that I can release you from the chains of the world. Be strong and have courage, because I AM always with you. My plan for you far outweighs any of the pulling from the world, because I love you and I will care for you. Do not be afraid, but rejoice that you have a Father who loves you so much. I want you to come to Me and draw life from Me. I will give you rest from all of the world's problems. You are in a sea of faces of those who do not know Me, and they follow the world. You follow Me and the world becomes very dim and all you see before you is My plan for you. You must learn My Ways, and I will mold you and shape you into the one who cares no more for the world but cares only for Me.

222

You should do good things on the Sabbath.

Matt 12:9 Going on from that place, He went into their synagogue, 10 and a man with a shriveled hand was there. Looking for a reason to accuse Yahshua, they asked Him, "Is it lawful to heal on the Sabbath?" 11 He said to them, "If any of you has a sheep and it falls into a pit on the Sabbath, will you not take hold of it and lift it out? 12 How much more valuable is a man than a sheep! Therefore it is lawful to do good on the Sabbath." 13 Then He said to the man, "Stretch out your hand." So he stretched it out and it was completely restored, just as sound as the other. (Luke 13:10-17, Ex 23:4-5)

My beloved, I gave the Sabbath Day to man to rest and be restored from his labors. During the time that I walked on Earth My people were so bowed down with excessive rules that there was no joy in living. Knowing Me brings joy. Knowing how to walk in loving kindness brings joy. Knowing how to love others bring joy. Excessive rules only bring bondage. My children were in bondage, and I came to set them free. I wanted to show them that doing good things on My Sabbath Day was not breaking the Sabbath. As long as you brought love to others, this would please Me. If you have a choice whether to work or rest on My Sabbath Day, then you should choose to rest. My healing will come on you on Sabbath and renew you for the week. If a crisis arises, then you must go assist whoever needs you, but this is not your usual day. You should spend time with your family and love them and study My words. You should teach your children My Words on Sabbath and build a foundation that will not shatter, then you will always rejoice over your children. Those around you may not celebrate Sabbath on the seventh day, but you are in My will and I will bless you. Some have not seen My Truth yet, and the enemy continues to deceive them. They have not searched the scriptures, because they would know that Sabbath celebrated on the seventh day is an everlasting ordinance and a sign to the world around you that you are My remnant-My unique and treasured people.

223

You should not speak careless words about others.

Matt 12: 36 "Make a tree good and its fruit will be good, or make a tree bad and its fruit will be bad, for a tree is recognized by its fruit. 34 You brood of vipers, how can you who are evil say anything good? For out of the overflow of the heart the mouth speaks. 35 The good man brings good things out of the good stored up in him, and the evil man brings evil things out of the evil stored up in him. 36 But I tell you that men will have to give account on the day of judgment for every careless word they have spoken. 37 For by your words you will be acquitted, and by your words you will be condemned." (Eccl 12:14, Rev 20:12)

My beloved, speak only loving and kind words to others. Do not allow evil words to come out of your mouth. If you want to hurt others with your words, then ask yourself why you want to be mean to others. What is causing you to want to hurt others? Are you in sin and the weight of the sin is so much for you to bear that you are crushed and only pain comes out of your mouth because you are not repentant. Have you not forgiven someone who has wronged you, and the pain inflicted by the person caused great wounds inside of you and you spill your pain onto others by the words of your mouth? Have you listened to My voice? If not you are resisting My will and all is going wrong in your life. You are so frustrated that you become angry and your anger spills out onto others. Do not allow your hurt and pain to spill onto others, but instead be cleansed by My Spirit and repent, forgive, and yield to My Spirit, and then you can deliver words of healing to others instead of pain and suffering. You can bring happiness to others instead of pain. Does your mouth flow over with mean words before you have a chance to consider their harm? Pray for self-control over your words, but more than this, pray for inner healing so you can be whole and not filled with wounds. I want you to be totally healed, so you can bring strength to others and not destruction.

224

You should do the will of your Heavenly Father.

Matt 12:48 He replied to him, "Who is my mother, and who are my brothers?" 49 Pointing to his disciples, He said, "Here are my mother and my brothers. 50 For whoever does the will of my Father in heaven is my brother and sister and mother." John 15:14 You are my friends, if you do whatever I command you. Lev 18:4 You must obey my laws and be careful to follow my decrees. I am YHUH your Elohim.

My beloved, do My will for you and you will be blessed. Do not resist what I tell you to do. Do you not know that I will only give you good things? I want you to have the best while you are here on Earth, but this does not mean wealth, fame or power, but it means all your needs for food, water, shelter, clothing and all your spiritual needs are met, so you have a strong faith and can stand in the last days. The most important thing is that you become mighty in the things of the spirit. I will send you testing and trials to produce a strong faith, so you will depend completely on Me. You must trust Me to care for you. You must know that I will guide you along the right path, so you can grow in Me and give generously to others. Be strong and bold, and do not allow the Evil One to deceive you. If you cling to Me, I will reward you in My kingdom. You are My child and heir to My throne. You will be given all My authority, so you can rule over nations and tell them about your heavenly Father. You will testify of My loving kindness and tender mercies. I wrapped you in flesh and placed you on Earth, so you can prove to all that you are worthy of bearing My Name. You are greatly loved, so do My will and see how greatly I reward you.

225

You should ask for understanding into the Scriptures.

Mark 4:10,33 When He was alone, the Twelve and the others around Him asked Him about the parables. 33 With many similar parables Yahshua spoke the word to them, as much as they could understand. 34 He did not say anything to them without using a parable. But when He was alone with his own disciples, He explained everything. Ps 119:34 Give me understanding, and I will keep your law and obey it with all my heart. Ps 119:169 May my cry come before you, O YHUH; give me understanding according to your word.

My beloved, I want you to read My Words that I have given you, and then if you do not understand My Words, ask Me to explain them to you. My disciples always asked Me to explain My parables to them. They did not understand many things I said until I left them and went to take My place in My Heavenly Kingdom. They had many questions, but I gave them understanding. I will give you understanding and wisdom if only you ask Me. Do not read My words and say "This is boring" or "This is too difficult to read" or "This is for another time, not today." Read My words with the desire to dig out the meaning of each and every word, and then you will be wise. You will have a strong foundation, so when trials and tribulations come you will not fall away. When worries of the world and fleshy desires come against you, then go to My words for strength, and then you will endure to the end and not be cast aside and thrown into the lake of fire with the others who turned against Me and would not keep My commandments. If you are lacking, call out to Me and I will help you. I AM never far from you. Those who call on My name I draw close to Me. I bend My ear to you, so I can meet every one of your needs. You are My beloved child, and I want you to understand My ways, so you can walk in righteousness and be saved from eternal darkness.

226

You should give up all you have to obtain the Kingdom of Heaven (eternal life).

Matt 13:44 "The kingdom of heaven is like treasure hidden in a field. When a man found it, he hid it again, and then in his joy went and sold all he had and bought that field. 45 Again, the kingdom of heaven is like a merchant looking for fine pearls. 46 When he found one of great value, he went away and sold everything he had and bought it." Prov 2:4 If you seek her (Wisdom) as silver and search for her as for hidden treasures; then you will discern the fear of YHUH and discover the knowledge of Elohim. (Rev 3:18)

My beloved, there is nothing of any greater value than to enter the kingdom of heaven and have eternal life. There is nothing on this Earth of any value. Everything on Earth will be burned. Nothing will last or have any eternal value. Nothing on this Earth was meant to be eternal. Earth is a temporary place used to test My children and prove to all that you are worthy of inheriting My kingdom. In this way you are proven faithful to Me, and all will respect the power and authority that is given you because you are My child. You must be able to endure to the end and love Me with all your heart. Some look at the Earth as a place to horde up treasure, but this is a place to be a servant to others and show loving kindness towards them so your love can be an example to them of My loving kindness. You must be able to give up everything that hinders your walk of righteousness. If you give it all up-all that is of the world-then you can walk in righteousness and obtain eternal life. Eternal life is a special gift given only to My children who prove to all that they are worthy of bearing My name-the name a father gives his child. If a child has no name, then who is his father? You have My name only if you are at one with Me-in unity with Me–and give up all for the sake of Me.

227

You should not focus on the little you have, but what miracle YHUH can do for you.

Matt 14:16 Yahshua replied, "They do not need to go away. You give them something to eat." 17 "We have here only five loaves of bread and two fish," they answered. 18 "Bring them here to Me," he said. 19 And He directed the people to sit down on the grass. Taking the five loaves and the two fish and looking up to heaven, He gave thanks and broke the loaves. Then He gave them to the disciples, and the disciples gave them to the people. 20 They all ate and were satisfied, and the disciples picked up twelve basketfuls of broken pieces that were left over. John 14:12 "Truly, truly, I say to you, whoever believes in Me will also do the works that I do; and greater works than these will he do, because I am going to the Father." (Deut 8:18)

My beloved, when I was with My disciples I taught them to do many things, and they became strong in the faith. I taught them not to limit Me, but to trust Me. When I fed the crowds of people, I wanted them to see how I could supply not only for them but for many. I AM Creator. I can create food and multiply food and make sure you and your family is fed. I sent My people bread from heaven in the desert, and I sent My prophets bread delivered by ravens. You do not have to be afraid as long as you call on My Name, I will help you. I AM your Father. Would I not supply for you what you need? You must believe that I will do the unlikely and the impossible. Is your faith strong? Read My words and pray and fast. You have no answer to your prayer, because of the sin in your life. Repent and ask forgiveness. Make restitution if you need to and be on good terms with all your brothers in the faith. Be fair and just to all men. Love others and do not say mean words to others. Be brave and bold and tell others about Me and My salvation. I have given to all who trust, believe, and cling to Me. You must be able to look past the natural and see the spiritual realm, because all things are possible in the spiritual realm.

228

You should guard over what comes out of your mouth.

Matt 15:10 Yahshua called the crowd to Him and said, "Listen and understand. 11 What goes into a man's mouth does not make him 'unclean,' but what comes out of his mouth, that is what makes him 'unclean.'" 15 Peter said, "Explain the parable to us." 16 "Are you still so dull?" Yahshua asked them. 17 "Don't you see that whatever enters the mouth goes into the stomach and then out of the body? 18 But the things that come out of the mouth come from the heart, and these make a man 'unclean.' 19 For out of the heart come evil thoughts, murder, adultery, sexual immorality, theft, false testimony, slander. 20 These are what make a man 'unclean'; but eating with (ceremonially) unwashed hands does not make him 'unclean.'" (Ps 49:3, Prov 12:18, Prov 17:27)

My beloved, I tried to tell My disciples that it was not the food you eat that makes you unclean, but what comes out of your heart that condemns you. The argument was over ceremonial hand washing as to whether the absence of the ritual made you unclean or not. It is important to wash your hands before eating, but washing your hands up to your elbows is excessive. It is important to eat only the clean foods that I have given you so your body will not be polluted, but the words from your mouth expose the spiritual state of your heart. If you speak kind and loving words, then your heart is kind and loving. If you speak mean words, then you have a heart filled with hatred. Look at yourself. Do you need to forgive someone? Do you need to make restitution? Do you need to correct some wrongs? Are you in sin and resisting the conviction of My spirit? Do you hate others? Where is My love inside of you? If you truly are My child, you would be filled with love for others. If you really wanted to serve Me, you would serve others. If you love those around you and bring encouraging words to others, then others will see the Light of My presence. Do you want to reflect Light or darkness? Anyone can serve the world. The path is easy. You just do whatever you want to do. Only a few can serve Me and walk in My ways, but great are their rewards.

229

You should walk away from blinded spiritual leaders.

Matt 15:12 Then the disciples came to Him and asked, "Do you know that the Pharisees were offended when they heard this?" 13 He replied, "Every plant that my heavenly Father has not planted will be pulled up by the roots. 14 Leave them; they are blind guides. If a blind man leads a blind man, both will fall into a pit." Is 9:16 Those who guide this people mislead them, and those who are guided are led astray. (Jer 14:14)

My beloved, do not be deceived by men who say they are "men of god" or "called by god to preach," if they do not preach the Truth. Each man has been trained to teach in his own denominational church, so he has been taught in error by his denominational leaders to follow a certain doctrine. Men who speak My words do not follow doctrine, but every word that proceeds out of My mouth. So many times these men who call themselves "servants of god" do not listen for My voice and follow My instructions, but they follow man-made laws and traditions. They are caught in a trap, because they do not search for the truth, so they are blinded in their sins. Beware of these men who teach lessons written by church leaders based on their doctrine. Look for a man who teaches from My words-the whole context of My words. If his bible is worn and he prays and fasts to find truth, then listen and judge and discern. If he walks righteously, then you know he is a good teacher who follows close to Me. Watch out for blind teachers and stay far away from them. What if you say, "I do not want to give up my church family," then I will say to you, "What do you value more The Truth or friends?" You must make a decision. People will not like you when you give up man-made laws and traditions. They will mock you and exclude you. Even your church family will shun you if you turn away from their doctrines. If you find Truth, you are released from bondage and given peace in Me.

230

You should believe that through faith nothing is impossible.

Matt 17:20 He replied, "Because you have so little faith. I tell you the truth, if you have faith as small as a mustard seed, you can say to this mountain, 'Move from here to there' and it will move. Nothing will be impossible or you." Matt 19:26 Yahshua looked at them and said, "Humanly this is impossible, but with Elohim everything is possible." Genesis 18:14 "Is anything too hard for YHUH?" Jer 32:27 "I am YHUH, the Elohim of all mankind. Is anything too hard for Me?"

My beloved, everything is possible through Me. Whatever you ask in faith believing that I will do it, then I will do it for you if you ask from a pure heart. If you ask of fleshly desires, then your heart is not pure. I hear the prayers of a righteous man. I hear the prayers of a sinner who is repenting. A sinner who mocks Me or an arrogant man who says he serves Me is an abomination to Me. If you ask in My name, ask humbly and in reverence for Me, then I will hear you. I want to do the miraculous for My children, but I do not see faith. I see very few of My children with faith. Who will cancel all your insurance and trust in Me to care for you and protect you? Who comes to Me for healing instead of a doctor? Who comes to Me for a child instead of a fertility doctor? Who comes to Me to lose weight or lose a bad habit? Who comes to Me to teach your children My ways? Who comes to Me for guidance or wisdom? Who comes to Me for correction or repentance? Who comes to Me to cure your cancer? Who comes to Me to release you from debt or demons? Who comes to Me instead of the world system? Where is your trust? People who have much trust little, but people who have little trust in Me for much.

231

You should humble yourself like a child.

Matt 18:2 He called a little child and had him stand among them. 3 And He said: "I tell you the truth, unless you change and become like little children, you will never enter the kingdom of heaven. 4 Whoever humbles himself like this child is the greatest in the kingdom of heaven." Ps 25:9 He guides the humble in what is right and teaches them his way. Ps 149:4 For YHUH takes delight in his people; He crowns the humble with salvation.

My beloved, humble yourself and learn from Me like a little child learns from his parents. A child must submit to the will of his parent and obey him, because the child lacks wisdom and the parent knows what is best for the child. The child may want his own way, and the parent will have to discipline the child. After a child is disciplined and learns from the error of his ways, he is a wiser child and can submit to the authority of his parents. You must submit to My authority and fear Me knowing that I have all authority and I can give to you or take away from you. I can bless or curse. I can see clearly into you and know exactly what you need at the time you need it. Rejoice and be glad that you have a father who loves you so much to correct you and make you see clearly how to walk in My ways. Be strong and of good courage, because I AM always beside you and will never fail you. Do not lead the little children astray, because if you do you will be punished severely by Me. Bless the little children and teach them My words. Do not depend on someone else to teach your children, but teach your children My words. Pray with your children and love them and show them an example of faithfulness. Show them an example of love and compassion to others. Love those around you and your child will learn to love others and walk in righteousness.

232

You should love little children and not despise them.

Matt 18:10 See that you do not look down on one of these little ones. For I tell you that their angels in heaven always see the face of my Father in heaven. Matt 19:14 Yahshua said, "Let the little children come to Me, and do not hinder them, for the kingdom of heaven belongs to such as these." Ps 103:13 As a father has compassion on his children, so YHUH has compassion on those who fear Him. Ps 127:3 Sons are a heritage from YHUH, children a reward from Him.

My beloved, do not despise the little children, but let them come close to you and teach them My ways. Children learn by example and you must be an example at all times of loving kindness, so your children can walk in love. Allow your children to learn at your knee the words of life that I have given you. Teach them My words-My scriptures about My commandments and My words of wisdom as I walked on this planet. Do not expect other people to teach your child about Me. Do not say that the church will teach My child the Commandments. Do not lay this responsibility on others. This is your responsibility to teach your children about Me. You will be held responsible for what you teach your children, so bring them Truth. Do not push them aside for others to care for them, but put them in your lap and read them My words and teach them to pray and walk in faith. The days grow increasingly darker. Darkest will cover the earth except where My children are living. A light will be in the midst of them. and they will be warm in winter and shaded in summer. My little ones are always in My presence. I never turn them away from Me. I expect you never to turn children away from you. Invest yourself into your children and love them and hold them close to you being watchful, because the enemy is always close at hand to prey upon My little ones and steal their innocence. Beware and guard your children very carefully

233

You should establish every matter based on the testimony of two or three witnesses (not only one witness).

Matt 18:15 "If your brother sins against you, go and show him his fault, just between the two of you. If he listens to you, you have won your brother over. 16 But if he will not listen, take one or two others along, so that 'every matter may be established by the testimony of two or three witnesses.' 17 If he refuses to listen to them, tell it to the church; and if he refuses to listen even to the church, treat him as you would a pagan or a tax collector." (Deut 19:15)

My beloved, if your brother sins against you, then go to him and tell him that he has wronged you and you have come to resolve the problem. If he owes you restitution, then he must pay it. If he has borrowed an item and he has not returned it, then go ask your brother for what he borrowed. If he has insulted you, then go to him and find out why he insulted you. If a man has wronged your family and said harsh words against your family members or has wronged a member of your family, then take the person he has wronged with you and go to the person and ask the person to correct the wrong. If the person will not listen to you, then if there are any witnesses to what happened, then take the witnesses with you to talk to the man so he can correct the wrong against you. If the man will still not listen to reason and will not repent, then lift him up to the believers in your area. If he repents, you have saved your brother. If he does not repent, you should separate yourself from him, because he has separated himself from Me and no longer wants to serve Me. Resolve your conflicts quickly, and let there not be any division between you and your brother. Love your brother and do good things for him, then your light will shine brightly to all those around you. They will praise Me for all your good works. I will bless you so you can give generously. Give and be a blessing to others.

234

You should agree with another for what you ask for in prayer.

Matt 18:18 "And so I tell all of you: what you prohibit on earth will be prohibited in heaven, and what you permit on earth will be permitted in heaven. Again I say to you that if two of you agree on earth concerning anything that they ask, it will be done for them by My Father in heaven. 20 For where two or three are gathered together in My name, I am there in the midst of them." (Deut 19:15)

My beloved, whatever you ask in My name believing in Me according to My will, I will give you. If you agree with two or three witnesses, you have pledged with these witnesses that this is good for Me to do this for you. What hinders your prayers? It is the darkness within you, the lack of Truth, the sin that you will not repent from, or the love of the world. The people who walk in darkness have no favor in My eyes. I look for the righteous man. His prayers carry much weight in My kingdom. If you agree with another in prayer asking Me for a righteous act, then I will hear you and act on your behalf. You can stop what you want on Earth and begin what you want on Earth. You can pray against evil and stop it, and you can pray for righteousness to begin on Earth. The man who stands against evil, I will reward. I look for a man who will fast and pray against evil. I look for a man who will fast and pray on behalf of righteousness. You can begin and end by the words of your mouth. The enemy fears you and will try to stop your prayers, but your prayers come up as flaming fires if you walk in righteousness. The enemy cannot stop their surge into My kingdom. Great are the prayers of those who love Me and obey My commandments.

235

You should obey the commandments YHUH gave to Moses.

Matt 19:17 "If you want to enter life, obey the commandments (given to Moses)." 18 "Which ones?" the man inquired. Yahshua replied, "Do not murder, do not commit adultery, do not steal, do not give false testimony, 19 honor your father and mother, and love your neighbor as yourself." Matt 5:17-19 "Do not think that I have come to abolish the Law or the Prophets; I have not come to abolish them but to fulfill them. 18 I tell you the truth, until heaven and earth disappear, not the smallest letter, not the least stroke of a pen, will by any means disappear from the Law until everything is accomplished." (Ex 20:1-17, Lev 19:18)

My beloved, I have given you laws to live by, so you will have eternal life and not death. If you will follow the commandments I gave Moses, then you will have an abundant life and you will be blessed. If you do not keep My commandments, you will face death and destruction. Life is in the commandments. They will teach you to love others and love Me. In them I tell you how to worship Me and please Me. You will be greatly blessed if you keep all My commandments. Where are these commandments? I gave the commandments to Moses. I wrote them on stone tablets, so Moses could take them to My people to read and follow. You must remember that My people did not keep the commandments, and they were punished and driven out of their home land-the Promised Land. They were scattered among the nations until they did not know who they were or where they lived. Now it is time to open the eyes of My children, so awake My little ones and receive your inheritance. What is your inheritance? The laws I have given you, so you can walk in righteousness and be blessed. If you will walk in My ways, I will take you to great heights so you can see ahead clearly and know the way you are going. If you draw close to Me, I will draw close to you. I will wrap you in My arms of love and comfort you during this time of testing on Earth, so you can overcome and be victorious in the last days.

236

You should be a servant to others.

Matt 20:25 So Yahshua called them all together and said, "You know that the rulers of the heathen have power over them, and the leaders have complete authority. 26 This, however, is not the way it shall be among you. If one of you wants to be great, he must be the servant of the rest; 27 and if one of you wants to be first, he must be your slave-28 like the Son of Man, who did not come to be served, but to serve and to give His life to redeem many people." (Luke 22:26, Prov 17:2)

My beloved, do not go the way of the world, but go the way of those who love Me. If you want to be first in My kingdom, then you must be last here. You must be a servant to all and love others. If you look at others as being less than you, then you are in error. You must love all men as equal not loving the sin in them, but loving their soul-the part of them that when released from their body will stand before Me at Judgment Day. The flesh can come in all sizes and colors, but the soul is what is of value. A man is very valuable to Me, if he wants to serve Me. He must also want to serve others. He must be humble and cannot be proud. He must be a man who loves to obey Me and follow after Me. He cannot follow after the things of the world and Me also, but he must only want to follow My ways. I AM jealous. I know who loves Me and wants to serve Me. Only those who want to serve Me will enter into My kingdom. If you have a servant's heart you will not want your own way, but you will want to follow after Me. Ask yourself if you will do whatever I ask of you. If you can answer yes to this, then your heart has turned towards Me. You are at one with Me, and you can be a servant to all.

237

You should not doubt YHUH.

Matt 21:21 Yahshua replied, "Truly I tell you, if you have faith and do not doubt, not only can you do what was done to the fig tree, but also you can say to this mountain, 'Go, throw yourself into the sea,' and it will be done." James 1:6 But when you ask, you must believe and not doubt, because the one who doubts is like a wave of the sea, blown and tossed by the wind. Num 14:11 Then YHUH said to Moses: "How long will these people reject Me? And how long will they not believe Me, with all the signs which I have performed among them?"

My beloved, you should have faith in Me that I can do all things. If you doubt Me, then you are hindering your faith. I can only move through a person who trusts in Me. If you are lacking, then believe in Me that I can provide what you need. As long as you trust Me I can do good things for you. If you doubt that I will help you, then you will not be able to receive anything from Me. There may be areas in your life that you trust Me completely, but there may be areas where you are weak and cannot trust Me completely. I will test those weak areas, so you will become stronger. If you wonder why difficulties come your way, it is because I must make you stronger in that area. Watch as you learn to trust Me. If you become strong in that area, then I will no longer test you in that area. I want you to completely trust in Me, so you can be strong in these Last Days. The days will grow darker and you must hear My Voice and trust Me to guide you. I may ask you to move quickly or I may give you advance notice. Whatever way I choose to guide you listen to Me and I will show you the way. You cannot doubt Me at this time. There should not be any fear in you. You must trust Me. If there is sin in your life, then repent and I will forgive you. Come before Me clean and pure and ready to hear My Words. I will help you in whatever way you ask Me. I am faithful.

238

You should pay your taxes and what you owe the government.

Matt 22:15 Then the Pharisees went out and laid plans to trap him in his words. 16 They sent their disciples to him along with the Herodians. "Teacher," they said, "we know you are a man of integrity and that you teach the way of Elohim in accordance with the truth. You aren't swayed by men, because you pay no attention to who they are. 17 Tell us then, what is your opinion? Is it right to pay taxes to Caesar or not?" 18 But Yahshua, knowing their evil intent, said, "You hypocrites, why are you trying to trap Me? 19 Show Me the coin used for paying the tax." They brought him a denarius, 20 and he asked them, "Whose portrait is this? And whose inscription?" 21 "Caesar's," they replied. Then He said to them, "Give to Caesar what is Caesar's, and to Elohim what is Elohim's." 22 When they heard this, they were amazed. So they left Him and went away. (Rom 13:7, Prov 24:21)

My beloved, My people were under a heavy tax when the Romans controlled them and governed them. I told them to pay the tax, because they do not need to rebel against the government. I brought this government to rule over them to punish them for past sins. This was their burden and punishment to have their enemies live in their land and control it. It was shameful to have such pagans in their land, but they had to be punished for their sins. Today you live in a land where you have to pay taxes and the amount of taxes increases and the burden is harder to bear. You are also in exile and under a burden of your ancestors' sin. As you walk out from under the man-made laws the church has adopted for you and come to My words and search for Truth for yourself and find it and teach your children My laws and not man-made laws, then I will release you from debt. You will see clearly and be released from all bondage. Your eyes will be open to Truth. Others may not see the Truth, because their hearts are dark, but if you truly want to know Me you will search for Me and find Me. I AM hidden and only reveal Myself to others who really search for Me. They love My words and search for Truth and they find it. They never put themselves in the bondage of debt or sin, but they are free to be led by My Spirit.

239

You should love your neighbor as yourself.

Matt 22:39 "And the second is like it: 'Love your neighbor as yourself.' 40 All the Law (given to Moses) and the (Old Testament) Prophets are dependent on these two commandments." John 13:34 "A new command I give you: Love one another. As I have loved you, so you must love one another. 35 By this all men will know that you are my disciples, if you love one another." Lev 19:18 Love your neighbor as yourself. I am YHUH.

My beloved, I AM the purest form of Love. I want all My children to be filled with love and give love to others. I want My children to reflect who I AM. I AM LOVE. If you love Me, you will love who I AM and I AM LOVE. If you know Me, you will know I AM LOVE. If you want to be like Me, you will love others. Who are these others? It is easy to love your family, but not so easy to love those who live around you. What about the poor? Do you love them and do good things for them? Do you love the needy, the aged, and the sick? Do you help others who need help? Do you seek out the wealthy to be your friends or do you seek out the poor to be your friends? If the poor are in sin and do not repent, then separate yourself from them. If the poor are trying hard to change their life and want to work hard and have a better place to live and better things for their children, then you should help them with their goals. If you see a mother who has children and her husband left her and she has no means of support, help her to start again and be able to support herself. If you can do this, then you can change a life and you will be rewarded. Love all those around you and do good deeds, so all will see My love within you.

240

You should not take the titles "Master" or "Father" for yourself.

Matt 23:8 But you are not to be called 'Rabbi,' for you have only one Master and you are all brothers. 9 And do not call anyone on earth 'father,' for you have one Father, and He is in heaven. 10 Nor are you to be called 'teacher,' for you have one Teacher, Yahshua. 11 The greatest among you will be your servant. 12 For whoever exalts himself will be humbled, and whoever humbles himself will be exalted. Is 64:8 Yet, O YHUH, you are our Father. We are the clay, you are the potter; we are all the work of your hand.

My beloved, I told My people not to set one man higher than the other. Do not call one rabbi and exalt him above the others or teacher and exalt him above the others. You are all brothers and no one should be exalted above the others. If you do this, then man will follow Me and only Me. This is what has happened with My children. They follow what their pastor, priest, or rabbi says and do not follow My words. Listen only to Me! Do not call a man "Father." I AM your only Father. I watch over and care for you better than any earthly father. I know what you need before you ever ask. Call on My name and I will give to you whatever you ask, because I want to give good gifts to My children. If you call on My name and you are in sin, then repent first because your sin separates us and we cannot be as one. If you love Me, you will obey My commands and do as My Spirit leads you to do. Do not listen to man, because he will lead you astray. Remember a man or anti-Christ will deceive the world and only the elect will escape his delusion. Only those who are searching My words for Truth and want to know Me will hear My voice. Awake My child and repent and turn from your sins. The days grow dark, and if you wait too long you will also be deceived with the masses by the Evil One. You must have Truth in your heart and know the signs to watch for and be led by My Spirit, otherwise you will be utterly destroyed.

Which Commandments Should I Obey?

241

You should be on your guard against greed and self-indulgence.

Matt 23:25 Woe to you, teachers of the law and Pharisees, you hypocrites! You clean the outside of the cup and dish, but inside they are full of greed and self-indulgence. 26 Blind Pharisee! First clean the inside of the cup and dish, and then the outside also will be clean. Prov 5:22 The righteousness of the upright will deliver them, But the treacherous will be caught by their own greed. (Luke 12:13-15)

My beloved, beware of men who say they serve Me, yet they are not humble towards others. Beware of men who say they follow My commandments, yet say the Old Testament is no longer of value. They say you no longer have to keep those laws, because when Yahshua came he gave us new laws to follow. Beware of men who dwell in churches and teach you to give all your money to the church. This is an abomination to Me. You should give to the poor, needy, widows, and orphans and to teachers who teach My commandments—including those found in the Old Testament. I plainly said when I came to earth that I did not come to take away My commandments but to fulfill the prophecy about Me in the Old Testament. I came to teach My disciples how to walk in My laws and not the laws of men. I gave them freedom, liberty, and took a burden of man-made laws off their back, so they could hear My voice and follow Me. If you are greedy for money, you will be punished. If men who teach My laws are greedy, stay far away from them. If they keep asking for your money, then do not listen to them because they are not of Me. I take care of those who love Me and serve Me. I send My Spirit to call on your heart to give to the men who serve Me and provide for them. Listen to My call to give, but do not allow men to blind you with false doctrine. Search My words for yourself and find Truth.

242

You should be careful that no one deceives you.

Matt 24:4 Yahshua answered: "Watch out that no one deceives you. 5 For many will come in my name, claiming, 'I am the Messiah,' and will deceive many. 23 At that time if anyone says to you, 'Look, here is the Messiah!' or, 'There He is!' do not believe it. 24 For false messiahs and false prophets will appear and perform great signs and miracles to deceive even the elect if that were possible." Luke 16:8 For the people of this world are more shrewd in dealing with their own kind than are the people of the light. (Jer 29:8)

My beloved, be careful not to be deceived, because many will come saying, "I am the way to eternal life, peace, and happiness." Others will say, "I am the one in whom you seek. I am the one you have waited for to come again." These will come with signs and wonders. They will say angels brought them messages for a new way to live in peace. No angels will come to anyone. You must not focus on angels. You must not worship angels, but only Me. If you focus on angels; you do not worship Me, but them. Men will try to deceive you by bringing a new religion to you-one you do not know. Be careful. The only Truth is in My words. No new truth will come to you. Cling to My words and you will not be deceived. If you hear that I have come to a certain place, do not believe it, because all men will see Me come at once as lightning flashes through the sky. I won't come out of a space ship or appear to a few people. I will reveal Myself to all the world at once, and they will know that I have returned. The Evil One will come and say that he is the one, and he will take advantage of the weak by performing signs and wonders, but these are only illusions. Do not be deceived by his witchcraft, but trust in Me. The time is near for My return so prepare yourself by reading My words and clinging to every one of them, and then you will not be deceived.

243

You should keep alert and watch for the Second coming.

Matt 24:42 "Therefore keep watch, because you do not know on what day your Master will come. 44 So you also must be ready, because the Son of Man will come at an hour when you do not expect Him." Num 8:11 Aaron is to present the Levites before YHUH as a wave offering from the Israelites, so that they may be ready to do the work of YHUH. Ex 19:10 Have them wash their clothes and be ready by the third day, because on that day YHUH will come down on Mount Sinai in the sight of all the people. (Matt 24:36-51, 25:1-13, Luke 12:35-40)

My beloved, be ready! Stay united and alert because I AM returning soon. Stand firm. Do not give into the temptation of the Evil One. He will show you the world and make it glitter and say it is all you ever wanted and you will be satisfied. You can never satisfy the flesh. You must submit your flesh to My Spirit within you, and then you will be satisfied. If you are miserable and you do not like your life, then you need to make some changes. You need to look at every area of your life and find the sin in it and repent and get your life going in the right direction. Maybe you are not listening to My Voice and once you begin to listen all will go well with you. Rejoice that you have a Father who points out your sin and even helps you change your life, so you can sin no longer. If you associate with drunkards and adulterers or fornicators, repent and let your friends be those you can trust-those who love Me and want to serve Me. Do not want to cling to those who love the world, but hold onto those who want to walk in righteousness. When hard times come, you will have friends who will support you and encourage you. You need only to trust Me. I will provide all you need until the last days. You are My beloved, and I will protect you from all the disasters. I will lead you to shelter and protect you from your enemies. Do not worry or be afraid, because I will care for you. Men of the world will die from terror, but you will rejoice at My coming.

244

You should be a faithful and wise servant to Yahshua until He returns.

Matt 24:45-51 "Who, then, is a faithful and wise servant? He is the one that his master has placed in charge of the other servants to give them their food at the proper time. 46 How happy that servant is if his master finds him doing this when he comes home!" Prov 14:35 A king delights in a wise servant, but a shameful servant arouses his fury. Prov 28:20 A faithful person will be richly blessed, but one eager to get rich will not go unpunished.

My beloved, be a faithful servant and continue to walk in My ways-the path of righteousness. You must always be at peace and rest in My presence. You must take each day one at a time listening for My voice and willing to do whatever I tell you to do. You should always try to please Me- ready, prepared, and waiting for My return. You should always be loving and kind and wanting to help those in need. Remember you are helping Me when you help others. My servants are My arms and legs. You are extensions of Me. When one of your brothers need help, then go to him and help him so he can have all that he needs. Do not allow your brothers to go lacking as you sit idle and do not help him. Think of your brother and how he needs you and do not turn him away, but give him all he needs. Go to others who are sick and pray for them. Go to those in prison and comfort them. Go to those who are mourning and give them words of cheer. Be kind and loving to others, and in this way you please Me. Be wise and do not be deceived. Many will say that I will not return soon, but the days are short so you must always be ready and make sure your children are well taught in My ways. Your children will face dark days ahead, and they must have a firm foundation or they will fall.

245

You should use your talents for YHUH.

Matt 25:14-28 Again, it will be like a man going on a journey, who called his servants and entrusted his property to them. 15 To one he gave five talents of money, to another two talents, and to another one talent, each according to his ability. 1 Peter 4:10 As each one has received a special gift, employ it in serving one another as good stewards of the manifold grace of YHUH. Ex 31:6 Also I have given ability to all the skilled workers to make everything I have commanded you. (1 Cor 7:7)

My beloved, if I give you a talent then use it for Me, because I have created you for a reason. I made you with a divine purpose. My hand molded you from the beginning to give you abilities and talents to complete your purpose. If you sing, then sing for Me. If you play an instrument, play for Me. If you draw, then draw for Me. If you have a good rapport with people and know how to lead them, then lead them down the path of righteousness. If you can teach, then teach others about Me. If you can interpret the Truth in My words and you are given revelations by Me of their meaning, then teach My words to others so they can understand My words. If you can fast and pray, then do this unto Me so walls of darkness can be broken down. If you can dance, then dance for Me. If you have the ability to act or perform, then do it unto Me. If you care for children and know how to nurture them and teach them My ways, then care for them as unto Me. If you can cook, then cook unto Me. If you can clean, then clean unto Me. If you serve others, then smile and serve then with loving kindness as unto Me. If you nurse, then nurse unto Me. If you heal others with your hands or words of encouragement, then do it unto Me. If you give counsel or advice, then give My wisdom to others and I will bless you. Whatever you do unto Me giving your best, I will honor and bless you greatly.

246

You should minister to others as you would to Yahshua Himself. Feed the hungry, clothe the naked, shelter the homeless, and comfort those in distress.

Matt 25:34-46 "Then the King will say to those on His right, 'Come, you who are blessed by my Father; take your inheritance, the kingdom prepared for you since the creation of the world. 35 For I was hungry and you gave Me something to eat, I was thirsty and you gave Me something to drink, I was a stranger and you invited Me in, 36 I needed clothes and you clothed Me, I was sick and you looked after Me, I was in prison and you came to visit Me.' 40 The King will reply, 'I tell you the truth, whatever you did for one of the least of these brothers of mine, you did for Me.'" (Is 58:7, Ezek 18:7)

My beloved, if your brother is in need, then give to him. Who is your brother? He is anyone who calls on My name-who believes in Me and clings to Me. If you see your brother in sin and he has fallen and he needs help with food or clothes or shelter, then give to him and help him get back on his feet so he can serve Me once again. You may see those who love Me go to prison for My sake, because they believe in Me. Go to him and comfort him there and make sure they have all they need and you will be giving to Me because they are My children. Whatever you do for those who love Me will be counted to you as righteousness. In the last days you will need to be aware of your brother's needs. Stay together and help each other and I will shelter you from the enemy. I will help you to overcome and be the victor. The Evil One will perish and be no more, but you will be safe in My Hands. Do not be fearful of the coming days for I have prepared an escape for you for all who hear My voice. Some will take up weapons and fight the Evil One, but he will be killed. Some will refuse the Evil One's system and be put in prison or killed by the world. A few will hear My voice and flee for the wilderness. There I will comfort you with My presence and care for you. Until then serve others and love them and do good things for them just as you would for Me, and I will bless you for your good works. Everyday whatever you do, do it unto Me and do your best and I will bless you.

247

You should remember the sacrifice of Yahshua at Passover.

Luke 22:19-20 (7 Then came the Day of Unleavened Bread, on which the Passover lamb had to be sacrificed.) And He took unleavened bread, and when He had given thanks, He broke it and gave it to them, saying, "This is my body, which is given for you. Do this in remembrance of Me." 20 And likewise the cup after they had eaten, saying, "This cup that is poured out for you is the new covenant in my blood." Ps 78:4 We will not hide them from their descendants; we will tell the next generation the praiseworthy deeds of YHUH, his power, and the wonders He has done. (Ps 111:4)

My beloved, I called My disciples and gave them direction where to go to prepare the Passover meal. This is a meal all My children have in order to remember your ancestors' flight from Egypt and how they left in haste and suffered in the desert for 40 years before they were allowed to go to the Promised Land. Together I broke bread with My disciples and called upon each of them to be strong and brave, because it was the last meal with them before I was taken from them. I grieved to leave them, but I knew if I left them I could spend My Spirit to help all My children not just My disciples. If you celebrate Passover and the Feast of Unleavened Bread as I have commanded you to do, then I will bless you. Anyone who partakes of My Passover meal will be called blessed, because they have honored My laws and praise Me for the great miracles I have performed for you and your ancestors. If you say, "How do I keep this meal?" You must carefully study from My Word what is necessary and allow the man who studies My laws to guide you. Most of all you should remember Me as you take the cup and break the bread. Remember what I have done for you. Praise Me for delivering you from Egypt or today you would have no people because they would all die in slavery. Many tribes have been taken off this planet and their ancestry line has ceased, but My twelve tribes have flourished, because I protect you and hover over you so I can bring you to My Kingdom in the last Day.

248

You should become fishers of men.

Mark 1:17 And Yahshua said unto them, Come ye after Me, and I will make you to become fishers of men. Jer 16:14-16 "However, the days are coming," declares YHUH, "when men will no longer say, 'As surely as YHUH lives, who brought the Israelites up out of Egypt,' 15 but they will say, 'As surely as YHUH lives, who brought the Israelites up out of the land of the north and out of all the countries where he had banished them.' For I will restore them to the land I gave their foreathers." 16 "But now I will send for many fishermen," declares YHUH, "and they will catch them." (Luke 5:4-11)

My beloved, I want you to seek out those who do not know the Truth and tell them about Me and My ways. Look around you. You have friends who do not know the Truth. Wake them up and tell them about My love for them and how I died for them, so they can see clearly their sins, confess their sins, turn away from their sins, and be saved from the fire of destruction on the Last Day. If they have not heard the Truth, they may receive it gladly or they will reject Me. They do not reject you, but they reject Me. Do not have fear or feel like you have been insulted. They have insulted Me and they must pay for their sins. Tell others about Me and pull them out of the world like a fisherman pulls a fish out of the sea. The fisherman eats the fish or sells the fish and he is satisfied. If you pull a man out of the world, you will feel joy and you will be satisfied. I told My prophets that I would send fishermen and hunters to come looking for My scattered children across the nations, so I sent bold strong men to tell them about My act of love for all men. If you are following Me, you will share with others My love and the gift of salvation. You must seek them out and find them. You will know them. The seed of righteousness is easy to spot within another. Look deeply, and you will see it amidst all their wounds and scars from sin.

249

You should hear YHUH's word, accept it, and prosper.

Mark 4:1-20 The farmer sows the word. 15 Some people are like seed along the path, where the word is sown. As soon as they hear it, Satan comes and takes away the word that was sown in them. 16 Others, like seed sown on rocky places, hear the word and at once receive it with joy. 17 But since they have no root, they last only a short time. When trouble or persecution comes because of the word, they quickly fall away. 18 Still others, like seed sown among thorns, hear the word; 19 but the worries of this life, the deceitfulness of wealth and the desires for other things come in and choke the word, making it unfruitful. 20 Others, like seed sown on good soil, hear the word, accept it, and produce a crop-thirty, sixty or even a hundred times what was sown. (John 8:47, Lev 26:15-16)

My beloved, I spoke in parables-stories that had to be interpreted to see the meaning. Many of the people did not understand them unless I explained the stories to them. Even My disciples lacked understanding. I spoke to My disciples and explained all the parables so they could write them down and explain them to you. I want you to know how the enemy works to steal My words from you, because My words are Truth. Man also rejects My words, because his heart is so hard or he is not of My seed and his heart cannot receive My words. There is no soil to receive the seed. Sometimes My children receive My words, but then they allow worries and cares of this life to choke out My words and they fall into sin because they are too weak to stand firm. You must have My words firmly planted within you and build a strong foundation or you will fall into sin. You must read My words, believe in My words, and follow My words so that you walk in My ways and serve Me with your whole heart. Men will mock you and criticize you for how you serve Me, but stand firm and I will prosper you. Expect for the world to hate you, but My people will receive you. You must walk away from the people of the world and do not conform to the image that the world wants you to become. The world says, "Do what you like" or "Do whatever it takes to succeed and have wealth." Do not listen to their words. You must love those around you, and let your light of love penetrate the lost dying world around you. Rejoice, because I love you and will protect you.

250

You should tell others what YHUH has done for you.

Mark 5:18 As Yahshua was getting into the boat, the man who had been demon-possessed begged to go with Him. 19 Yahshua did not let Him, but said, "Go home to your family and tell them how much YHUH has done for you, and how He has had mercy on you." 20 So the man went away and began to tell in the Decapolis how much Yahshua had done for him. And all the people were amazed. Ps 66:16 Come and hear, all you who fear YHUH; let me tell you what He has done for me.

My beloved, I saw a man tormented by demons-bound all his life by oppressive demons who tried to harm him every day. Everyone in the town knew of his torment and tried to help him by chaining him up, but the demons within him were too strong and broke the chains. When I saw his torment I had mercy on him, and I released him for his misery and drown the demons into a herd of pigs that ran into the ocean and escaped My Hand of wrath. The man begged to come with Me and be My disciple, but I told him to go tell the region of what I had done for him-the miracle I had performed to set him free from a legion of demons. There are many around you suffering from the oppression of the evil one. Tell those around you of My love and My Mercy that I have had on you. Tell them that I can set them free from all darkness, so they can have peace and joy. Be strong. Be brave. Tell others around you of what I have done for you. If you are afraid to speak, pray for boldness and I will rise up inside of you through My Spirit and speak. Do not be afraid to share My love with others, but if they do not want to listen then walk away from them. Do not try to persuade them. If they are of the righteous seed, they will receive the Truth. If they are My children, they will hear and receive. Only My children want to hear My voice and receive My Truth.

251

You should not teach man-made laws.

Mark 7:1-13 So the Pharisees and teachers of the law asked Yahshua, "Why don't your disciples live according to the tradition of the elders instead of eating their food with 'unclean' hands?" 6 He replied, "Isaiah was right when he prophesied about you hypocrites; as it is written: 'These people honor Me with their lips, but their hearts are far from Me. 7 They worship Me in vain; their teachings are but rules taught by men.' 8 You have let go of the commands of Elohim and are holding on to the traditions of men." (Is 29:13)

My beloved, listen to My words and not the words of man. Man wants to make his own rules on how to serve Me, but I do not need any man to add rules to My laws. My laws are perfect and if a man follows My laws, then he will follow the ways of eternal life. If a man is trapped by serving the laws of man, then he is burdened by bondage of trying to keep laws and not serving Me with his whole heart. The Talmud is a set of man-made laws, and it is an anchor around My people's neck if they try to keep all these laws. These laws are perverted and not pure and sacred like My laws are. My laws bring liberty, but man-made laws bring death. The churches each have their own set of man-made laws-when to worship, how to worship, when to give, who to give to, who comes to the church, and what man will govern the body of believers. These laws are all bondage. My laws tell you when to keep My Sabbath day in which you should rest. My laws tell you what feasts to celebrate and how to celebrate them. You must know that you look to Me for direction-not your pastor, priest, or rabbi. You must be led by My Spirit not a man with his own ideas. If I speak through a man, then I will also confirm this to you in another way. Do not be deceived by false prophets, but trust only in Me. Look in My words for the laws, and do not allow any man to lead you into bondage.

252

You should be last if you desire to be great in the Kingdom of Heaven.

Mark 9:33 They came to Capernaum. When He was in the house, He asked them, "What were you arguing about on the road?" 34 But they kept quiet because on the way they had argued about who was the greatest. 35 Sitting down, Yahshua called the Twelve and said, "If anyone wants to be first, he must be the very last, and the servant of all." 36 He took a little child and had him stand among them. Taking him in his arms, He said to them, 37 "Whoever welcomes one of these little children in my name welcomes Me; and whoever welcomes Me does not welcome Me but the one who sent Me." (Jer. 45:5. Ps 131:1)

My beloved, My twelve disciples thought I would bring My kingdom to Earth while they lived on Earth, but they were in error. They argued among themselves who would be given more power to rule on Earth, but they did not even see what I had to suffer and endure. They did not realize I would leave them, and they would have to be strong without Me and gather My children and prepare them for the last days. My disciples were expecting splendor and power, but instead they endured persecution. My people on this planet will suffer, because they love Me. If they serve Me, many will hate them. If they serve Me, then they must serve others and love others. If you want to have great rewards in My kingdom, then you must put your desires last and you must think of the needs of others. Welcome others in your arms and love them. Be kind and giving to others, and you will be greatly blessed in My kingdom. If you love others and do not expect anything back in return, this is the purest form of love. This is the love I seek from My children. If you love Me with all your heart, then you will rejoice in giving all you can spare to others. I will bless you and reward you for your good works. So lift up your eyes to Me, and I will show you the way to walk in loving kindness and you will have great rewards in My kingdom.

253

You should not forbid others to preach Yahshua. You should not oppose other believers in Yahshua who are not in your group.

Mark 9:38 "Teacher," said John, "we saw a man driving out demons in your name and we told him to stop, because he was not one of us." 39 "Do not stop him," Yahshua said. "No one who does a miracle in my name can in the next moment say anything bad about Me, 40 for whoever is not against us is for us." (Josh 5:13, Matt 12:30)

My beloved, I look at My people and they become powerless as they continue to build a church ,and then the church splits and you have two smaller churches. The problem with these churches is that they are not established on a firm foundation, because when they have problems they fall apart because they are not founded on Me. A group of believers should pray and fast and let Me tell them what to do. They should not fight among themselves as to what is right, and then get mad and leave if things do not go their way. You must love each other and come together, and then your prayers will have power and you can rock mountains if you so desired. So if your brothers who believe are ministering in My name, do not stop them but encourage them. Brother should encourage brother, but I see My children fighting among themselves about doctrine. I said to love each other and hold fast to your brother, so you can build together and not tear apart. Mend and not tear. Heal and not wound. If you have a brother that you have argued with concerning doctrine and now you have anger for your brother because of his words, then go to him and let your words of love heal your brother. Do not hate each other over the meaning of My words. Instead love each and do good things for each other, and pray together over My words and fast together over My words. Be hungry for the Truth and not about whether you are right or wrong, and then you will be blessed and have power.

254

You should believe that YHUH is one and there is no other One but Him.

Mark 12:28-34 One of the teachers of the law came and heard them debating. Noticing that Yahshua had given them a good answer, he asked him, "Of all the commandments, which is the most important?" 29 "The most important one," answered Yahshua, "is this: 'Hear, O Israel, YHUH our Elohim, YHUH is one.'" (Deut 6:4, John 1:1-2)

My beloved, there is only one Elohim-I AM. There is no other. I AM Creator. I created all things. I have no beginning. I have no end. I AM the Life-giver. All the evil ones who set themselves up as gods are created and therefore are not gods. I have no mother or father and no children. I create My own children and you are My child-chosen by Me. I have placed My stamp of approval on you. You are sealed by My Spirit and you are at one with Me when you communicate with Me through My Spirit. I can commune with millions of My people at once, because I AM sprit and fill all things—both great and small. I continue to create and breathe life into babies and give joy to their parents. I see that it is good. I draw life out of the person when their days are complete. All men have a certain number of days assigned to this planet. At the end of their days as recorded in My book, My angels come to take you away from this planet. You must trust Me that while you are here, I will protect you, guide you, and show you the way. I AM the only true Elohim and you should serve only Me. When others serve another god or say, "All gods are equal" or "We should have freedom to choose any god we want," they are deceived. You should cling to Me and stay far from pagan gods. They will oppress you and deceive you, because they are spirits of darkness. You must be separate and love only Me, and then I can bless you and give you guidance. Be careful to keep your ears open and reject all lying spirits.

255

You should not be alarmed when you hear of wars or rumors of wars.

Mark 13:5 Yahshua said to them: "Watch out that no one deceives you. 6 Many will come in my name, claiming, 'I am He,' and will deceive many. 7 When you hear of wars and rumors of wars, do not be alarmed. Such things must happen, but the end is still to come. 8 Nation will rise against nation, and kingdom against kingdom. There will be earthquakes in various places, and famines. These are the beginning of birth pains." Ps 27:3 Though an army encamp against me, my heart shall not fear; though war arise against me, yet I will be confident.

My beloved, man has always been at war or preparing for war. Man is a conquering being who wants power and wealth. Kings have been put in power by Me to be used by Me to pass judgment on wicked nations and pass judgment even on My own people. If you think that I do not bring wars on My own people, you are wrong. If My people do not serve Me, then they will be punished until they repent. My people were even driven out of their land and scattered all over the world, and they even forgot who they were because they had been out of their land for so long. If you do not serve Me, I will punish you until you open up your eyes and see your sins and repent. War brings repentance to the nation who is conquered. If you think you will escape war in your life, you are wrong. If you serve Me, I can protect you through the war. Even now your nation is at war-a silent war- and brings troops to fight a war not declared as war but as a conflict. Men are dying every day for the ideals of your nation–that all men should be free and your nation is protected from nuclear attack-or so your leaders tell you. In reality it is struggling for world power and putting nations who do not submit to their rules under their feet. You will see nations rise up against nations until the end comes and world "peace" will come. It really will not be peace, but a takeover of all of your rights. A dictator will arise and the world will receive him. Go hide My beloved for he is an antichrist and he will hate you, but I will keep you safe.

256

You should be baptized in the name of Yahshua.

Mark 16:15 He said to them, "Go into all the world and preach the good news to all creation. 16 Whoever believes and is baptized will be saved, but whoever does not believe will be condemned." Acts 2:38, "And Peter said to them, 'Repent, and let each of you be baptized in the name of Yahshua for the forgiveness of your sins; and you shall receive the gift of the Ruach HaKodesh.'" (Lev. 6:4,23-24, 2 Kings 5: 1-14, Ezek 16: 9)

My beloved, I set an example for My people when I asked John to baptize Me in water. I set an example to those who did not believe in Me that John had come before Me to prepare the way for Me. He was killed on account of Me and his rewards are great. He will sit beside Me in My kingdom. If you hesitate about what It means to be baptized, then you must look at My example. I went to the river and was immersed in water. The water covered Me over as a sign of true repentance. When you repent all signs of the sin is washed away and will return no more. True repentance is when you are sick of the sin, and do not ever desire to be a part of the sin again. You become ill just thinking about the sin. This is true repentance. Sometimes people are sorry they are caught in the sin and are rebuked, but they really did not want to leave the sin. Search for true repentance and let baptism be a symbol of washing away your sin that you have truly repented. You do not have to have a rabbi, pastor, or priest to baptize you, but let one of your family or even yourself cover you over with water so you can be released or the sin can be cut away. Baptism makes you stronger and ready to put all hindrances far away from you. If you are in a debate over what kind of baptism you should have and being baptized by what person, then look at My example. I was baptized by a family member.

257

You should not blaspheme the Ruach HaKodesh (Holy Spirit). But whoever blasphemes against the Holy Spirit will never be forgiven; he is guilty of an eternal sin.

Matt 12:32   Anyone who speaks a word against the Son of Man will be forgiven, but anyone who speaks against the Holy Spirit will not be forgiven, either in this age or in the age to come. (Luke 12:10, Ex 22:28, Num 11:17, Ps 106:32-33)

My beloved, I said that anyone that rejects Me also rejects My Son and also rejects My Spirit. If you reject Me, then you will go to the Lake of Fire and be consumed. You will be no more. You will no longer be remembered. You have turned against Me and rejected My love and compassion for you. You have wanted your own way-the way of the evil one. You have wanted to harm others and not love them or care for them or help them. You have chosen to make yourself a "god" and do as you please. You worship yourself and do whatever you want to do not caring for others and how they are affected by your actions. You are wicked and evil, and do not want to walk in the ways of the Light. You have scorned My Name and lifted up yourself. You have mocked Me and turned away from Me. You have blasphemed Me and for this there will be no forgiveness. If you want to serve Me, then you must lift up My Name and draw close to Me. You must put aside your fleshly desires and walk hand in hand with Me. Your flesh will pass away, but your spirit will live forever. If you value your flesh more than your spirit, then you are deceived. Don't you know that your flesh is dying every day? Don't you know that you will be judged according to your spirit and how you have grown in Me and reflect My Image? You are deceived if you think that you are immortal, or that you can continue on after you are dead without serving Me. If you are following a false god, then repent and I will forgive you. Draw close to Me and I will show Myself to you. I am merciful and compassionate. I will show you the way to life. Lift up your voice and rejoice that I can give you so much. Look to Me and rejoice that I can wash you clean, and you will see with new eyes-eyes of gold. Rejoice that I love you so much, and I will enter into covenant with you and you will be at one with Me forever.

258

You should speak in new tongues.

Mark 16:17 And these signs will accompany those who believe: In my name they will drive out demons; they will speak in new tongues; 18 they will pick up snakes with their hands; and when they drink deadly poison, it will not hurt them at all; they will place their hands on sick people, and they will get well. Is 28:11 Very well then, with foreign lips and strange tongues YHUH will speak to this people. (Acts 2:1-4, Acts 19:1-7)

My beloved, I sent My Spirit to My people and I allowed My people to speak in new tongues-heavenly tongues through My Spirit. The Spirit knows how to pray for you and others, so if you allow your Spirit to pray through you, then you know you do not pray in vain. If you say, "How can I do this?" Just call on My name and ask Me to help you yield your tongue to My Spirit within you, so you can pray like My Spirit gives utterance. Yielding to My Spirit is a good thing not a bad thing. The evil one does not want you to pray through My Spirit, so he lies and tells others who do not understand what exactly is happening that it is from him-the evil one. This makes some of My people afraid to pray through My Spirit. They are afraid to yield their tongue to My Spirit within them. This should not be so My little ones. The evil one wants to kill you and he may bring all sorts of traps for you, but I will protect you from animals, snakes, sharks, poison, soldiers, and all sort of traps. You must be led by My Spirit, and I will tell you what to do to remain safe. Do not allow fear to cripple you, but do exactly what I tell you so you can escape destruction and plagues. Judgment will come, but I will keep you from it all if you listen to My voice.

259

You should seek YHUH before choosing leaders.

Luke 6:12 One of those days Yahshua went out to a mountainside to pray, and spent the night praying to Elohim. 13 When morning came, He called his disciples to Him and chose twelve of them, whom He also designated apostles: 14 Simon (whom he named Peter), his brother Andrew, James, John, Philip, Bartholomew, 15 Matthew, Thomas, James son of Alpheus, Simon who was called the Zealot, 16 Judas son of James, and Judas Iscariot, who became a traitor. (Deut 3:28, 1 Sam 16:13)

My beloved, I spent the night in prayer being at one with My Father, because we are one and carefully considered all those who followed Me-who accepted My teachings-before I decided on those twelve who would be My inner circle of disciples. These twelve would be told things that others would not hear. These twelve were given authority and power from My kingdom. They did not know at the time what responsibility I had placed on them, but they knew that they had found the One they had been searching for. I struggled with the flesh in selecting these twelve, because I did not want Judas to be part of the twelve but he must be near Me to betray Me. I carefully considered all those in My midst before I selected them to be near Me. You must also carefully consider and ask Me to help you make decisions before you take a step forward. I can keep you from making a mistake. You must guard over your family, marriage, money, and home before you make decisions concerning these. You must come to Me for advice, so I can guide you. If you never ask Me for help when you make a decision, then you go your own way and you will encounter obstacles. Many pray, "God help Me," and then do whatever they please. You must stop and present the decision to Me and wait for an answer. I will give you an answer and guide you.

260

You should rejoice when men hate you on account of Yahshua.

Luke 6:22 Blessed are you when men hate you, when they exclude you and insult you and denounce you as a criminal on account of the Son of Man. 23 Rejoice in that day and dance for joy, because great is your reward in heaven. For that is how their fathers treated the prophets. (John 15:18-19, John 17:14-16, Acts 5:40-41, Prov 8:36)

My beloved, rejoice and be glad when men do not like you because you serve Me. The evil one hates you, because you are My children and heirs to the kingdom. One day you will rule over angels, and the evil one cannot bear to have you rule over him. Therefore he decided to destroy you. He tells all his followers that you are evil, so they will hate you also. My beloved, do not be afraid when men hate you, but be glad because your light is exposing their sins. If you have fewer friends because you want to walk in righteousness, then you know your friends are following the ways of the world and not following My ways. Teach your children that the world will despise them because of Me, so they will understand and not be sad. They must realize that light cannot associate with darkness and find any satisfaction. You must realize that if you continue to associate with those of the world, then you will be drawn into their darkness and suffer loss. The evil one is a deceiver, and he slowly deceives you by taking away the Truth a little at a time until you have no Truth at all. If you understand the concept, you will fight to keep Truth and not give up even a little of it; compromise with darkness is never good. Stand on My words. Do not depart from My laws. Obey Me and I will bless you. Stay close to Me and I will bring only good things to your door.

261

You should pray for those people who are mean to you.

Luke 6:28 Bless those who curse you, pray for those who mistreat you. Matt 5:44 But I tell you: Love your enemies and pray for those who persecute you. (Lev 19:18)

My beloved, this world is filled with evil men who hate you. They will want to harm you and belittle you. Even though these people are evil you must be a light to them. Pray for the people who are mean to you and mistreat you. Pray for those who persecute you. Pray for the wicked people who seek to harm you, and I will hear your prayers. I will judge this person that harms you and bring punishment to him. As long as you forgive him and continue to be kind to him even though he mistreats you, I will look into his heart and judge him according to his ways. I will stop his hand of mistreatment towards you. Sometimes I use mean people to test you to see if you will continue in love. If you can love those around you that are mean to you, then you can love all men. You should be an example to the people around you. You will be a shining light. They will see you love others, and this will encourage them to love others. My people are looking for someone to stand up and do what is right. They want to join in with others that want to love those around them. If you have someone who you cannot forgive, ask Me to help you forgive him. I will give you the ability to love him in spite of his meanness. If you love those around you, I will bless you greatly. You are My Hands and Feet, and only through you do the people of the world see Me. Arise and walk in love. Arise and give love generously to others. Your hands will be blessed by Me, and you will prosper in all you do.

262

You should lend to others without expecting any return.

Luke 6:34 And if you lend to those from whom you expect repayment, what credit is that to you? Even 'sinners' lend to 'sinners,' expecting to be repaid in full. 35 But love your enemies, do good to them, and lend to them without expecting to get anything back. Then your reward will be great, and you will be sons of the Most High, because He is kind to the ungrateful and wicked. Deut 23:19 Do not charge your brother interest, whether on money or food or anything else that may earn interest.

My beloved, do good things for all men whether they are good men or evil men. Do good things for others and you will be a light to others. You will show others how to live a life worthy of bearing My Name. You will be able to look past the flesh and into the hearts of men and love them no matter their condition. You should hate the sin, but love the man. Lend to those in need expecting not to be paid back. I will pay you back for your generous gifts. You must only think of what I would do for men if I walked on this Earth. I would give generously to those in need. If you give to someone in need, do not take what your family needs but only take what you know you can live without in case the person cannot pay you back. If you must use the money or the item for your family, then do not lend it to someone else, because you would put your family in peril and this would not please Me. Love those around you, giving to others when you can and not expecting to be paid back for your services. If you love Me, then you will love others because I AM love and I love all men, even those who are wicked. I look at life and all I created, and I AM pleased. The evil one tries to harm others, but I bring new life to others. I bring rain and food to the good and evil alike. I give generously to all until the Judgment Day when all men will pay for their sins.

263

You should be merciful.

Luke 6:36 Be merciful, just as your Father is merciful. Matt 5:7 Blessed are the merciful, for they will be shown mercy. James 3:17 But the wisdom that comes from heaven is first of all pure; then peace-loving, considerate, submissive, full of mercy and good fruit, impartial and sincere. (James 2:12-13, Dan 9:9)

My beloved, be merciful to others. Be kind to those who are not kind to you. Forgive them for their sins against you, so I can punish them Myself. Do not take revenge on others, but love others. Cast your love upon them, so it can be as fiery coals upon their heads. They will see your love for others and feel guilty that they have been so unkind to you. Many men will hate you, because you love Me. The evil one deceives them and tells them that you are a threat to the peace of all men by what you believe. Nations will rise up against you, but I will keep you close to Me. You should never be afraid, but you should be on guard and aware so you can hear My voice when I say depart quickly. If you love Me, you will cling to Me and My ways. I deal kindly with the wicked. I bring rain and sun upon the wicked and righteous. I bring good things to a land that has wicked and righteous living in it. I shine My face on the righteous, and I turn My face against the wicked. I do punish the wicked for their sins. Allow Me to punish the wicked and not you. I AM the judge, so allow Me to judge righteously among men. If you will treat others with respect and kindness and be merciful to those who do not even deserve your mercy, I will bless you and uphold you during the darkest of days and carry you through. You will be stronger than you ever thought you would be, and you will bring the gift of love and mercy to others.

264

You should not condemn your brother.

Luke 6:37-42 Do not judge, and you will not be judged. Do not condemn, and you will not be condemned. Forgive, and you will be forgiven. Rom 2:1 You have no excuse, you who pass judgment on someone else, for at whatever point you judge another, you are condemning yourself, because you who pass judgment do the same things. (Ps 94:21-23)

My beloved, I said not to judge your brother. Do not condemn your brother, but forgive your brother and I will forgive you. I want you not to be hard on your brother, but be forgiving knowing that all men struggle. If your brother is sinning against Me and he is in disobedience to Me, then go to your brother and confront him about his sin. It is your duty to go to your brother. If you know your brother is lying or stealing or in adultery, go confront him about his sin and tell him to repent and turn aside from his sin. If your brother repents, then forgive him and love him. He needs your support. If he is turning to idols and celebrating pagan holidays and not keeping My feast days or Sabbath, then confront him about his sin. Do not condemn him, but go to him in love with compassion. Warn him about the danger he is in and how I will punish him for this sin. You must know that I will judge him and correct him. You do not have to judge him harshly. You must love him and help your brother overcome. If your brother loves his sin and will not depart from it. then you must turn aside from your brother. He has chosen the ways of death, and you must separate yourself from him. If you love Me, you will walk in My ways and do My will. You will love those around you, and only do good things for them. Do not condemn your brother, but love him and bring him to the right path again.

265

You should give generously to others.

Luke 6:38 Give, and it will be given to you. A good measure, pressed down, shaken together and running over, will be poured into your lap. For with the measure you use, it will be measured to you. Prov 19:17 Whoever is kind to the poor lends to YHUH, and He will reward them for what they have done. Prov 11:25 A generous person will prosper; whoever refreshes others will be refreshed.

My beloved, give generously to others and love others. You could be the one that your love changes their heart towards Me, and they turn towards Me. They will want to find the love that you have within you. Give to others, and I will give to you over and above what you gave. If you love others, you will want to give to others. You will want to help the poor and needy and try to help the children who are neglected and abused. Your heart will be towards them, and you will want to help them. Where does love like that come from? It comes only from Me. If you love Me, you will also love others and want to do good things for them. If you do not love Me, then you will have no love for others and will not want to give to others. Be kind and loving to others, and I will bless you. Watch for those in need, and give when you see the need. If you give to others in need, I will give back to you more then you give. If you watch carefully, I will send others to you so you can support and encourage their emotional, physical, financial, and spiritual needs. You may have to help them with all of those needs, but they may only need spiritual guidance or a friend to talk to. You can give them sound advice as you pray together seeking Me. Give and be ready to give, and I will bless you.

266

You should build a firm foundation on the Rock.

Luke 6:47 I will show you what he is like who comes to Me and hears my words and puts them into practice. 48 He is like a man building a house, who dug down deep and laid the foundation on rock. When a flood came, the torrent struck that house but could not shake it, because it was well built. 49 But the one who hears my words and does not put them into practice is like a man who built a house on the ground without a foundation. The moment the torrent struck that house, it collapsed and its destruction was complete. 2 Sam 22:3 YHUH is my rock, in whom I take refuge, my shield and the horn of my salvation. Ps 127:1 Unless YHUH builds the house, those who build it labor in vain. (Ps 95:1, Ps 18:46)

My beloved, come to Me and I will tell you what to do. Come to Me and I will show you the way. Come to Me and follow My words and be obedient unto My laws and you will be strong, unbending, and ready for any storm in your life. You may suffer disaster around you, but you will not be touched because your foundation is strong and cannot be broken. Others may fall, but you will not give way to temptation and fall into sin. All around you are people who want you to do wrong. "Come let's have fun. Let's party. Let's do whatever we want to. No one can stop us. No one will know. We will not get caught. We can do as we please." These people are deceived. These will be judged for their sins. Stay far away from these people. Search for those who want to do right. Search for those who long to please Me. Search for those who follow My laws. These are the ones who will encourage you to stand strong and do my will. Be very careful to listen to Me, and follow Me and do all I tell you to do. Stay away from the things of the world. Stay away from their sin. Keep yourself pure and set apart, and then it will be easy to be unbendable. The world will eat at you and destroy you. Do not be a part of it. Be separate. Be different. You are unique-chosen from the other peoples as my own unique treasure. I AM preparing you to be My Priests to rule nations. You must be firm and not bend to sin. Continue standing on the Rock of your foundation.

267

You should seek the secrets of the Kingdom of YHUH.

Luke 8:9 His disciples asked Him what this parable meant. 10 He said, "The knowledge of the secrets of the kingdom of Elohim has been given to you, but to others I speak in parables, so that, though seeing, they may not see; though hearing, they may not understand." Ps 25:14 The secret counsel of YHUH is for those who fear Him, and He reveals His covenant to them. Dan 2:22 He reveals deep and hidden things; He knows what lies in darkness, and light dwells with Him.

My beloved, I came to earth and I taught in parables so only My children could understand the hidden things from Me. Even My disciples did not understand the parables, but I explained the parables to them so they could have understanding. They rejoiced to know the meaning of the parables. They could not understand why I could not explain them to the crowds, but this people did not deserve to hear the truth. Their hearts were hard, and they would not receive the truth. They would only scorn the truth, so I chose not to have My wisdom mocked by them. They even scorned My acts of love and compassion and tried to trap Me every day, so the world could not hear the truth and be saved. I send My disciples all over the world, and the truth is preached to everyone so all can be saved. Many reject the Truth, but only My true children receive Me gladly. Only My children repent of their sins and enter the Kingdom of Heaven. If you have a hard heart today, pray for a new heart ready to be filled with the things of Me-joy, peace, love, mercy, compassion-so you can walk in oneness with Me. You must always check yourself and make sure no sin is in your heart, so you can remain close to Me. If you are angry with someone, then go to him and solve the problem between you. You may be able to share My love for him. Do not be deceived, but stand firm and the secrets to the Kingdom of Heaven will be yours.

268

You should give to those who preach the Kingdom of YHUH.

Luke 9:3 He told them: "Take nothing for the journey-no staff, no bag, no bread, no money, no extra tunic. 4 Whatever house you enter, stay there until you leave that town. 5 If people do not welcome you, shake the dust off your feet when you leave their town, as a testimony against them." 1 Cor 9:14 In the same way, YHUH has commanded that those who preach the gospel should earn their living by the gospel. Deut 18:1 The priests, who are Levites-indeed the whole tribe of Levi-are to have no allotment or inheritance with Israel. They shall live on the offerings made to YHUH by fire, for that is their inheritance.

My beloved, I sent my disciples into the world to search for the lost tribes of Israel. I wanted them to find them and tell them the truth about Me and My laws. I wanted to tell them that I had fulfilled the prophecy given by the prophets. I wanted to give them eternal life and a gift of My Spirit to comfort them until I returned or until death brought them to Me. My disciples went out preaching about Me and healing the sick and driving out demons and telling of all My miracles. They were My hands and feet. I first chose twelve disciples. Later I chose seventy two disciples who I sent out in pairs to tell others about Me. I told them to stay only in those people's houses that had My peace and wanted to hear the truth about Me. When a teacher of My laws comes to you, give him shelter and food. Allow him to stay as long as My spirit guides him. He will not stay longer than I want him to stay, if he is My true follower. How will you know? My Spirit inside of you will tell you and give you peace. He will cling to My words and teach from My scriptures. He will be well versed in the Torah and know where all My commandments are. He will keep the seventh day Sabbath- not Sunday the first day. He will say My laws have not changed. The rules for the priest are not used today, but will be used in the last day. They are not to be forgotten, but they should be remembered until the Temple is rebuilt. Rejoice that I have given laws that need not be changed, but are constant because they are perfect in all ways.

269

You should say "No" to yourself. You should take up your cross (execution stake).

Luke 9:23 Then He said to them all: "If anyone would come after Me, he must say, No, to himself and take up his cross daily and keep following Me. 24 For whoever wants to save his life will lose it, but whoever loses his life for Me will save it. 25 What good is it for a man to gain the whole world, and yet lose or forfeit his very self?" Titus 2:12 It teaches us to say "No" to ungodliness and worldly passions, and to live self-controlled, upright and godly lives in this present age." 1 Sam 15:22 "Does YHUH delight in burnt offerings and sacrifices as much as in obeying the voice of YHUH? To obey is better than sacrifice, and to heed is better than the fat of rams." (Luke 14:25-33)

My beloved, do not try to go your own way seeking the pleasures of the flesh. The flesh is lazy and loves to have pleasure and fun and do whatever it wants to regardless of what My laws say. The flesh is unruly and is greedy and always wants more. The flesh is never satisfied. The flesh says, "If only I have this, then I will be happy," but the flesh can never be happy unless it is ruled by My Spirit. Only My children with My righteous seed can ever be happy. The only happiness you will find in this world that brings satisfaction that does not flee from you is serving Me with your whole heart and loving Me and wanting only to please Me. You must say, "No" to your own flesh and make your flesh weak, so your spirit can be strong. Teach your flesh not to have all it wants. Deny yourself or fast at least once a week. At least fast one thing you like every day for a week, then your flesh will be under control. If you are overweight, your flesh is not under control. If you are lazy and do not work and make money for your family so you can get out of debt, then your flesh is not under control. If you break the laws of the land, then your flesh is not under control. If you lie or gossip or criticize others, your flesh is not under control. If you say mean things about others, your tongue (a part of your flesh) is not under control. Say "No" to yourself and live a life of righteous-ness, so you can be at one with Me and hear My voice.

270

You should not be ashamed of Yahshua or His words.

Luke 9:26 If anyone is ashamed of Me and my words, the Son of Man will be ashamed of him when He comes in his glory and in the glory of the Father and of YHUH's angels. Ps 19:46 I will speak of your testimonies also before kings, and will not be ashamed. (2 Tim 1:8-9, Rom 1:16)

My beloved, do not be ashamed of My words and what they say. You must believe that they are divinely inspired by Me, and they carry great weight for My children. Do not be ashamed to say you believe in Me and want to walk in My ways. People will not understand why you do what you do, because they have no understanding into Me and My ways. They do not know Me. They are not of the righteous seed-My children. How can someone who has as his father the evil one be able to understand Me? What can Light and Darkness have in common? They are seeking darkness-evil-and you are seeking good-righteousness. You must realize that only those who love Me will accept you. Be brave and strong and do not be ashamed of what you have in Me, but rejoice and be glad. Hold fast to the faith. You may have men hate you because of Me, but they hate Me not you. They hate the Light within you. They do not understand Me and cannot serve Me. You must love those no matter what they say about you, but hate the sin-the rejection of Me. Forgive them, because they only hate Me. They want their own way, and they want to have what the earth can give. They will pass away and the earth will be destroyed, but you will live forever with Me. I will reward you for your faithfulness and all your acts of love. I will prepare for you a house filled with treasures, because you are My child–heir to the throne. You will be greatly blessed because you are Mine.

271

You should proclaim the Kingdom of YHUH.

Luke 9:59 He said to another man, "Follow Me." But the man replied, "King, first let me go and bury my father." 60 Yahshua said to him, "Let the dead bury their own dead, but you go and proclaim the Kingdom of YHUH." Ps 145:11 They will tell of the glory of your kingdom and speak of your might, 12 so that all men may know of your mighty acts and the glorious splendor of your kingdom. 13 Your kingdom is an everlasting kingdom, and your dominion endures through all generations. (Ps 103:19)

My beloved, do not allow anyone or anything to hinder you from telling others about Me and My wondrous love for them. If you allow excuses to keep you from sharing truth, this displeases Me. You should tell others about your love for Me and if they will listen, then tell them all about Me. Some people will not listen because they love the world and do not want to serve Me. They think that their life would be horrible to give up all earthly pleasure to serve Me, because they do not realize that knowing the Elohim of the universe in an intimate way is total satisfaction. I have made you to be at one with Me, and no man will be satisfied with the world. Sin will make a man happy only for a season, and then his emptiness will overtake him and he will not be happy. Only I can fill the void, because I have created you in a way that only I can fill you and bring you satisfaction. You must be brave and strong and stand firm and tell others about Me. If they will not listen, leave them. Do not force anyone to listen or beg someone to change. Change is an individual choice, and you cannot force someone to change. You can pray for them and My Spirit can press on them and convict them of their sins, and then they may listen and change. All you are responsible for doing is telling others about Me.

272

You should not look back to the past.

Luke 9:62 Yahshua replied, "No one who puts a hand to the plow and looks back is fit for service in the kingdom of YHUH." Phil 3:13 Brothers and sisters, I do not consider myself yet to have taken hold of it. But one thing I do: Forgetting what is behind and straining toward what is ahead, press on toward the goal to win the prize for which YHUH has called me heavenward in Yahshua. (2 Chron 30:7)

My beloved, look ahead to what I tell you to do. Keep your eyes focused on Me and listen for My Voice. I will guide you down the right path. Do not look at your past sins. Ask Me to forgive you of your sins, and I will forgive you. No sin is so great that you cannot ask Me to forgive you. You must forgive yourself of what you have done wrong. You may look at your life and think about all the things you did wrong. You cannot go back and correct what you have done. You have made mistakes, but do not allow your past mistakes to cripple you and keep you from going forward. You may have been in rebellion and did not want to follow Me. If you are sorry for your sins and want to change your life, I will help you turn your life around. It is not too late to make changes. I want you to listen to My Voice and focus on Me. I will show you a new life where you can live in liberty and not in bondage to sin. If you have harmed others in the past, then ask them to forgive you and make restitution to them. I can heal all relationships, if you ask Me to intervene. I have the ability to change the person's heart. Only I can change a heart and heal a relationship. Continue to look forward and do not fall into self-pity. I will cleanse you from the past and create in you a new creature. Do not desire to go back to the sins of the past. Stand firm, and do not give into sin. I will help you overcome!

273

You should pray that YHUH would send laborers for the harvest.

Luke 10:1 After this YHUH appointed seventy others, and sent them on ahead of Him, two by two, into every town and place where He Himself was about to come. 2 And He said to them, "The harvest is plentiful, but the laborers are few; pray the Master of the harvest to send out laborers into his harvest." (Matt 9:37, John 4:35)

My beloved, I AM opening the eyes of My children-those lost in exile for years. Like animals that hibernate all winter and awake for spring, so My children are opening their eyes and seeing truth for the first time. When they see it, they know it and cling to it. This is the time to pray for those who know the truth about Me to share it with others. If a person wants to find truth, it is very easy. The internet and television has all sorts of options where you can find truth and listen to the truth. More information is available to you today than ever before. You are free to search all sorts of data, but that is only for a season. The evil one will eventually cut off all truth, and anyone who tries to speak truth he will kill or take into captivity. He is wicked and wants all to be wicked with him. His goal is to rule earth and destroy all truth, so he can set himself up as "god," but he will not succeed. He is only allowed to continue to test My children and show everyone that they are faithful and worthy of being My children. This will make sure that there will be no one to oppose them when I allow them to rule over others and help others learn about Me and My ways. Only My children are tested by fire and found true to Me. The others are destroyed in the Lake of Fire. Even the evil one will no longer exist. Pray that My children will rise up and bring the truth to others while they still can.

274

You should take power over the enemy.

Luke 10:18 He replied, "I saw Satan fall like lightning from heaven. 19 I have given you authority to trample on snakes and scorpions and to overcome all the power of the enemy; nothing will harm you." Ps 91:13 You will tread on the lion and the cobra; you will trample the great lion and the serpent. Is 14:12 How you have fallen from heaven, morning star, son of the dawn! You have been cast down to the earth, you who once laid low the nations!

My beloved, I have put the evil one under your feet, so you have power over him. I have given you My name, because you are My child and whenever you speak in My name you have authority over the evil one and all his forces. If demons come to you, command them to leave in My name and they must submit to you. The only way they would stay is if they have grounds to stay-legal rights to stay. Are you in sin? Do you have a curse on you because your ancestors sinned? Repent and be cleansed, and they can no longer torment you. Do you have a portal opened in your house where uncleanness pours out filth into your home? Pornography, TV, movies, video games, and unclean books can pollute your house and have demons attached to them. Do you have pagan idols or any symbols that are worshipped by pagans in your house? Maybe you purchased an artifact from another country and do not know its source. Be careful what you bring into your house. Do not bring into your house any statues or foreign symbols. Do not allow your children to see unclean material, and do not look into unclean material. Do not look into the sexual activities of the gods of Hollywood. Do not imitate or long for any of their greed or wickedness. They are worshipped, and they should be rebuked for their sins. Wake up and cleanse your house and yourself, so you can have power over the enemy.

275

You should rejoice, because your names are written in heaven.

Luke 10:20 However, do not rejoice that the spirits submit to you, but rejoice that your names are written in heaven. Ps 69:28 May they be blotted out of the book of life and not be listed with the righteous. (Rev 20:12-15, Rev 21:10-27)

My beloved, rejoice and be glad that I have chosen you from the beginning and have placed My seed of righteousness within you, so your names can be written in heaven on the Lamb's Book of Life that lists all those who will have eternal life and live in My kingdom forever. Rejoice and be glad, and do not allow the sorrows of the world to overtake you so you lose sight of your destiny. You are chosen. I send My angel to watch over you and care for you, so no harm can come to you. If you go into rebellion and sin against Me, then you open a door for the evil one to come in and cause you harm. If you are in sin, then my shield of protection is not on you. You must always be on guard not to fall into sin. The times are dark, and you need to be obedient to My voice. Sacrifice your flesh and obey Me, so you can walk under My shield of protection. The evil one comes into heaven to condemn you once you walk into sin, and then I must punish you for your sins. I do not rejoice in punishing you, but as a parent spanks his child when he disobeys so I too spank My child when he does not obey Me. I know that the child will learn from this correction and change this ways of living. You must be faithful to correct your children and teach them how to walk in My ways, so when they grow up you can rejoice in their good works and know I have also written their names in My Book of Life in heaven.

276

You should be a good neighbor. You should not be prejudice towards others.

Luke 10:27-37 Yahshua answered, "'Love YHUH your Elohim with all your heart and with all your soul and with all your strength and with all your mind'; and, 'Love your neighbor as yourself.'" Rom 15:2 Each of us should please our neighbors for their good, to build them up. Lev 19:18 Love your neighbor as yourself. I am YHUH.

My beloved, if you see a need or hear of a need, then you should have compassion and act in mercy so you can help the person in need. If each person would help a person in need, there would be no poor among you. There would be no needy. You sit in your rich houses while others starve and are lacking. They are sick and in pain and no one cares for them. The medical system is set up so only the rich will have the best care. Those who cannot pay for it will not have the care they need. Everything in your country is set up so only the rich can have the best. You have an abundance of food in your markets, but only the rich can buy all they want. Others have to eat the least expensive food and cannot buy the better cuts of meat and vegetables. They make sacrifices, but the rich make no sacrifices. So what will happen in the last days? The rich are preparing places to live to protect them from coming disaster, but the poor will perish. Only My children will be covered by My Hand of protection. Then all will know that I AM Elohim. In the meantime be compassionate and help those in need. If they are in sin, then ask them to repent and pray with them. If they reject My mercy towards them, then you need not give them mercy again. My love and compassion have come to their door, and they shut the door. If this happens, take My love to another house and maybe the one inside will receive freely and be blessed by Me.

Which Commandments Should I Obey?

277

You should not be distracted from hearing YHUH's Word.

Luke 10:38 As Yahshua and His disciples were on their way, He came to a village where a woman named Martha opened her home to Him. 39 She had a sister called Mary, who sat at YHUH's feet listening to what He said. 40 But Martha was distracted by all the preparations that had to be made. She came to Him and asked, "Master, don't you care that my sister has left me to do the work by myself? Tell her to help me!" 41 "Martha, Martha," YHUH answered, "you are worried and upset about many things, 42 but there is only one thing that is essential. Mary has chosen the right thing, and it will not be taken away from her." (Luke 12:29, John 6:27, Is 55:1-3)

My beloved, I entered a house and I was teaching My words to them and all in the house were enjoying the Truth from the words I spoke. Their hearts were light and they were filled with joy to hear such Truth. Only Martha was worried about preparing food for her guests and making the meal ready, so she missed My words of Truth. I told her that she worried about unimportant things and she should search for Truth and hold on to it. She did not understand My words, but Mary understood and her heart was filled with joy. I could not take that away from her. Are you too interested in the affairs of the world to even notice the Truth I want to give you? Do you search your bible for Truth? Do you call on My name for insight? Are you blinded and cannot see, because you do not search for Truth? Truth is everywhere, but you must seek it to find it. I do not give Truth to anyone, but they must be searching for Me and desiring to walk in righteousness. You must love Me and want to follow My commandments and follow the leading of My Spirit. You must turn from the world and all its distractions and focus on Me. What are your distractions? TV, movies, games, friends, work, sports, children...What keeps you from spending time with Me? If you really loved Me, you would delight in reading My words. You would want to hear My words and look for My Truth. Rejoice when you find Truth, because you are blessed.

278

You should ask Yahshua to teach you to pray.

Luke 11:1 One day Yahshua was praying in a certain place. When He finished, one of his disciples said to Him, "Master, teach us to pray, just as John taught his disciples." James 5:16 The prayer of a righteous man is powerful and effective. Ps 34:15 The eyes of YHUH are on the righteous, and his ears are attentive to their cry. (Rom 8:26-27, James 5:16)

My beloved, come to Me and I will teach you to intercede for others. I will show you how to allow My Spirit within you to pray through you. Allow your voice to lend itself to My Spirit within you. Just as you use your voice to speak in tongues, then use your voice to speak the prayers that My Spirit within you utters for you. You will see how you can pray for yourself and others as led by My Spirit. You must allow Me to show you the problem in others' lives so you can pray specifically. You will begin to have a desire to pray all the time and for everyone all day long. You have allowed My Spirit within you to be unleashed or uncovered, so you can see clearly. You will cry out for others to Me for their salvation, healing, or release from sin. So many of My children run from interceding for others. Take up your staff, and be a leader who prays for others. You will become more sensitive to My Presence, because I will lend My ear to you to hear your every prayer. Your prayers will come up as lights towards Me. The more you pray, the more I hear and answer. You must not forsake your brothers and sisters and turn your face away from their troubles, but you must pray for them and support them. If someone walks out of your life, do not forget about him but continue to pray for him. Your intercession will break down darkness. Come to Me, and I will teach you to pray.

279

***You should ask in Yahshua's name for whatever you
need.***

Luke 11:9-13 So I say to you: Ask and it will be given to you; seek and
you will find; knock and the door will be opened to you. John 16:24 Until now you have not asked for anything in my name. Ask and you will
receive, and your joy will be complete. (1 Kings 18:36-37, Gen 32:9)

My beloved, ask Me and I will give to you. I AM a generous Father, and I love
to give good gifts to My children. I love to give to those who love Me and obey
Me. If you seek for Me, you will find Me in every moment of your day. You will
find Me in My scriptures. You will begin to know who I AM. If you think you
can find Me completely while you are in the flesh, then you are wrong. The flesh
is a veil that keeps you from seeing Me and knowing Me in oneness. You can be
at one with Me to a point that you are led by My Spirit every moment of the day
and that is all you need. You do not have to go to man to guide you, just call on
My name and I will show you the way. The biggest error My children make is to
lean on the advice and teaching of man as opposed to leaning on Me. Lean your
head on My shoulder, and I will whisper direction, guidance, advice, wisdom
and conviction of sin. I will keep you in the right path free from sin, and you will
not be deceived by the evil one. If you go to a man to have him guide you, you
miss out knowing Me and understanding who I really am. If you really want to
be righteous and walk in My ways, then you will seek Me all day. My Spirit is a
gift to all who call on My name and confess Me as their Elohim and love Me. It
is the best gift anyone can receive.

280

You should be careful that the Light within you may not become dark.

Luke 11:33 "No one, after lighting a lamp, puts it away in a cellar, nor under a bushel, but on the lamp stand, in order that those who enter may see the light. 34 The lamp of your body is your eye; when your eye is clear, your whole body also is full of light; but when your eye is evil, your body also is full of darkness. 35 Then watch out that the light in you may not be darkness. 36 If your whole body is full of light, with no dark part in it, it shall be wholly illumined, as when the lamp illumines you with its rays." (Is 5:20)

My beloved, if you are filled with Light, then you are filled with My nature-who I AM. You are My child and you should resemble your Father. You should be loving and kind and giving generously to others. Joy cannot come to you unless you give to others and love them. If you are selfish and not giving, then you will not be filled with Light. Be careful that the Light within you is not selfishness and have a desire for worldly possessions. Cling not to the world, but cling to Me and My ways. Men will come to you saying they love Me, but if they do not treat others fairly and do not give generously to others and do not love those around them, then beware because they may not love Me at all. Beware of those declaring the faith yet have no fruits of righteousness. Beware of those deceivers and be glad and rejoice that you are a Child of the King-the only King-the Creator of all things-the Author of wisdom-the Giver of Life. I even gave life to Satan-the deceiver, knowing he would test the faithful. I knew that it was only for a season, and then he would be no more. No one rejects Me and lives on eternally. Either you love Me and show allegiance to Me, or you don't. You will be judged and sifted, and who endures to the end will be saved from the Lake of Fire. You will rejoice on that day. Beware. Keep the Light within you free from selfishness, greed, and unforgiveness. Have the Light of love within you always.

281

You should beware of hypocrisy.

Luke 12:1 He turned now to his disciples and warned them, "More than anything else, beware of these Pharisees and the way they pretend to be good when they aren't. But such hypocrisy cannot be hidden forever. 2 It will become as evident as yeast in dough. 3 Whatever they have said in the dark shall be heard in the light, and what you have whispered in the inner rooms shall be broadcast from the housetops for all to hear!" (Matt 23:27-28, Job 36:13)

My beloved, beware of those teachers who proclaim to be righteous-honest and just-obeying all My commandments-and secretly they are wicked. All sins will eventually be exposed. If you look carefully, you can judge them by the fruits they bear. Do they love people and try to help them, or do they love money and love only what money can bring? Do they live in mansions, or do they live in a modest house? Do they have fine expensive clothes, jewelry, and cars? Do they long for being "prosperous," or do they long to be righteous? Do they long to be "blessed" with money, or do they want to give money to others? Look at these teachers and discern their heart and what they really teach. No man can serve himself and Me also. He has to give up one or the other. He must do as I desire-as I guide him-as I command him-or he does not serve Me at all. You must discern who says they are good and really are not. Many righteous men fall due to the love of money and greed. Do not allow money to consume you, but allow your life to be one of sacrifice-or denying yourself. Your sacrifice will be a flaming light before Me, and I will answer all your prayers. If you are in an assembly of believers and the man who teaches you does not walk in righteousness, then he will lead all of you into the ditch. Beware of the man who wants to build a large expensive church and a fine mansion for himself. Look for a man who encourages giving to the poor and needy, and then you will have found a righteous man.

282

You should not fear people.

Luke 12:4-7 I tell you, my friends, do not be afraid of those who kill the body and after that can do no more. 5 But I will show you whom you should fear: Fear Him who, after the killing of the body, has power to throw you into hell. Prov 29:25 Fear of man will prove to be a snare, but whoever trusts in YHUH is kept safe. Ps 118:6 YHUH is with me; I will not be afraid. What can mere mortals do to me?

My beloved, do not fear men. What can they do to you? They can kill your body, but they cannot touch your spirit. The world hates you, but I love you and will protect you from the Evil One. Some of you may suffer persecution for My sake. You will confess Me before men and be persecuted in the last day. Great is your reward to die for Me, because you have confessed your love for Me. Many will be slain by the sword and many more will be put in prison, but many will escape into the wilderness and be set free from the hand of the evil one. Listen carefully to My Voice. All those who love Me will listen and follow My voice of guidance and go to the wilderness where I will care for you just as I did in the days given to Moses. I will feed you and clothe you during the great tribulation. No man can harm you. Fear Me and follow in My ways, and you will escape the fires of judgment. Fear Me and love others and walk in My commandments, and I will deliver you from the Lake of Fire where no man returns. This will be his final end. The evil one will go there and be no more. He knows his end is coming, and he tries very hard to take as many of My children as possible with him to destruction. Not one of My little ones will be lost. Not one will enter destruction. Only I know My little ones-well hidden from the evil one. I will gather you, My child, and keep you in My arms and take you to My kingdom and bring you to the house I have prepared for you from the riches of the universe.

283

You should confess Yahshua before men.

Luke 12:8 I tell you, whoever acknowledges (confesses) Me before men, the Son of Man will also acknowledge him before the angels of Elohim. 9 But he who disowns Me before men will be disowned before the angels of Elohim. 10 And everyone who speaks a word against the Son of Man will be forgiven, but anyone who blasphemes against YHUH's Spirit will not be forgiven. Ps 111:1 Praise YHUH. I will extol YHUH with all my heart in the council of the upright and in the assembly. (Matt 10:32)

My beloved, confess that you love Me before men. Confess to others My love for you and all the miracles I have done for you and your ancestors. Do not do as the religious leaders do who say you must keep all these man-made laws to enter My kingdom. Man made up these laws. It was not Me. My laws are from the foundation of the earth. They were established by Me, and they are fair and just. Any time someone tries to make a man keep his man-made laws, this is an abomination to Me. I want men to search My Words and find My laws for themselves. Torah teachers can help them understand the laws, but men should read the laws for themselves and follow them and teach their children how to walk in My ways. If you are shy and do not want to talk about Me to others, then ask for boldness from Me and I will give it to you. There are dark days coming, and you will have to make a choice. Who do you serve? You must be ready to stand firm or flee to the wilderness, so I can take care of you. The world will hate you, because you love Me and do not confess to serve their god. You must be ready to face the dark days ahead. Prepare and make your children ready. Let them know that they must serve Me by standing up for Me. No man can be double minded at this time and enter My kingdom. You must confess Me and My love for you to all men, and you will be counted worthy to enter My kingdom.

284

You should sell your possessions and give to the poor.

Luke 12:32 Do not be afraid, little flock, for your Father has been pleased to give you the kingdom. 33 Sell your possessions and give to the poor. Provide purses for yourselves that will not wear out, a treasure in heaven that will not be exhausted, where no thief comes near and no moth destroys. 34 For where your treasure is, there your heart will be also. Sell your possessions and give to the poor. Prov 19:17 He who is kind to the poor lends to YHUH, and He will reward him for what he has done. (Deut 15:7, Matt 19:21-24)

My beloved, give to the poor. This is what I command you to do. Sell your possessions if necessary, so you can give generously to others. Give, and I will give back to you. The poor will always be among you, and you should give to them and not be selfish. Do not hoard up riches for yourself, but give to those in need. If you say, "I do not know any poor person or I do not know where to give," then ask Me where you should give and I will show you. If you know a local place that feeds the poor, this is a good place to start giving your food or money. If you see men who are in need of work and you can supply them a job, then help the men out so they can feed their families. If the men are lazy and do not work, then do not help them even if they are poor. You have given them a chance to succeed, and they have turned away from it. If you hoard up possessions, then you sin because how many possessions do you need? Give away what you do not need to the poor. If you have numerous shoes and clothes, give away to others, so they can have clothes and shoes also. I will send your possessions to the right places. You do not really need numerous possessions, and you will be set free if you are released from the bondage of numerous possessions. Give away to others and you will be blessed.

285

You should humble yourself.

Matt 23:1-12 For whoever exalts himself will be humbled, and whoever humbles himself will be exalted. Prov 29:23 Pride brings a person low, but the lowly in spirit gain honor. 1 Peter 5:6 Humble yourselves under YHUH's mighty hand, that He may lift you up in due time. (Luke 14:7-11, Luke 18:9-14)

My beloved, humble yourself and I will exalt you. Humble yourself, and I will lift you up. Do not think you should be given the best of everything, but look at yourself and know your faults and you weaknesses and see yourself how you really are-totally unworthy of My blessings. In My Mercy and compassion I will bless you, if you love Me and call on My name for help. Some cannot call on My name, because they are not humble towards Me. Humble yourself and repent. Others do not want to accept responsibility for their errors and do not want to say they have made a mistake. They do not want to make restitution and reconciliation. They want to ignore their offenses and say they have done nothing. The proud want people to admire them and praise them, because of what they have accomplished or the wealth they have. Others want no one to take notice of their good deeds. If you do a good deed, keep it hidden and I will reward you. If you will secretly do kind things for others, I will bless you and raise you up. Stay humble before Me always confessing your sins and going to others quickly who you have angered or who have something against you. Do not allow hatred to grow, because it comes imbedded and festers and causes great wounds. Go to someone who has something against you whether you wronged the person or not and make things right between you and your brothers, so you both can dwell in peace.

286

You should help those who can't repay you.

Luke 14:12 Then Yahshua said to his host, "When you give a luncheon or dinner, do not invite your friends, your brothers or relatives, or your rich neighbors; if you do, they may invite you back and so you will be repaid. 13 But when you give a banquet, invite the poor, the crippled, the lame, the blind, 14 and you will be blessed. Although they cannot repay you, you will be repaid at the resurrection of the righteous." (Prov 19:17, Matt 10:42)

My beloved, if you invite your friends who love you and those who have wealth to come to your house, they will repay you and ask you to come to their house. If you ask the needy to come to your house to eat, then you know they will be blessed and they cannot repay you, but I can repay you with blessings. When you sit at your table and you have abundance, share it with others who need extra help at this time. Maybe they are suffering and are in pain from the events of their life. Your meal and your love will brighten them. If there is one who is searching for truth, bring him to your table to eat and share the truth with him. He can never repay you for the truth you have given him. If you are lonely and have no friends, reach out to those in need of My love and give compassion to them. If you are not lonely and have many friends, make room for those who have no friends and needs someone to help them. Do not always think of yourself and how others can bless you, but think of how you can bless others-those who really need your help. If you will reach out to others, I will reach out to you and shine My face upon you. Do not be mean to others, but always show your love to others. Even those who reject Me, always show your love to them and this will convict their very soul.

287

You should count the cost of following Yahshua.

Luke 14:28 "Suppose one of you wants to build a tower. Will he not first sit down and estimate the cost to see if he has enough money to complete it? 29 For if he lays the oundation and is not able to finish it, everyone who sees it will ridicule him, 30 saying, 'This fellow began to build and was not able to finish.'" (John 5:41-44, Gen 11:4. Prov 24:27)

My beloved, does a man decide to build a house without first counting the cost of the house? If he does not have the cash, he secures a loan so he can complete the house and have a shelter for his family. If you follow Me, you should count the cost of what you will have to give to Me to serve Me. I want you to be willing to give up anything I ask you to give up. I may not say to give a thing up for Me, but if it hinders you from drawing closer to Me or if it is of the world system, then you must give it up. What is polluting your life? Every time you turn on a TV or go to the movie theatre, do you see things that pollute you and contaminate you from the world? Do not look at these any more. Are you willing to do this? If you are turning away from these things, you are sacrificing your flesh as a burning sacrifice to Me that gives a pleasing aroma. What else contaminates you? People who do not serve Me, but love the world? A body of people who say they serve Me, but walk in man-made doctrine? Books that do not teach you about Me, but entertain you or pollute your mind with filth? Video games with spirits, spells, and demons? What do these things do for you? How can they bring you closer to Me? Do you long to see what is happening in Hollywood? They do not serve Me. They are wicked and sinful, so do not look at what they do. The Evil One pulls you into the world in all sorts of ways, so beware. Wake up and give up all these things and serve Me.

288

You should repent of your sins.

Acts 3:19 Repent, then, and turn to Elohim, so that your sins may be wiped out, that times of refreshing may come from Yahshua. Ps 19:12 But who can discern their own errors? Forgive my hidden faults. Is 43:25 I, even I, am He who blots out your transgressions, for my own sake, and remembers your sins no more. Jer 36:3 Perhaps when the people of Judah hear about every disaster I plan to inflict on them, they will each turn from their wicked ways; then I will forgive their wickedness and their sin. (Luke 15:3-24, Mark 1:14-15)

My beloved, repent of your sins and be happy. Repent and your life will be blessed. Do not think you can continue in sin and not be punished. You will be punished for every one of your sins. I will balance the scales. I will send My Spirit upon you to convict you of your sins and if you reject Me and will not listen, then you will pay the penalty for your sins-every one of them. Do not think you will escape, because I will punish you. If you ask Me to forgive you, then I will if you are sincere and turn from your sins. If you say, "Forgive Me" and the next day you do the same sin again, then you mock Me. You are not repentant. You do not want to live in righteousness. Think about your life and be strong. Sin will destroy you, but righteousness will make you strong-strong enough to overcome any situation. The days are growing darker. Now is the time to repent. Do not delay and tell others to repent also, so they may experience My love and compassion. If you are in sin, My presence is not upon you, but I will be faithful to convict you. If you reject Me, then you reject My Spirit and punishment will come upon you. You will become sick, or your money will be taken from you, your possessions will break and fall apart, your children will follow your example and sin also and cause you grief, your family will be taken from you, your animals will die, and your house and land will be lost. You will look to heaven at last and repent. Do not wait until this happens, but repent today.

289

You should not envy others.

Luke 15:25-32 "But he answered his father, 'Look! All these years I've been slaving for you and never disobeyed your orders. Yet you never gave Me even a young goat so I could celebrate with my friends. 30 But when this son of yours who has squandered your property with prostitutes comes home, you kill the fattened calf for him!' 31 'My son,' the father said, 'you are always with Me, and everything I have is yours. 32 But we had to celebrate and be glad, because this brother of yours was dead and is alive again; he was lost and is found.'" 1 Cor 13:4-5 Love is patient, love is kind. It does not envy, it does not boast, it is not proud. Prov 14:30 He that cools his anger is a healer of his heart, and envy is the decay of the bones. (James 3:16)

My beloved, I told a story about a brother who took his inheritance and left his father's house and lost all his inheritance by sinful living. He wanted the things of the world, and the things of the world devoured him. Once he repented of his sinful ways, he wanted to come home to his family. He humbled himself and returned home. His brother could not rejoice that this brother had repented and returned to them. He was still angry with his brother for leaving and taking his inheritance and leaving his father sad and worried. He could not forgive him for his sins, so he was angry and resented his brother. When his brother was given a feast to rejoice that he had returned, he was furious. He could not rejoice that his brother had repented. His brother still had no inheritance and he was still poor, but he had the love of his family which was a great blessing. The brother wanted his father to celebrate him, because he had remained with him and worked with him and had been a delight to his father. My beloved, do not be angry when others are celebrated and lifted up. If they have repented, rejoice with them and share their celebration. If they are honored or if they earn a large sum of money or whatever their blessing may be-a child, a marriage, a new home, a new job-do not be jealous, but instead be happy for your brother.

290

You should not seek the praise of men.

Luke 16:15 He said to them, "You are the ones who justiy yourselves in the eyes of men, but YHUH knows your hearts. What is highly valued among men is detestable in YHUH's sight." John 12:42 Yet at the same time many even among the leaders believed in Him. But because of the Pharisees they would not confess their faith for fear they would be put out of the synagogue; 43 for they loved praise from men more than praise from YHUH. (John 5:41-44, 1 Sam 16:7)

My beloved, do not seek the praise of men, but seek Me and do My will for you. If you try to please men, you will never make all men happy. Some will not like what you are saying or doing . If you try to seek Me and walk in My ways , then you will be satisfied in Me. You will find no satisfaction in trying to please men. Once you please them, then you will have to do other favors to please them, and it will be endless. You will never keep them satisfied unless you continue to do all they want you to do. They will begin to use you and take advantage of you, because they know you want to please them. If you fall into this trap, you will become very unsatisfied. Only complete satisfaction comes in serving Me. You will feel My love for you, and My presence covering you telling you how pleased I AM with you. If you seek the praise of men, seek My praise instead because it is much more gratifying. You will always feel satisfaction when you obey Me. You will feel strong and confident in Me. If you disobey Me and seek the world, then you will be miserable and always seeking happiness and never reaching it. You must look into My eyes and be led by My Spirit every day, so you can go to great heights and succeed in all you do. You will at last find full satisfaction.

291

You should not divorce and remarry.

Luke 16:18 "Everyone who divorces his wife and marries another commits adultery, and he who marries one who is divorced from a husband commits adultery." **Mal 2:16** "I hate divorce," says YHUH Elohim of Israel. **1 Cor 7:27** Are you married? Do not seek a divorce.

My beloved, it is better for a man not to marry than to marry after he divorces his wife. You should think clearly before you marry someone and before you divorce someone. I tell you that I hate divorce. Once you give your oath to someone that you will love him and care for him for as long as you live, then you must keep your oath that you made before Me. You must keep your vow that you made before men not to separate yourself from your mate. You must ask yourself a question in the beginning, "Is this a person who serves Me and wants to live a life filled with love for others? Does this person want to live a selfish life and serve himself only?" If you cannot answer this question, then you need more time before you marry. If you are concerned that the person may be a selfish person, then know that you will have to live with a very selfish person for the rest of your life. Choose wisely and let Me guide you. Let Me deliver you from the temptations and lust, so you will not be hasty in your decision. Men come and go and women come and go, but only My purpose will stand for you. I want you to have a life of happiness, so ask Me before you marry. My choice for you will not bring you disaster. Divorce is an abomination to Me, but to marry again is worse. Your sins are multiplying, and your blessings are falling away from you.

292

You should not tempt others to sin.

Luke 17:1 "There will always be temptations to sin," Yahshua said one day to his disciples, "but woe to the man who does the tempting. 2 If he were thrown into the sea with a huge rock tied to his neck, he would be far better off than facing the punishment in store for those who harm these little children's souls. I am warning you!" (Mal 2:7-9, Matt 18:6)

My beloved, the Evil One sets many traps for you. If you are not careful, you will fall into the traps. You must not allow others to fall into them either, so watch your brother and if he falls into sin rebuke him and tell him to stop his sin. If you go to him in love, he will listen to you and may stop his sin. If you go to him and show him that there is no love or compassion in your heart for him, then he will not listen but reject your words. If you are the one who falls into sin and then you try to make others sin with you, then you will be punished for your wickedness. You will be made to pay for your sins against others over and above your own sins. If you say to younger children, "Come let us sin; this will be fun," then you are the trap and I will punish you for enticing young children to sin when they are innocent. Eve was deceived by the Evil One and she was innocent, but the penalty of her sin was borne by mankind for thousands of years. Your sin against these little ones may cripple them for years, and I will hold it against you. Do not ask younger children to break the law or perform sexual acts. Do not contribute to minors by giving them alcohol, cigarettes, or drugs. This is an abomination in My sight. If they ask you to buy one of these for them, do not do it. This is wrong in My eyes. I will not let you escape your punishment. If you will guard over the little ones, I will bless you greatly.

293

You should privately rebuke a brother and if he repents forgive him.

Luke 17:3 So watch yourselves. "If your brother sins, rebuke him, and if he repents, forgive him." Prov 17:10 A rebuke impresses a man of discernment more than a hundred lashes a fool. (Prov 15:31-32, Eccl 7:5)

My beloved, if you see your brother in sin, then go to him privately and tell him in love about his sin. If you talk to him in love showing concern for him, then he will listen to your words and he may repent. If he does not repent, bring one or two others who love your brother and in love tell him about his sin and ask him to repent. If the brother will not repent, then you must expose his sin to the congregation and humiliate your brother so he will repent. If he does not repent, send him out of your fellowship until he can come back and repent in front of the congregation and start anew. Otherwise have nothing to do with the person until he can repent. Do not forget about him, but pray for him to come to his senses and see clearly his sin. Do not give up on him, but continue to pray for him and then your rewards are great. You may not think he will ever turn back to Me, but My Hand is on him. I can make his life miserable until he changes his ways and repents and follows Me. I know what a man needs to bring him to repentance. I know how to humble him until he looks up and cries out to Me. I know what My children need to bring repentance. I will not allow My children to sink in sin, but I will pull them up and put their feet on a strong foundation. Be patient with your brother and be there for him when he needs support.

294

You should continue to forgive your brother.

Matt 18:20 Then Peter came to Yahshua and asked, "Master, if my brother keeps on sinning against Me, how many times do I have to forgive him? Seven times?" 21 "No, not seven times," answered Yahshua, "but seventy times seven." Luke 17:4 "If he sins against you seven times in a day, and seven times comes back to you and says, 'I repent,' forgive him." Jer 31:34 Declares YHUH, "For I will forgive their wickedness and will remember their sins no more." Matt 6:15 But if you do not forgive men their sins, your Father will not forgive your sins.

My beloved, forgive your brother when he sins against you, if he repents and turns from his sins. If he continues to sin, then go to him and talk to him privately about his sins. Tell him of his danger if he does not repent. Be wise and do not cling to a man who continues to sin, but separate yourself from the man. Many traps will be set for My little ones by the Evil One. He will come at you from all sides and want you to reject Me or turn aside from Me. If you hold fast to Me, then I will raise you up at the last day and you will dwell with Me eternally. The man who contuses to sin will go to eternal darkness. If you do not forgive the man who has sinned against you, then you hold onto anger and bitterness and you harm your own soul. These are the sources of hatred and My children should love others and not hate them. Be kind and giving to others and allow yourself to know that all men are not perfect and they will sin from time to time. If a man sins and then turns from his sin, then accept the man and hold him close to you. Even a friend may sin against you and hurt you. The friend may not even know he has hurt you. Go to your friend and tell your friend of his sin, so healing can come between you. Do not allow hurt to grow or you will have anger against your friend, and soon you will have hatred. Forgive quickly, so you can always walk in love.

295

You should be an obedient servant.

Luke 17:7-10 "So you also, when you have done everything you were told to do, should say, 'We are unworthy servants; we have only done our duty.'" Rom 6:22 But now that you have been set free from sin and have become slaves to YHUH, the benefit you reap leads to holiness, and the result is eternal life. 1 John 5:3 This is love for YHUH: to obey his commands. And his commands are not burdensome, 4 for everyone born of YHUH overcomes the world. (Deut 30:17, Is 1:19)

My beloved, you are My servant, My beloved servant, and I ask you to do certain tasks. Listen for My voice, and do as I ask you to do. I will send My Spirit to convict you and show you when you are not obeying Me. Do not reject My Spirit, because this is blaspheming My Spirit. When you say, "No" to Me you blaspheme Me, and you will end up in eternal darkness and be no more. You must listen and get ready to serve Me. An eager trustworthy servant is always ready and listening for My voice, so you can eagerly serve Me. If you want to do what you want to do and not care about others and helping them, then you are not My servant. You serve yourself and are a product of the deception of the Evil One. Beware of his lies. He says, "You should have fun and pleasure, laugh and sing, dance and party. This is what life is all about–doing what you want to do and having pleasure all the time." This is a lie. This is not your purpose for this life. You are put here to test your faith. If you are faithful to Me, then you are worthy to enter My Kingdom of Light. If you fail the test, then you are not allowed into My Kingdom. Only My faithful servants are allowed to enter. You must be born again-allowing My Spirit to fill you before you will ever say to Me, "I am your servant and I have only done my duty for you."

296

You should not desire to go back to the things of the world.

Luke 17:32 Remember Lot's wife! 33 Whoever tries to keep his life will lose it, and whoever loses his life will preserve it. Luke 9:62 Yahshua replied, "No one who puts his hand to the plow and looks back is fit for service in the kingdom of Elohim." (1 Kings 19:19-21, Phil 3:13)

My beloved, remember Lot's wife how she desired to go back to Sodom and was destroyed because she was not faithful. Look at yourself. Are you faithful to Me? Do you continually seek Me and cry out to Me? Do you continually read My Words and seek My Truth? If you are of Me, you will want to learn from Me. You will want to obey Me. You will love Me and not desire the things of the world. Are you in a situation like Lot where you are living in a perverted city and your children are suffering because of the perversion? Do not wait until judgment has come to your city, but go to another city and raise your children in peace. If you live in exile, there will be few around you who want to follow Me. Rejoice that I have called you out, and pray that I will release you from exile and send you back to My Beloved City-My Land. In the Land I have chosen are many blessings and I will care for all My children. I will pour out an abundance of blessings on you. When you are holding fast to Me, you will have success in your life. If you are in the bondage of debt and you feel like the weight of the world is too heavy for you and you have no resistance to sin, then cry out to Me and I will help you overcome and have faith. You will be able to rejoice at last, once you are released from your bondage.

297

You should be persistent when you are praying. Keep asking and do not give up.

Luke 18:1-7 And will not Elohim bring about justice for his chosen ones, who cry out to him day and night? Will He keep putting them off? 8 I tell you, He will see that they get justice, and quickly. Ex 22:23 If you do and they cry out to Me, I will certainly hear their cry. Ps 88:1 YHUH, you are the Elohim who saves me; day and night I cry out to you. 1Thess 5:17 Pray without ceasing.

My beloved, ask and continue to ask for what you need, and I will supply all you need. If someone is treating you unfairly and will not give you justice, then call on Me and I will hear you and change the situation so you can be treated fairly. You must call on Me day and night and all your prayers will be heard. I bend My ear to those who call on My name. If your prayers meet up with resistance, then I send My heavenly angels to fight for you and tear away the darkness. If you are praying against ancient gates, then you must pray and fast with others and your prayers will be as lights before Me. I will destroy the ancient gate and bring a flow of righteousness to you. Ancient curses may be hindering your walk with Me. You must discern as you are praying and fasting with your family. Is there a spirit that has been there since you were a child? Search and look for your weak areas and attack them with prayer and fasting until you are strong in the spirit, then you will be able to stand in the darkest of days. You may be able to remember times when you gave up. There is no longer time to give up and walk in sin or allow the weight of the hindering spirit to cause you to stumble. There is no longer time to fall down and get up, but you must remain in prayer and fasting and do not give in to temptation, but remain firmly planted and you will be ready for the last days.

298

You should make restitution for your sins.

Luke 19:1-8   But Zacchaeus stood up and said to Yahshua, "Look, Master! Here and now I give half of my possessions to the poor, and if I have cheated anybody out of anything, I will pay back four times the amount." 9 Yahshua said to him, "Today salvation has come to this house, because this man, too, is a son of Abraham. 10 For the Son of Man came to seek and to save what was lost." (Num 5:5-7)

My beloved, I came to eat at the house of a tax collector. Everyone hated the tax collectors, because the taxes the people paid were imposed by the Romans and were a hardship for My people. The tax collectors not only collected the required tax, but took in money for themselves. They had to have a set amount to collect for their city or region, so they collected it any way they could not thinking of widows or the poor and needy. They pressed down all the people and the people hated them and called them the chief of sinners. When I went to eat at any house owned by a tax collector, the people were furious. I came to show love, and I wanted My people to know that I forgive those who repent and want to make restitution for their sins. If you sin and ask for forgiveness, then you must restore what was taken from the person you wronged. If you stole property, or neglected something in your care, or damaged someone's property, or you borrowed something and did not return it, then you must restore and make right with the person that you wronged. If you damaged a person with your words, then restore the person with your words and go to others and restore the person's reputation. If you take from others, I will punish you unless you repent and give back to the person what you stole plus a gift of 20% of the value of what you stole. You must restore others trust in you. You cannot treat your brothers like the world treats each other, but you must love your brother and treat him with fairness and kindness.

299

You should beware of the teachers of The Law who are not humble.

Luke 20:45 While all the people were listening, Yahshua said to his disciples, 46 "Beware of this kind of teachers of the law. They like to walk around in flowing robes and love to be greeted in the market-places and have the most important seats in the synagogues and the places of honor at banquets. 47 They devour widows' houses and for a show make lengthy prayers. Such men will be punished most severe-ly." Ps 147:6 YHUH sustains the humble but casts the wicked to the ground.

My beloved, beware of those who say they are teaching My Words, yet they are not kind to others. How can they even begin to interpret My Words, if they do not live a life of love? They must be the foremost example of loving kindness to My people, if they are going to teach My words to others. If the teachers are not humble, they want men to praise them for their religious actions Beware! Do you want a haughty arrogant man to interpret My words for you? Let it not be so. Look for a teacher of My laws to focus on My laws-My instructions for life. Look for a man who has compassion and mercy in his heart for others. Look for a man who wants you to know the truth about Me and focus on seeking for the truth. Beware of teachers who live in mansions with many material possessions. Where does all this money come from? It comes from gifts from My people who wanted to build up a ministry, but instead are building up a man's wealth. This is not of Me-this is an abomination to Me. A man that follows after Me lives on only enough to care for his family, and the rest goes to help the poor and needy-the widows and orphans-to buy bibles and send out laborers to gather in the harvest. Do not be deceived by such ministers. Stay far away from them.

300

You should be a cheerful giver.

2 Cor 9:6 Remember this: Whoever sows sparingly will also reap sparingly, and whoever sows generously will also reap generously. 7 Each man should give what he has decided in his heart to give, not reluctantly or under compulsion, for Elohim loves a cheerful giver. Prov 22:9 The generous will themselves be blessed, for they share their food with the poor. (Ex 25:2, Deut 15:10, Luke 21:1-4)

My beloved, I told My disciples that a person who gives out of his wealth can easily give to Me. A person in poverty cannot spare any money, so when he gives to Me he has made a sacrifice. When you give to Me, is it a sacrifice or not? When you give do you wish you didn't have to give to Me-then don't. I don't need your money. I could rain down money, if I wanted to do so. You must know that I own all things, so I need nothing. You need to learn how to give to others. You need to open your heart to the poor and needy, so you will not look down at them, but you will have compassion on them. Be brave and strong, and put aside your longing for material possessions. If you long to serve Me, then you will let go of your money and give to Me. I want you to give to Me happily and with joy, because you love Me. When you buy your child a gift you are happy to do so. I want you to feel the same way when you give to Me. Find an agency where you enjoy giving your money- an agency that you know helps others in your local area-a place where you can volunteer your time and know your money goes to feed the hungry and help the needy. Then you can give with a joyful heart.

301

You should watch for the signs of His Return.

Luke 21:25 "And there will be signs in the sun, the moon, and the stars. On earth whole countries will be in despair, afraid of the roar of the sea and the raging tides. 26 People will faint from fear as they wait for what is coming over the whole earth, for the powers in space will be driven from their courses. 27 Then the Son of Man will appear, coming in a cloud (of angels) with great power and glory. 28 When these things begin to happen, stand up and raise your heads, because your salvation is near." Joel 2:31 The sun will be turned to darkness and the moon to blood before the coming of the great and dreadful day of YHUH. (Is 5:30)

My beloved, be alert and stay on guard because you are in the season of My return. Put aside your fleshy desires and get ready to see Me face to face. You must be set apart as I AM set apart and walk in My ways. You will have blessings come to you, if you walk in My ways and follow My laws. If you rebel against Me, then you will suffer loss. You will suffer and not be able to enter My kingdom. Watch for signs in the heavens. Watch for changes in the weather. Watch for changes in countries so that wars begin and men fight against men and many are killed and countries are left in ruin. Watch for disasters that will be all around you, floods, famine, storms, earthquakes, lightening, hail. You will see strange weather as the Earth wobbles and quakes and tilts on its axis. You will see the Earth almost collapse under the weight of the stress on it as foreign objects enter its atmosphere and pulls on it. These foreign objects that come from outer space and cross the path of Earth were sent by Me to bring stress on the Earth and fear to man. Men will die from fear, but My chosen ones will know that I have told them of these things and they will look up and know that your deliverance from this planet is near and I AM faithful to return as I have said.

302

You should be careful not to become too involved in feasting and drinking.

Luke 21:34 "Be careful not to let yourselves become occupied with too much feasting and drinking and with the worries of this life, or that Day may suddenly catch you like a trap. For it will come upon all people. Be on watch and pray always that you will have the strength to go safely through all those things that will happen and to stand before the Son of Man." Prov 23:20 Do not join those who drink too much wine or gorge themselves on meat. (Eccl 9:12)

My beloved, be careful to guard over yourself that you do not become dull and enter into the things of the world. Be careful not to sin against Me, but hold fast and you will find fulfillment in Me. If you do not cling to Me, you will fall back into the world. The world says, "Let's have fun. Let's find pleasure. Let's do what we want to do," but I say, "Put aside the tings of the world and focus only on Me and My ways, so you can do well." I will bless you, if you turn aside from the fleshy desires. The flesh is strong and weighs on you, but as you resist the evil one you will become stronger. Just as a man builds muscles, so consistent resistance to the temptations of the evil one will make you stronger and overcoming. Be glad that you have the ability to resist evil, because I have given you My Spirit to help you overcome. Only My children are allowed to receive My Spirit and be filled with joy and peace. If you are not walking in joy and peace, you are not receiving your blessing. You ask, "How can I have joy while I live in exile with all the pagans?" You do not depend on those around to do the right things, but you depend only on Me. If you depend only on Me, you will live in joy and peace. Men around you will be getting drunk and celebrating pagan festivals, but My people will rejoice only in My festivals and be sober at all times.

303

*You should eat bread and drink wine in remembrance
of Yahshua at Passover.*

Luke 22:14 When the hour came, Yahshua and his apostles reclined at the table. 15 And He said to them, "I have eagerly desired to eat this Passover with you before I suffer. 16 For I tell you, I will not eat it again until it finds fulfillment in the kingdom of Elohim." 17 After taking the cup, He gave thanks and said, "Take this and divide it among you. 18 For I tell you I will not drink again of the fruit of the vine until the kingdom of Elohim comes." 19 And He took bread, gave thanks and broke it, and gave it to them, saying, "This is my body given for you; do this in remembrance of Me." 20 In the same way, after the supper He took the cup, saying, "This cup is the new covenant in my blood, which is poured out for you."(Ex 12:25-28, Deut 4:9)

My beloved, before My death I called My disciples together and said, 'Let us eat the Passover Meal together." I sent My disciples to prepare the meal and find a place to celebrate. I told My disciples about what would happen to Me and to remember My act of love-the giving of My life for others. To remember this, I said to drink the wine and eat the bread in remembrance of Me at the Passover celebration. You may not know how to keep the Passover, but I will teach you so you can realize that I AM the Passover lamb slain for you. I will pass over you and not send the death angel to you to destroy you on the Day of Judgment. Anyone who keeps My Passover is pleasing in My sight. It does not have to be a big feast, because you are remembering how I took you out of Egypt and delivered you from the bondage of sin when I laid down My life for you. They led Me to slaughter-innocent without sin-and they mocked Me and tormented Me. They inflicted stripes upon Me and tore My flesh. They hung Me up and exposed Me for all to see. I rebuked the sinners by turning the sky dark and tore open the dirt. I showed Jerusalem who they had crucified. I tell you not one man there could ignore the signs of My displeasure. You should pick up yourself and read My words to understand My Passover, so you can remember Me with your bread and wine. If you do this, then blessings will be upon you and your house.

304

You should preach repentance and forgiveness of sins in the name of Yahshua.

Luke 24:45 Then He opened their minds so they could understand the Scriptures. 46 He told them, "This is what is written: The Messiah will suffer and rise from the dead on the third day, 47 and repentance and forgiveness of sins will be preached in his name to all nations, beginning at Jerusalem." Ps 51:13 Then I will teach transgressors your ways, so that sinners will turn back to you. (Luke 5:27-32, Is 2:3)

My beloved, there is only one name above all other names-Yahshua. Speak in My name about the message of good news-the message of repentance and the forgiveness of sin though My name. If you trust in Me and believe that I will save you from eternal darkness, then you should repent and be released from all your sins. Sin is bondage and death, but forgiveness that comes from repentance is a release from all bondage-deliverance. You are set free from death. When you go out, proclaim to others about My mercy and grace. Tell others that I have the power to forgive, if only they will repent and turn away from their sin. Look up and praise Me that you have such a wonderful Elohim. You are blessed to have such grace and mercy placed upon you. Be brave and turn away from all your wickedness. Be strong and run from sin. Many want to run to sin and love the pleasure of sin, but you must shun all forms of evil. You must turn away from the bondage of sin and be set free, so you can walk in unity with Me. Otherwise you will not prosper in Me. You can do whatever you please, but if you serve the world you will die with the world. You will be punished for your sins and will suffer loss. Why would you want such a yoke of bondage put on you? Walk in righteousness and let others see your good works, and tell them about My wondrous love for them. All you must do is repent and ask forgiveness in My name, and then you will be blessed.

305

You should be clothed with power from on high.

Luke 24:49   I am going to send you what my Father has promised; but stay in the city until you have been clothed with power from on high. Is 32:15 Until the spirit be poured on us from on high, and the wilderness be a fruitful field, and the fruitful field be counted for a forest. (Is 59:21)

My beloved, I sent My disciples out after I had gone back to My kingdom's throne. I told them that I would give them My Spirit that would cover them with power from My kingdom and give them authority to speak in My name, because you are My sons-My very precious possession. You are the only ones I have given My authority to on this planet, so whatever you ask Me to do for you in accordance with My will I will do. First, My beloved, you must receive My Spirit by receiving Me and My ways, then you will have power through My Spirit. You will be able to overcome, because I give you the ability to see clearly what I desire for you and understand how I do things-the rules of My kingdom. Understanding makes your faith strong, so the evil one takes away understanding from My people by extracting the truth from My words. He has been doing this for years, and he delights in it. I AM bringing truth back to My people in these last days. You must search for it, and you will find it. My beloved, if you walk in truth covered in My Spirit, then you will not be shaken even in the last days. You will stand strong and not waiver. You are My beloved, and I will allow no one to harm you. The evil one will release all sorts of evils on the planet, but you will not be touched by these things. You will be hidden by My Hand. Just trust in Me to take care for you.

306

You should believe that Yahshua was raised from the dead after three days.

John 2:19 Yahshua answered them, "Destroy this temple, and I will raise it again in three days." 20 The Jews replied, "It has taken forty-six years to build this temple, and you are going to raise it in three days?" 21 But the temple He had spoken of was his body. 22 After He was raised from the dead, his disciples recalled what He had said. Then they believed the Scripture and the words that Yahshua had spoken. (Matt 28:5-7, Matt 12:40, Jonah 1:17)

My beloved, you must believe that I was crucified by the Romans, and I died for you so your sins could be forgiven. You must believe that I was dead, placed in a tomb, and on the third day I was raised to life and overcame death. You should not believe those who say I died on Friday and arose on Sunday, because this is not three days. You must believe that I was three full days in the tomb and arose at the end of Sabbath, because I AM King of the Sabbath. The women came to find Me on Sunday, because they could not violate the Sabbath and did not go out in the night to find Me. Early Sunday morning they came to find Me, but I had already been dead for three days. If you do not believe this, then you have no share in Me. If you do not believe My words are true, then you are lacking and without. Do not think that I would deceive you. All My words are true and you must accept them as true. Men want to have holidays to celebrate all sorts of things, but My days of celebration are the only true days when I want you to worship Me. If you keep My chosen days of celebration, I will bless you. Some people are confused about Easter, but do not keep man-made holidays. Turn to the Truth and find truth in My words, and then you will be delivered from the bondage of this world.

307

You must be born again.

John 3:1-18 Now there was a man of the Pharisees named Nicodemus, a member of the Jewish ruling council. 2 He came to Yahshua at night and said, "Rabbi, we know you are a teacher who has come from Elohim. For no one could perform the miraculous signs you are doing if Elohim were not with him." 3 In reply Yahshua declared, "I tell you the truth, no one can see the kingdom of Elohim unless he is born again from above." (Ezek 36:26)

My beloved, I came to earth not to judge the earth, but to save the earth. I came to bring salvation to all mankind. I came to walk among My people and teach them My ways. They had their life twisted by captivity. My words were misrepresented to My people by their leaders. There was no more truth, but only a heavy burden of laws. I came to give life and restore the laws I gave to Moses, so they could have an abundant life. You must not focus only on the laws I give you. Focus on your love for Me, and then you will want to please Me. You will be able to keep My laws with great joy, and they will be grafted into your heart so you will not sin against Me. I told Nicodemus that he must be born again, but he did not understand until later what I meant. He became one of My disciples and suffered persecution on behalf of Me. Today you must also be born again. You must receive My Spirit within you, so your spirit becomes alive-is born a new-is afresh-cleansed-made one with Me. If you believe in Me, you will call out to Me and ask Me to be a part of you, so we can dwell as one. You are My child, and I give good gifts to My children who love Me and obey My commandments. What are My commandments? I want you to love others and to love Me above all other things or people. Only then can you enter My kingdom and not be utterly destroyed.

308

You should worship YHUH in spirit and in truth.

John 4:23 Yet a time is coming and has now come when the true worshipers will worship the Father in spirit and truth, for they are the kind of worshipers the Father seeks. 24 Elohim is spirit, and his worshipers must worship in spirit and in truth. Deut 6:5 Love YHUH your Elohim with all your heart and with all your soul and with all your strength. (Matt 4:8-10)

My beloved, I AM Spirit and I AM Truth. Come to Me and I will teach you how to worship Me, because My Sprit within you will cry out in praise to Me. Lift up your voice and praise Me, but walk in truth. You must walk in My Words. You must walk in the commandments I have given you. Do not be deceived, because men will try to tell you that the commandments are no longer for today. What is truth will stand forever. My words are forever. If you cannot believe that My words are true, then you cannot worship Me in truth, and you will be deceived. Do not let man deceive you, but hold fast to My truth. Many will come wanting you to listen to their half-truth, but beware. Listen to My voice and not the voice of a man. Read My words and search for truth. Do not depend on a man to teach you, but be taught by My Spirit, and then you will be free from the bondage of doctrine. Some men cannot believe that all My words are true or unchanging or relevant for even today. Beware of these men. I gave you My laws at the beginning, so you could have a good life. The evil one tears away at My laws and the hearts of men, so he can pull all men from Me. If you absorb yourself with the things of the world, you will be led astray. Be firm and stand. Walk in My truth and worship Me in My Spirit.

309

You should pray that your eyes are open to the lost around you.

John 4:34 "My food," said Yahshua, "is to do the will of Him who sent Me and to finish his work. 35 Do you not say, 'Four months more and then the harvest?' I tell you, open your eyes and look at the fields! They are ripe for harvest.   36 Even now the reaper draws his wages, even now He harvests the crop for eternal life, so that the sower and the reaper may be glad together. 37 Thus the saying 'One sows and another reaps' is true. 38 I sent you to reap what you have not worked for. Others have done the hard work, and you have reaped the benefits of their labor." (Is 43:5, Is 49:12, Is 60:4)

My beloved, open your eyes and see the souls in need of salvation. Call upon My name that I may send reapers to those who have heard the word and need someone to help show them the way. Pray that I will send someone to sow the seeds of truth and plant the truth in the children of men. Be brave and be bold and see how ripe the harvest is. I will be calling My children home from all over the Earth to come to My Land soon. There will be wars and rumors of wars and the earth will quake and shake and men will tremble from fear. Grown brave men will panic and be afraid, but My children will be safe in My arms. I will bring them to a safe place and cover them from My wrath and coming judgment. The evil one will try to harm you, but if you come to My Land I will show you a place to retreat into the wilderness where you can flourish and no man can harm you. I will give you safe passage there and surround you with My love. Tell others that the time is short. The time is now to repent and worship Me. Gone are the days of mercy, but now are the days when all men must stand in righteousness to escape the horrors that fall on the Earth. Call on My name and I will help you prepare for the days to come. You should not be afraid, but you should trust Me to guide you and protect you.

310

You should honor the Son (Yahshua).

John 5:19-23 Moreover, the Father judges no one, but has entrusted all judgment to the Son, 23 that all may honor the Son just as they honor the Father. He who does not honor the Son does not honor the Father, who sent Him. (Is 11:10)

My beloved, I AM the righteous judge yet if you do not believe in and receive My Son as your Savior-the one who died for you so you could live-then you are not worthy to enter My kingdom. I walked among you in flesh. I covered Myself with flesh and walked among you, so I could teach you the laws-the laws that Moses gave you- and correct them. Many had perverted the law and made it a burden for My children to bear, but I came to show you a new way to look at it. I wanted to keep it simple. Love others around you and do good things for others. I wanted all the many laws that man had made up for the people to keep to be simplified, so they could know freedom in My love. I walked among you in the flesh and I had mercy on you and healed those who would listen. Those who listened received Me and will not stand before Me on Judgment Day as not worthy to enter My kingdom. Those who received My Son-the one I sent-will receive Me and will be saved from execution on the Judgment Day. If you honor My Son-you honor Me-the One who set Him and only through My Son-accept Him as the Messiah, the Savior of mankind-will you be spared the Lake of Fire. Awake My children! Judgment is coming, and you must be righteous before Me.

311

You should not work for material things, but for spiritual things.

John 6:26 Yahshua answered, "I tell you the truth, you are looking for Me, not because you saw miraculous signs but because you ate the loaves and had your fill. 27 Do not work for food that spoils, but for food that endures to eternal life, which the Son of Man will give you. On Him Elohim the Father has placed his seal of approval." (1 Cor 15:58, Phil 2:12-13, Is 55:2)

My beloved, do not work for wealth, but work for the kingdom. Do not allow your focus to be on worldly things, but on the things of Me. I want you to work hard and make money for your family and take care of their needs, but I do not want you to live only to make money-only for your job-your position-so all you consider is this. I want you to provide for your family, but I do not want your whole life to be focused on how you can make money. Focus on your work if you are in a helper's position where you heal the sick, or save lives, or teach others about Me. If you are helping others, then you love others and your focus is a good one. This pleases Me when you devote your life to helping others and show love for others. If your job or position supports a business or promotes a business, then you need to find ways to help others so you can rejoice and be glad. Man is created to help others and he feels compete when he helps his brother in need. If you love others around you and have compassion on them, then you feel the satisfaction of being My servant. If you live only to serve yourself, then you live an unsatisfied selfish life. You must learn to serve others and meet their needs. If you work for the temporary things in this life, then your rewards will be temporary. If you work for those things that are of My kingdom, then your reward will be permanent. No one can take these rewards from you, because they are Mine to give.

312

You should believe in Yahshua.

John 6:28 Then they asked Him, "What must we do to do the works Elohim requires?" 29 Yahshua answered, "The work of Elohim is this: to believe in the One He has sent." Deut 18:18 I will raise up for them a prophet like you from among their fellow Israelites, and I will put my words in his mouth. He will tell them everything I command him. (John 14:6, John 3:16-18, John 20:29, Acts 16:30-34)

My beloved, I came to the world to redeem the world. I came to save My little ones from eternal destruction. I forgave their sins and paid the price for their sins. I did not come to be king of the world, but to teach My little ones My ways. I wanted them to live a life of peace and be free from religious leaders who put a heavy burden of laws upon them. I have given you all the laws you need, and man does not need to add to them or subtract from them. If you live your life according to My laws, then you will prosper and be blessed. I have blessings attached to My laws, so if you keep them you will prosper. I came to bring you life in abundance. If you believe in Me and cling to Me, then you will be able to walk and be strong and no one can harm you. Blessed are you who believe in the One you have not seen, yet you know Me because we are intimate and at one with each other. Sin in your life keeps us from drawing close to each other, so you must repent and walk a life of righteousness. Those who believe in Me and follow after Me are different and separate from the world. They stand above the rest. Others do not understand them and their love for Me. Others cannot see how they want to walk in righteousness, but the light of your presence will minister to others. You will not be able to blend in with the world. You will feel different, because you are different. Rejoice because you believe in Me.

313

You should not grumble among yourselves.

John 6:41 At this the Jews began to grumble about Him because He said, "I am the bread that came down from heaven." 42 They said, "Is this not Yahshua, the son of Joseph, whose father and mother we know? How can He now say, 'I came down from heaven'?" "Stop grumbling among yourselves," Yahshua answered. 44 "No one can come to Me unless the Father who sent Me draws him, and I will raise him up at the last day." (1 Peter 4:9, Num 14:27)

My beloved, I talked to the spiritual leaders, because they were so blinded that they could not understand My words. They began to argue among themselves and grumble about Me and who I may be, but they did not come to Me to be taught by Me. You see so many churches, and they all believe many different things. If a church cannot decide on what they believe, then the church splits and forms a new church. This is all an abomination to Me. This is not a church who seeks Me. They are not coming to Me to be taught by Me. They are following man-made doctrines, and they are losing ground in the faith. Be careful, if you are part of one of these churches. If church members grumble against each other, or if they grumble against other brethren who love Me, or if they grumble against My words and the interpretation of My words, judge clearly. Do not stay in a church that discards any section of My scriptures or says these books are not for today. If a church does not teach the Law I gave to Moses or the prophets, you should search for another church. All of My ways are built on the Laws I gave to Moses, and all the future events are prophesied through My prophets. You should all learn the words I said when I taught on Earth, but what I said was already given to Moses. I only tried to correct their misinterpretations. I will teach you My words, if you ask Me to do so. Do not grumble among yourselves, but come reason with Me.

314

You should not love your life in this world.

John 12:23-26 Yahshua replied, "The hour has come for the Son of Man to be glorified. 24 I tell you the truth, unless a kernel of wheat falls to the ground and dies, it remains only a single seed. But if it dies, it produces many seeds. 25 The man who loves his life will lose it, while the man who hates his life in this world will keep it for eternal life." Eccl 2:17 So I hated life, because the work that is done under the sun was grievous to me. All of it is meaningless, a chasing after the wind. (Matt 6:24, Eccl 1:14)

My beloved, anyone who loves his life in the world will not receive the gifts of the spirit. Anyone who hates his life here and hates to live in his fleshy body with its earthly desires and longs to live in My heavenly kingdom will inherit eternal life and live with Me eternally. Living in the flesh is an experience that tries you and tests you, so you can resist the evil desires of the flesh and want to live a righteous life. This is the way I have chosen to test you, so you can be found worthy to enter the kingdom of heaven. Your life here is a testimony of your love for Me and how you resisted the things of the world and chose to follow after My ways. You must resist all that sparkles in the world and know it is a trap to pull you away from Me. All that glitters is not righteous. If you look into it, you would find the wickedness in it. You must look for the Light and seek eternal things of the spirit, and then you will prosper and have success here on earth. If you follow your fleshy desire and sin against Me, then you lose all your eternal rewards unless you see your sin and repent and no longer go this path again. I have mercy on My Children, because they do live in flesh, but I expect you to learn and grow and see the wickedness of the earth and seek only Me and My righteousness.

315

You should pray that YHUH's name will be glorified in you.

2 Thess 1:11 With this in mind, we constantly pray for you, that our Elohim may count you worthy of his calling, and that by his power He may fulfill every good purpose of yours and every act prompted by your faith. **12** We pray this so that the name of our Adonai Yahshua may be glorified in you, and you in Him, according to the grace of our Elohim and Adonai Yahshua. (Is 24:15, Mal 1:11, John 12:27-28, John 15:8)

My beloved, I want you to fulfill the purpose I created for you. I want you to serve Me and do My will, and then you will bring glory or praise to My Name. When others see your kind deeds they will be thankful for you and praise Me for bringing you along their path. You should pray that I will show you your purpose clearly, so you can know the way to go. In whatever you do, you should love others around you and be kind. In all you do, you should lift up My name and praise Me for My wondrous works, and then others will praise Me also and magnify My Name. Bring glory to My name by the life you live. I came as an example for you, so you could walk in My ways. I came so you could see love in its purest form that I laid down My life for your mistakes-your sin-your rebellion against Me. No man has to pay for another man's mistakes, but I was willing to cover your sin with My blood and glorify the name of YHUH. Through My blood was My name lifted up and glorified. I gave up for you so much, and I did so with no regrets. If you will love Me with all your heart, then you will be able to bring glory to My Name. Arise, My little one, and put all sin behind you, so you can fulfill your purpose to walk humbly in My ways bestowing love, compassion, and mercy on others. Tell others of My wondrous love for them, so My Name can be lifted up and glory bestowed on it, so others can glorify My name.

316

You should walk in the Light of Yahshua.

John 12:35 Then Yahshua told them, "You are going to have the light just a little while longer. Walk while you have the light, before darkness overtakes you. The man who walks in the dark does not know where he is going. 36 Put your trust in the light while you have it, so that you may become sons of light." Prov 4:19 But the way of the wicked is like deep darkness; they do not know what makes them stumble. (John 8:12)

My beloved, walk in the Light of My presence. Make sure you stay far from darkness. Keep far away from those of the world, but cling to Me and listen to My Voice. You are a creature made of Light, because you are sons of Light. You are My children created in My image and sealed with My approval, so you come forth with the seed of righteousness within you. Only My children bear My mark of approval. I know all My children, but the Evil One does not know all My children. I have kept a record of all My children and from which tribe they come from, and I have kept each tribe preserved so all of Jacob's sons can come through the gates of My eternal city. No one will be lost. I have sent My angels to fight for you, and I have covered you with My hand. The battle is in the spirit in places you cannot see. The heavenly realm is closed to your fleshy eyes, but when your flesh falls away from you, then you can see clearly. I know you feel weighed in your suit of flesh and long for it to be removed from you, and soon it will be. Man's life is cut short-only 70 years, and then he can come live with Me. The end of this age comes soon, and I rejoice in it. I want My children to come live with Me and have no more suffering. You must be brave in the last days and love those around you. Search for the Light and walk in it, and your life will be blessed. You will then overcome the darkness around you even in the last days.

317

You should speak only what your Father tells you to say.

1 Peter 4:11 If anyone speaks, he should do it as one speaking the very words of Elohim. If anyone serves, he should do it with the strength Elohim provides, so that in all things Elohim may be praised through Yahshua. To Him be the glory and the power forever and ever. Jer 23:28 "Let the prophet who has a dream recount the dream, but let the one who has my word speak it faithfully. For what has straw to do with grain?" declares YHUH. (John 12:47-50)

My beloved, listen to My voice and speak only what I tell you to say. Do not grieve others by your harsh words, but let love flow through you from My spirit and speak love and kindness to others. You must not speak as the pagans speak out of a heart filled with greed, lust, perversion, and hatred. You are of the light, so your words should be seasoned with salt and bring healing, hope, and encouragement. Many men say they love Me, but their words do not reflect this. You must reflect My light as you speak. Just as a full moon reflects the light of the sun and illuminates the night, so I want you to reflect My light to others. If you reflect love and kindness, then others will be encouraged to be loving and kind to others. Humans imitate each other, and follow after each other just as sheep follow after each other. If one falls in the ditch, then they all fall in the ditch. You must be an example for your friends, co-workers, family, and your children of My love by being kind and generous to others. Guard over your words, so no man can condemn you by the words you speak. Do not judge others harshly and be critical towards others, but point out the good in man, so others can recognize the good. If you judge others harshly and speak evil of your brothers in the faith, then I will also judge you harshly. Be merciful, kind, and compassionate, and you will be pleasing in My sight. Be led by My spirit, and speak My words.

318

You should wash one another's feet.

John 13:12-17 Now that I, your Master and Teacher, have washed your feet, you also should wash one another's feet. 15 I have set you an example that you should do as I have done for you. 16 I tell you the truth, no servant is greater than his master, nor is a messenger greater than the one who sent him. 17 Now that you know these things, you will be blessed if you do them. Gal 5:13 You, my brothers and sisters, were called to be free. But do not use your freedom to indulge the flesh; rather, serve one another humbly in love. (Gen 18:4, Gen 24:32, Gen 43:24, Luke 7:44)

My beloved, as I celebrated My last Passover with My disciples I longed to give them a special gift, so I gave them the example of washing one another's feet. This is an act of love, and you must humble yourself to wash another's feet. You must lower yourself and wash the feet of the person and say to them, "I will help you in any way even to wash your feet. I am your brother and we are servants together of the Most High Elohim." If you feel that you cannot wash another man's feet, then repent and humble yourself and go do this as unto Me, and I will bless you. It is not a feast day, so on certain days you are not required to wash your brother's feet. As I lead you, then you are saying to your brother, "I am your brother. I will humble myself and wash your feet and do all within my power to help you triumph in your walk with Yahshua." My little one, remember you are here to serve others, not to exalt yourself above men. You are My servant, if you follow in My ways. You are called by My name. You must listen to My voice and obey. You must seek Me for guidance. A servant awakes listening for his master's voice to speak, so he can obey him and do all that he instructs him for the day. Are you My obedient servant? Do you open our eyes each morning and listen for My voice? If you aren't listening, you need to start listening every morning, because the days are dark and the Evil One is always present trying to deceive you and mislead you.

319

You should do the things that Yahshua did.

John 14:12 I tell you the truth, anyone who has faith in Me will do what I have been doing. He will do even greater things than these, because I am going to the Father. 2 Chron 20:20 Have faith in YHUH your Elohim and you will be upheld. Mark 16:20 Then the disciples went out and preached everywhere, and Yahshua worked with them and confirmed his word by the signs that accompanied it.

My beloved, I want you to walk in the same way I walked upon this earth-giving to others My words, healing, restoring, correcting, and teaching. If you will do these things, I will bless you. Be an empty vessel poured out for Me. I will bring healing through your hand and glory to My name. I will give you the ability to teach My words to others, so all the errors My people have been taught can be corrected. My people have been given lies, and I want My people to know the words of truth. You must speak truth, so healing can flow to them. There will be no healing unless there is repenting and restoring of relationships. You must put aside your bitterness and resentment and live a life of giving kindness, and then you will do the same works that I did. You have to love others, and even if necessary lay down your life for them if they are your brothers in the faith. You will have to stand shoulder to shoulder with them and fight the enemy together with them through prayer and fasting to tear down walls of darkness-ancient gates. If you fast and pray, I will be faithful to hear you, and give you what you ask. Ask and ask and ask, and I will see you seeking Me and pressing in for Me to direct you and open doors for you. There are many who scorn Me, but if you are faithful to Me I will give you power from My kingdom. You will put the enemy under your foot, and he will not oppress you any longer. Be brave and walk only in My ways, and do as I did.

320

You should obey Yahshua's commandments.

John 14:15-24 "If you love Me, you will obey what I command. 21 Whoever has my commands and obeys them, he is the one who loves Me. He who loves Me will be loved by my Father, and I too will love him and show Myself to him." Deut 5:33 Walk in obedience to all that YHUH your Elohim has commanded you, so that you may live and prosper and prolong your days in the land that you will possess. John 14:15 "If you love me, keep my commands." (Matt 19:16-19)

My beloved, if you love Me, you will keep my commands. Listen to what I tell you to do, and then do it. Do as I say, and I will guide you down the path of least resistance. I will guide you to good things. I will give you the best things, because you love Me. If you love Me, you will long to please Me in all your ways. I have given you My Spirit to dwell among you and guide you. My Spirit will comfort you for Me and will remind you of My words so you will not sin against Me. If you do not know My words, then your responsibility to Me is less, but you still must pay for the sin you commit even though your punishment is light. If you do know My words and yet you choose in your heart not to obey them, then you will receive your punishment of heavy lashes because you are a disobedient servant and you do not love Me with your whole heart. When your children disobey you, you are hurt. I AM also hurt, because you turn from Me and do not obey Me. I am joyful over an obedient servant and will celebrate with him on the last day. We will celebrate in My kingdom, and we will all be as one. We will live together eternally. You will have proven your loyalty to Me and your faithfulness. You will be found worthy to enter My kingdom. You will be My ambassador of love and peace to the entire universe. You will stand for Me and speak My authority as a ruler's son. You will be the children of the Most High Elohim.

321

You should live in peace.

John 14:27 Peace I leave with you; my peace I give you. I do not give to you the way the world gives. Do not let your hearts be troubled and do not be afraid. Num 6:26 YHUH lift up His countenance on you, and give you peace. Ps 29:11 YHUH will give strength to his people; YHUH will bless his people with peace. (2 Thess 3:16, Col 3:15, Phil 4:7, Rom 8:6)

My beloved, I AM your peace, so walk in Me and you walk in peace. If you are upset and nervous, then you are not at one with Me and your eyes are not set on Me and your faith is not in Me. If you walk in peace, you trust Me to care for you. Open your eyes and see! You do not have to live an anxious life worried about all sorts of little things. Be bold and brave and trust Me with all your heart, and let your faith be in Me. No one from the world can care for you like I can. I AM your Father and My love for you is greater than any earthly father. I know every molecule in your body and how you think and what your hopes are for your life. I have My Hand on you to guide you. All you have to do is reach out to Me. All you have to do is depend on Me. Ask Me if you need anything. and I will give it to you. You are My Child. I want you to have all you need and more. I want you to be blessed by Me. Peace is a blessing from Me. The men of the world have no peace, but My Children walk in peace, because I AM peace and they walk in Me. Do not be afraid of anything. Nothing is impossible for Me to do. Call on Me, and I will do whatever you need so you can rest in peace. Do not allow the world to tear at you, but let peace be your constant companion, so you can stay in good health and prosper.

322

You should stay united (married) to Yahshua.

John 15:1-7 I am the true vine, and my Father is the gardener. 2
He cuts off every branch in Me that bears no fruit, while every branch
that does bear fruit He prunes so that it will be even more fruitful. 3
You are already clean because of the word I have spoken to you. 4 Stay
united in Me, and I will stay united in you. No branch can bear fruit
by itself; it must stay united in the vine. Neither can you bear fruit
unless you stay united in Me. (Is 62:5)

My beloved, if you stay united to Me as you would unite to someone in marriage
and never divorce Me, then you will love Me and hold fast to Me and cherish
Me. You will begin to bear the fruits of love, kindness, mercy, compassion, forgiveness, long suffering, patience, and perseverance. You will resemble Me and
know My ways of loving kindness. The world does not know these things. All
they know is hatred, revenge, bearing a grudge, murder, lies, and greed. They do
not know My ways of giving and speaking blessings over others. You must always
encourage others and hold fast to My ways, so no one can deceive you. The Evil
One will bring all sorts of deceptions and some of My people will be deceived,
but those who know Me and hear My voice will not be deceived but will be led
by My Spirit. You must be born again of My Spirit-filled with my Spirit, so you
can be at one with Me. You must remain united to Me all your life-clinging to
Me-calling on My name-trusting in Me to make all things new, and giving you
all you need on this earth. We are one in the spirit, but the flesh keeps us apart.
Soon the flesh will fall away, and we will be united at last. We will always be at
one with each other. I will present you to My heavenly kingdom on the day of My
coming as My faithful one, because you have endured the testing of earth and did
not fall away. You held fast to Me and trusted in Me until the end, so you shall
have eternal life with Me forever.

323

You should bear the fruit of the Spirit.

John 15:8-16 This is to my Father's glory, that you bear much fruit, showing yourselves to be my disciples. 16 You did not choose Me, but I chose you and appointed you to go and bear fruit-fruit that will last. Gal 5:22 But the fruit of the Spirit is love, joy, peace, patience, kindness, goodness, faithfulness, 23 gentleness and self-control. Ps 1:3 That person is like a tree planted by streams of water, which yields its fruit in season and whose leaf does not wither-whatever they do prospers.

My beloved, you should bear fruit as an example of My love inside of you. You should be loving and kind, patient and longsuffering, merciful and compassionate. You should want to give to others-not selfish or stingy. These are the fruit that brings glory to My name. If you are angry and you say and do angry things, then you will not be an example of love to others. You must walk among others always bearing fruit and leaving the fruit as a testimony of your love for Me. Go among the others of the world and share the fruits of My love with others. Be loving and kind. Hate the sin, but love the person. Your love could be the light that awakens the seed of righteousness within the person. All My children are chosen-created by Me to serve Me-chosen before creation to be My Children. I appointed each of you a certain time to come to earth. A remnant was left throughout time-to know Me and My ways. I have led My Children through the desert-out of Egypt–to the Promised Land. I scattered them to the nations, but never forgot them. I never leave My Children, but I hold fast to them. If you feel deserted by Me, then arise and repent and wash yourself off-baptize yourself, and go and bear fruit so others can glorify My name. They will rejoice, because you give so freely to others and your loving kindness is a testimony to My wondrous love and compassion.

324

You should love others as Yahshua loves you.

John 15:12 My command is this: Love each other as I have loved you. 17 This is my command: Love each other. 1 Peter 4:8 Above all, love each other deeply, because love covers over a multitude of sins. (Lev 19:18)

My beloved, I have given you My love. I have given you Myself and I AM love. I dwell within you, so My love is within you, and you should love others with My love. If you love others, you are obedient to Me. If you do not love others, you do not know Me or any of My ways. My way is to love your brother, and do good things for him. I came loving others, and the world hated Me and killed My flesh. They played into My Hand, because I came to die for you. I died so the sin of the world can be washed from you, so you can be clean and sacred. I came to set you free. There is no greater love than to lay down your life for those you love. Men will put you to the test and say, "Renounce your God or you will die." Death is better than renouncing Me. In death only your flesh dies, but your soul lives on with Me for eternity. If you love Me, you may have to lay down your life for Me. If you love Me you may have to give up what you love in this world and sacrifice yourself, so your flesh will die and your spirit will reign supreme. Death to flesh is a hard road, but it leads to life in Me. Love those around you. Even if men are not kind in return, continue to love them. Your love will be a testimony to others of your love for Me. Your love will bring healing to others, set them free, and deliver them into My Hands of love. Love others around you.

325

You should be convicted of your sins.

John 16:7-15 But I tell you the truth: It is for your good that I am going away. Unless I go away, the Counselor will not come to you; but if I go, I will send Him to you. 8 When He comes, He will convict the world of guilt in regard to sin and righteousness and judgment: Job 36:10 He makes them listen to correction and commands them to repent of their evil. (Zec 12:10)

My beloved, I give you My Spirit to guide you, to comfort you, and to correct you. I will convict you of your sin. You will feel the grieving of your spirit when you are in sin. You will even feel My Spirit saying, "No, do not go this direction" before you even go the way of sin, when you are listening to My voice. The Spirit within you amplifies My Voice, so you can hear My Voice speaking to you. Truth comes through your spirit. If your flesh is strong, you will fall into lies and not Truth. You will know that I am showing you the way, because Truth will come to your house. Listen to the Truth and My Spirit will guard over it, and bring it to you when you need it. You must discern between Truth and lies. My Spirit within you will help you. I will tell you about the days to come, so you can prepare and not fall into sin because your foundation is too weak. You must be alert and on guard to all the attacks of the enemy. He will always try to attack your weak area, so stay focused on My Spirit within you. You must be alert. My Spirit will tell you what is lies and not Truth, so you will not fall into sin. Men will try to deceive you and lead you astray, but My Spirit will only bring you into Truth. My Spirit will bring the future into light, so you can see ahead and prepare for the things to come.

326

You should rejoice always.

John 15:10 If you obey my commands, you will remain in my love, just as I have obeyed my Father's commands and remain in his love. 11 I have told you this so that my joy may be in you and that your joy may be complete. 1 Thess 5:16 Rejoice always. Ps 68:3 But may the righteous be glad and rejoice before YHUH; may they be happy and joyful. (John 16:33)

My beloved, I created this world beautiful and a perfect place for My Children. The evil one hates My Children, because they are My heirs and will rule with Me over the many nations throughout the universe. He came to the Garden and deceived Eve-innocent Eve who did not know evil, and Adam who loved her and wanted to please her. Each of them had faults and the evil one saw the flaws. In his cunning he questioned them and tempted them, and found them weak. After they sinned they were ashamed. The sin had been done, and there was no salvation for them. I came Myself and shed My innocent blood, so Adam and Eve and all their offspring could be saved and not destroyed in the Lake of Fire. I have kept My Children safe. I know each of My Children by name, because I created you and know your inner parts and what you think and how you feel and when you sin. I know all things about you, so I hold you in My Hand and protect you. You should never be sad, but be joyful that you are My Child-heir to the throne. You will rule over nations. You are My beloved precious child. I came to die and to regain authority over the Earth. I came, so I would overcome all the evil one's plans. Rise up, and rejoice. Be glad! This is a good day for all who love Me.

327

You must believe that Yahshua was sent by YHUH.

John 17:3 Now this is eternal life: that they may know you, the only true Elohim, and Yahshua the Messiah, whom you have sent. John 14:6 Yahshua answered, "I am the way and the truth and the life. No one comes to the Father except through Me. 7 If you really knew Me, you would know my Father as well. From now on, you do know Him and you have seen Him." Is 53:11 As a result of the anguish of His soul, He will see it and be satisfied; by His knowledge the Righteous One, My Servant, will justify the many, as He will bear their iniquities.

My beloved, you should know Me as a Father who loves you-not as a god who is very far away. I AM near, and I want to be at one with you. I want to commune with you all day. I want you to know My ways and keep all My commands. If you love Me, you will respect My commands and keep all of them. You can be an obedient child never rebelling, but always wanting to please Me by obeying all I ask you to do. If you know Me, you will see how I give you all My commands so you can have an abundant life. You will treat others with justice and fairness and loving kindness. You will honor and respect the rights of others and not be selfish-wanting your own way in spite of the rights of others. If you know Me, you will see the world the way I see it. You will pull away from the world and cling to Me. You will want only the gifts that I can give–peace, love, joy, and satisfaction in Me. You will walk in My presence all the day and the world will not devour you with fears and worry, but My peace will cover you and you will be complete in Me. You will walk hand in hand with Me and I will tell you secret things about you and your future that will help you as you live your life on earth. Your life is short and a period of testing for you, but if you know Me you will understand why you have come to earth-your purpose-and you will desire to walk in My presence every day and know Me more.

328

You should call on Yahshua's name for protection.

John 17:11 I will remain in the world no longer, but they are still in the world, and I am coming to you. Father, protect them by the power of your name-the name you gave Me-so that they may be one as we are one. 12 While I was with them, I protected them and kept them safe by that name you gave Me. None has been lost except the one doomed to destruction so that Scripture would be fulfilled. Ps 17:8 Keep me as the apple of your eye; hide me in the shadow of your wings. (Acts 12:5-11, Ps 27:5)

My beloved, call on My name, and I will protect you. Call on My name, and I will heal you. Call on My name, and I will guide. Call on My name, and I will strengthen you. There is great power in My name, but you must call on My name before I can help you. That is why I say to you to ask, and continue to ask, and I will help you. Whatever your need may be, no matter how small, I AM not too busy to help you. You are My child, and whenever a child cries out for help his father comes to help him. Whenever you cry out for help, I will always help you. If you are in sin, repent and turn away from your sins. Do not go that way again, and then cry out to Me, and I will help you. If you really love Me, you will obey Me and not sin against Me. You must want to commune with Me all the day. You must want Me to guide you and protect you from the evil one. All day I use My angels to protect you, so you are not harmed. If you listen to My Voice, I will show you where to go to escape. Do not run into trouble. If you know a land is in war, then go to another place that I will show you. If you know a land is in drought or has a high crime area, why should you go there? Let Me show you a good place to live, so you can dwell in peace and rest in My Presence. I do not want My Children to suffer from war and its destruction or famine or wicked people. If you call on My name for protection, I will guide you to live in a safe place.

329

You should be sanctified by His Word.

John 17:17 Sanctify them by the truth; your word is truth. 18 As you sent Me into the world, I have sent them into the world. 19 For them I sanctiy Myself, that they too may be truly sanctified. Lev 11:44 For I am YHUH your Elohim: ye shall therefore sanctify yourselves, and ye shall be holy; for I am holy. Ps 119:11 I have hidden your word in my heart that I might not sin against you. (1 Thess 5:23, Acts 20:32)

My beloved, you should read My words, meditate on My words, and cling to My words. My words bring life, and cleanse you from all unrighteousness. If you will seek Truth, you will find it. I will sanctify you and purify you, so you can be free from all sin-all darkness. If you cling to My words, they will cleanse you from all unrighteousness. If you long for Truth, then Truth will come to you and bring you peace. If you are always listening to My Voice, I will give you the words of life, and you will be filled with My Spirit. What does it mean to be sanctified? If you are cleansed from your sin and you want to do only what pleases Me, then you have no rebellion in your heart. You cling to My words and you do not go the way of the world, then you are filled with the Truth and are sanctified. You are not perfect, but you strive for perfection and living a sin-free life. All of My children want to walk in the Truth and hate the ways of the world. You must be willing to give up everything that hinders your walk with Me. Do not allow darkness or perversion to enter your house. Be strong and bold. Do not allow any portal of darkness to be open in your house through TV, movies, games, pornography, music, or computers. Watch carefully over your children, and do not allow them to slip into darkness through any of these portals. Sanctify yourself and your children by clinging to the Truth-My Words.

330

You should be in unity with your brothers.

John 17:23 I united in them and You with Me. May they be brought to complete unity to let the world know that You sent Me and have loved them even as You have loved Me. Ps 133:1 How good and pleasant it is when brothers live together in unity! (Col 3:12-14)

My beloved, I want My People to live in unity-to be as one, but all I see from My People is different groups fighting over different things. Soon this will change when persecution comes. All My People will band together for survival, and all will help each other and be as one. Some of My People will resist the evil one and be slain quickly. Others will be captured and put in prison, because they saw persecution coming and did not flee their homes. Others will flee to the wilderness and depend only on Me to survive. I will help My Children-those in prison and those in the wilderness. Those in the wilderness who endure to the end through great trials will be given great rewards. You must be able to listen to My Voice and dwell in unity with your brothers. Man cannot live alone, but must connect with his brothers. If you lift up a brother when he is in need, then he will be there for you when you are in need. You must give to those who are struggling and those who are lacking and without. If brothers in your fellowship cannot see eye to eye, then pray together concerning the issue, and I will bring you the answer so you can do as I do. If there are brothers who oppose the body of believers, then you must pray with these brothers, and I will give them peace or remove them from your group. I do not want brothers who constantly want to stir up discord to continue to be part of your assembly. Talk with them, pray with them, and remove those who continue to oppose every effort to follow Me.

331

You should receive the Ruach HaKodesh (Holy Spirit).

John 20:21 Again Yahshua said, "Peace be with you! As the Father has sent Me, I am sending you." 22 And with that He breathed on them and said, "Receive the Ruach HaKodesh!" Job 33:4 The Spirit of YHUH has made me; the breath of the Almighty gives me life. (Eph 1:13-14, Acts 8:14-17. Ps 33:6)

My beloved I came to bring life to you. I first gave Moses My Commandments-instructions for life. Then I sent My Prophets to guard you against sin, so you would not live in bondage but have freedom. I came Myself to walk among you to restore My Commandments to you, so once again you could have life. I did not want you to be in bondage to a set of laws that were more of a weight than freedom. Truth will make you free, and I came to bring you Truth. I laid down My life, so you could no longer be in the bondage of sin. Then I gave you My Spirit, so you could have power over the enemy so no one could harm you. I gave you My Spirit to guide you, and comfort you, and show you how to have compassion and love others. It is My gift to you- My Spirit is inside of you. You will not love the world, but despise it and want release from all the elements of Babylon. You will want not to look into it, but you will want to focus on Me and My Words. The days are growing darker. Receive My Spirit. Ask and you shall receive. Be full of My Spirit, so you can know who I really am. You will be able to forgive others of their wrongs against you, because My love will be within you. You will release them from their sins, so I can punish them and treat them justly. If you do not forgive them, then you hold onto their sin and they cannot be corrected. You hold in your hand the keys to forgiveness. Forgive and set them free from their sins.

332

You should accept YHUH's purpose for your life.

Rom 8:28 And we know that in all things YHUH works for the good of those who love Him, who have been called according to his purpose. Eccl 12:13 Fear YHUH and keep his commandments, for this is the whole [duty] of man. Prov 19:21 Many are the plans in a man's heart, but it is YHUH's purpose that prevails. (Ps 57:2)

My beloved, I have called you for a certain purpose in this life. You were created and designed for a certain task. You each have gifts, and you should use them to build up those around you. I want you to be My Hands and Feet while you are on this earth. You have My Spirit inside of you, and you can give that spirit to others through your love and compassion. You must continue to be strong and mighty and not allow the evil one to draw your away from Me. He will try to make you want to hurt others and say mean words to others. You must forgive and love those around you. You must obey My Laws while you are on earth, so you can have a good life here. I have given you the instructions for living your life through My Laws. My Laws are for your good and not meant to be a weight to you. My Laws are a blessing to you and not a curse. If all men lived by My Laws there would not be any bloodshed or war. There would be peace with all men. The hearts of men are dark, but My Children walk in the light and are a ray of hope to a very dark world. You must continue to be that ray of hope to others. You must be the one who reaches out your hand to others and gives them the support they need in times of trouble. There will always be difficult days, so you will need to support each other and make each other stronger through your love. Accept My Purpose for you in this life to transform you into My Image through the difficulties in this life. You will emerge a glorious being full of light.

333

You should offer your body as a living sacrifice.

Romans 12:1 Therefore, I urge you, brothers and sisters, in view of YHUH's mercy, to offer your bodies as a living sacrifice, holy and pleasing to YHUH-this is your true and proper worship. Ex 29:38 "Now this is what you shall offer on the altar: two lambs a year old day by day regularly. The one lamb you shall offer in the morning and the other lamb you shall offer at twilight."

My beloved, your flesh does not want to walk in the ways of love and compassion. Your flesh can be very dark and want its own way filled with lusts and worldly desires. You must control your flesh and put it under your hand. Do not allow your flesh to control you. If you make your flesh die and your spirit arise, then you will become a man full of My Spirit. You will be able to overcome darkness and walk in the Light. As you make your flesh die it burns before Me as sacrifice and the aroma is pleasing to Me. Make your sacrifice in the morning and the afternoon just like My Priests made a sacrifice of flesh in the morning and afternoon on the altar in My Temple. Their act of obedience was a sweet smelling flagrance before Me. You make your morning and afternoon sacrifice when you stop what you are doing and lift your hands to Me in praise and adoration. I will receive your offering of praise, and I will bless you. If you stop at these times and lift your heart to Me and give thanksgiving to Me for all the blessings of the day, I will be there in your midst. We will commune together. We will be as one. I will smile on you as you walk in obedience to Me. I will see your sacrifice as a burning light before Me. Come before Me and I will give you peace from all the activities of the day. If you have problems, I will give you answers to your questions. I will give you wisdom how to go forward with whatever problems you may have. There is nothing too difficult for Me to do. Ask whatever you need for Me to do, and I will hear you and help you. I AM always with you. I never leave you. I love you so deeply. Make your sacrifice before Me, and I will meet you there.

334

You should use your spiritual gifts to serve others.

Rom 12:6-8 Having gifts that differ according to the grace given to us, let us use them: if prophecy, in proportion to our faith; if service, in our serving; the one who teaches, in his teaching; the one who exhorts, in his exhortation; the one who contributes, in generosity; the one who leads, with zeal; the one who does acts of mercy, with cheerfulness. 1 Peter 4:10 Each of you should use whatever gift you have received to serve others, as faithful stewards of YHUH's grace in its various forms. (Dan 2:6, Gen 41:15)

My beloved, I have given you a gift from My Spirit. Use this gift to build up others around you and encourage them. If you do not know what your gift is, then come to Me and let me show you what gift I have given to you. Do you like to give to others? You have the gift of giving. Do you like to teach others about Me? I have given you the ability to teach. Do you like to help others? I have given you the ability to serve others. Do you like to encourage others? I have given you the gift of exhortation. Do you like to be in charge of a group? I have given you the ability to lead others. Do you like to share the words that I have spoken to you with others? I have given you the gift of prophecy. Do you like to show mercy to others? I have given you the gift of mercy. Do you have faith to believe for others? I have given you the gift of faith. You may not have developed your gift yet. It may lie dormant inside of you. Arise from the ashes and draw near to Me, so you can come close to Me. As you draw close to Me the flesh will burn away and your gift will become apparent. You will strip away the flesh that hinders your gift, and you will walk in the spirit. Seek Me so you can find the gifts hidden within you and begin to use them to uplift the other believers around you. You are My Hands and Feet. You are the one who will speak My Words to others and encourage others and help others draw closer to Me. Lift up your head and look into Me, and I will show you hidden things.

Which Commandments Should I Obey?

335

You should obey the laws of the land where you live.

Rom 13:1-2 Obey the government, for YHUH is the one who put it there. All governments have been placed in power by YHUH. So those who refuse to obey the laws of the land are refusing to obey YHUH, and punishment will follow. 1 Peter 2:13-14 Place yourselves under the authority of human governments to please YHUH. Obey the emperor. He holds the highest position of authority. Also obey governors. They are people the emperor has sent to punish those who do wrong and to praise those who do right. (Prov 24:21, Dan 2:21)

My beloved, I know you live in exile, and you are appalled by some of the things that happen around you. You do not understand your government and how they can allow certain things to happen. I have placed you in this land for a reason. I have My Children all over the world each one being a Light to those around them. You are an example of love and kindness to those around you. Your light will bring hope to a troubled world. You will see many things that grieve you in this life, but you can bring love to those who need you as you travel through this world. If you will only trust in Me that I will care for you where I have placed you. You must follow the laws established by the government, so you can be under the protection of the government. I do not want My Children to rebel against the government where I have placed them. You must submit to their authority until I move you to another place. If your government is harsh to you and wants to harm you, then seek Me to show you a new place to live. I want you to live in peace and prosper. I want you to raise your children to serve Me and obey My Laws. If you are unable to obey My Laws where you live, then ask Me to help you escape to another place where you can serve Me wholeheartedly. I will make a space for you in another place just like I did for Abraham. I will go before you and provide for you, so you can live in peace with those around you. This world is a dark place filled with many evils, but I am the hedge around you. I place you in a strong tower that no enemy can penetrate. My Angels are around you protecting you. You should never be afraid. Keep the laws of your land or you will not become an enemy of the state and be thrown in prison. I want you to have your freedom. I want you to walk in My Presence and live in peace.

336

You should not get into debt. You should use your money wisely.

Rom 13:8 Do not owe anyone anything except to love one an-other. For the one who loves another has fulfilled the Law. **Prov 22:7** The rich rules over the poor, and the borrower is the slave of the lender. **Prov 21:17** Whoever loves pleasure will be a poor man; he who loves wine and oil will not be rich. **Prov 21:20** There is treasure to be desired and oil in the dwelling of the wise; but a foolish man spends it up.

My beloved, you should use the money that I give you very carefully. You should buy only what you need, and do not waste your money on things that you do not need. Save your money and build up an inheritance for your children, so you can bless them. Save your money, and do not fall into debt. If you are in debt, then work out a plan to get out of debt as soon as possible. If you have to take on one or two other jobs, release yourself from these obligations. My People should not be in debt to the world. They should not borrow from others, but they should give to others. My People should be an example to others of how to live their lives using their money wisely. You do not have to have a new car or house or fine clothes or shoes. You should use what you have been given by Me. I will guide you when you need to buy an item, and I will show you a good price. You must be led by Me in your buying and selling. If you look to Me first, then I can help you with your money and bless you. The world wants to acquire possessions. I want you to give away to others. I want you to keep only what you need, and give to those in need. A wise man watches over every coin he has knowing that I have given him that coin to go in a special place. Many people want to spend their money to have pleasure or adorn themselves. You should only want to live your life as a righteous example for those around you. Spending your money foolishly on worldly possessions is not an example of righteousness. If you have an old car and it runs, then be thankful for what you have. If you have an old house but it is clean and comfortable, then be happy for what you have. If you have clothes and shoes to wear that are comfortable and in good shape, then be happy for what you have. I will give you what you need when you need it. Look to Me before you buy anything. Look to Me and be wise with your money.

337

You should desire the spiritual gifts.

1 Cor 14:1 Follow the way of love and eagerly desire the gifts of the Spirit, especially prophecy. 2 Kings 2:9 And it came to pass, when they had crossed, that Elijah said unto Elisha, Ask what I shall do for you, before I am taken away from you. And Elisha said, Let a double portion of your spirit be upon me. Prov 21:21 Whoever pursues righteousness and kindness will find life, righteousness, and honor.

My beloved, desire to walk in the things of the Spirit. Desire to seek the gifts that My Spirit gives you. I give you gifts to edify the believers and encourage them. When you pray in the Spirit, you pray to Me. You edify yourself and encourage yourself. When you prophecy, you lift up others. I want you to minister to the other believers. You can give them a word of discernment or encouragement that can lift them up and help them be able to stand. I do not see My People using the gifts that I have given them, because they are lost in the traditions of men and cannot see clearly. They want to walk the same way that their fathers walked. I tell you that your fathers are deceived, and you need to find the Truth from My Words. You need to look deeply into My Scriptures and find true meaning. Your fathers have been taught lies, and you will be given Truth, if you seek Me and find Me in these words of life. Rejoice that I want to bring you Truth, so you can see clearly and turn away from the error of your ways. Seek Me, and I will give you the gifts of the Spirit, so you can minister to your brothers and sisters who want to walk in My Ways of loving kindness and tender mercy. Rejoice that you hear My Voice and can be led by Me. Be open to Me, and I will give you Truth. I will show you the path that leads to Me. Rejoice that I love you so much.

338

You should walk in the Spirit and not in the flesh.

Gal 5:16-17 So I say, walk by the Spirit, and you will not gratify the desires of the flesh. For the flesh desires what is contrary to the Spirit, and the Spirit what is contrary to the flesh. They are in conflict with each other, so that you are not to do whatever you want. Rom 8:5 Those who live according to the flesh have their minds set on what the flesh desires; but those who live in accordance with the Spirit have their minds set on what the Spirit desires. Ezek 36:27 And I will put my Spirit in you and move you to follow my decrees and be careful to keep my laws.

My beloved, walk in the things of the Spirit. Walk in loving kindness. Be forgiving and merciful to all men. If you walk in love, then you will walk in My Ways. Do not desire the things of the flesh. Do not desire to go your own way wanting to follow the things of the world. Seek the Light, and walk in the Light. Walk in My Ways, so you can be cleansed from the desires of the flesh. The more you read My Words the more you will be washed clean and be set free from the desires of the flesh. You are human and encased in flesh. You will battle with the flesh as long as you live. The closer you draw to Me, the stronger you will become and be able to have victory over the flesh. Focus on what you know is right to do, and do only those things. Focus on the weak areas that you have, and push yourself to become strong in these areas. It will not be easy. This life is not easy. I did not design this life on earth to be easy. I designed it to be difficult, and only a few will walk the narrow way that leads to Me. Only a few will want to follow Me and walk in Truth. If you have My Seed of righteousness in you, then you will long to have the Truth and walk in righteousness. You will be miserable, if you have My Seed of righteousness and do not walk in righteousness. You will long to know your Creator- the One who made you-the One who forms you into My Image. Rejoice and be glad that My Hand is on you so tightly. I will not allow you to walk down the wrong path. I will correct you until you turn and follow only Me. I will discipline you until you walk in My Ways led by My Spirit. Rejoice that I will not give up on you until the day you have turned totally to Me. I AM faithful to you.

339

You should use your time wisely.

Eph 5:15-16 Therefore be careful how you walk, not as unwise men but as wise, making the most of your time, because the days are evil. Eccl 9:10 Whatever your hand finds to do, do it with all your might. Prov 14:23 All hard work brings a profit, but mere talk leads only to poverty. Prov 10:5 The one who gathers crops in the summer is a wise son, but the one who sleeps during the harvest is a son who brings shame to himself.

My beloved use your time wisely. Do not seek the things of the world. Do not fill your time with entertainment, but fill your time with My Words and communing with My Spirit. If you seek after the world, you will be lost in darkness. You will not be able to see the Light. You will grow darker by the day. If you turn from the things of the world and follow close to Me, then you will be cleansed of the things of the world and not long for them anymore. Use your time to help others. Use your time to study My Words and allow Me to teach you hidden things. Use your time to research the answers to your questions. You may not find the answers through your studies, but I will bring the answers to you as you search for them. If you are new to My Words, then give yourself time. The answers will come to you. Use your time wisely to build up your family. Spend time with your family and teach them My Ways. Use your time wisely to give to the poor and not continue to buy for yourself. Do not set yourself up as a "god" that you must dress in beautiful clothing with beautiful sparkling accessories. Make yourself a humble servant, and give to others instead of yourself. Use your time to build up your marriage spending time with your mate and increasing your union. The enemy fights against the family and marriage to destroy both of them. Do not allow him to come in and steal from you, because you do not spend enough time with your family and mate. Use your time wisely to sing praises to Me and worship Me. Use your time wisely to teach others My Ways. Use your time wisely to pray for the believers and minister to the sick. Use your time wisely to be still, and listen to My Voice. Turn off the noises around you. In the stillness you will find Me.

340

A husband should love his wife. A wife should respect her husband.

Eph 5:33 However, each one of you also must love his wife as he loves himself, and the wife must respect her husband. 1 Cor 7:3 The husband should fulfill his marital duty to his wife, and likewise the wife to her husband. The wife's body does not belong to her alone but also to her husband. In the same way, the husband's body does not belong to him alone but also to his wife. (Gen 3:16)

My beloved, I have given you a mate to help you endure the trouble in life. Cling to each other, and do not stand against each other. If you are having difficulties getting along with each other, then repent and turn to Me to help you. You must begin your morning in prayer together. I will hear your prayers and heal your relationship. You must end your day in prayer together, and I will bless your marriage and give you peace. You must not hold bitterness in your heart against your mate. You must forgive and allow Me to change your mate. If your mate is not a believer and wants to leave you, then allow him to leave. I will deal with his heart. If your mate is a believer and wants to leave you, then continue to love your mate and intercede with your mate to keep your marriage covenant. You should never turn away from the marriage vow that you made. You must keep your oath to each other, because it is sacred in My Eyes. You must give yourself to each other in love and devotion always wanting to please your mate to bring comfort to him. Only if you stand together will you be able to stand against the evil one. The evil one roams around and tries to find a place to divide a marriage. He wants to destroy as many marriages as possible, because he knows that I hold the marriage vow sacred. He wants to destroy the vow and bring jealousy and adultery into the marriage. Do not fall into his trap, but guard your eyes from the lust of the flesh. Stay pure and righteous. Do not go to places where you know you are weak. Stay far away from these places. Praying together as partners will keep you in a hedge, and you will be able to fight the enemy together. You will be strong and powerful, and no one will harm you. Love and respect each other, and no power can overtake you. I am with you always. I will help you endure until the end.

Which Commandments Should I Obey?

341

You should fight against the devil.

Eph 6:10-13 Finally, be strong in YHUH and in his mighty power. 11 Put on the full armor of YHUH so that you can take your stand against the devil's schemes. 12 For our struggle is not against flesh and blood, but against the rulers, against the authorities, against the powers of this dark world and against the spiritual forces of evil in the heavenly realms. 13 Therefore put on the full armor of YHUH, so that when the day of evil comes, you may be able to stand your ground. 2 Cor 10:4-5 The weapons we fight with are not the weapons of the world. On the contrary, they have divine power to demolish strongholds. (James 4:7- 8, 1 Peter 5:8-9, Rev 12:9, Job 1:7)

My beloved, stand firm against the devil. Stand firm, and do not give into his schemes to trap you into doing evil. He wants to destroy all men. He wants to disgrace you in My eyes. He wants Me to change My Mind about you by showing Me that you are unworthy to enter My Kingdom. He was outraged that I would create a first born heir for My Kingdom, and he and his angelic realm would have to serve you and bow to your authority in the coming age. He wanted to remain the supreme leader and all others would remain under him. He craved power and dominance. He wanted to be like Me. He wanted others to worship him. He fell under a lie that he could be like Me. He created an evil plan to deceive My Children and get them to eat from The Tree of Good and Evil, so they would become evil and not good. He came to the garden and walked among them as many of the angels did. He wanted to see how he could deceive them. He questioned them and found that Eve was weaker. He deceived her and tricked her and she fell into sin. She turned to Adam and asked him to sin with her. He could not refuse the one he loved, so he fell with her. The evil one continues to this day to prove that you are unworthy to enter My Kingdom. You must stand firm and fight against him. Control your flesh and do not allow your flesh to control you. It is a battle that is within the mind. Drive away any evil thoughts and focus on Me. You will become stronger every day. You may be weak today and crying out for help. I will help you overcome whatever your weakness may be. I hear your prayers. I have not given up on you. You can overcome. It does not matter what sin you have fallen into, you can still get up and overcome your flesh. The evil one says that it is too late, but it is never too late to repent and turn to Me. Arise and be strong, and I will help you become an overcomer.

358

342

You should pray in the spirit.

Eph 6:18 With all prayer and petition pray at all times in the Spirit, and with this in view, be on the alert with all perseverance and petition for all the saints. Ps 88:1 O YHUH, Elohim of my salvation; I cry out day and night before you. Ps 77:3 I remembered you, YHUH, and I groaned; I meditated, and my spirit grew faint. (Col 4:2)

My beloved, pray in the Spirit and give thanks to Me at all times. Pray in the tongues of the Spirit. Allow the Spirit within you to pray for you, so you can be healed and restored. Only the Spirit within you knows what you need. Take time each day to pray in the Spirit that is within you. It is My Spirit that I have breathed inside of you. It is the Spirit that I have given you, so you can commune with Me. I know what you need and when you need it. Do not question My Timing. Do not question what I give you whether it is good or bad. Do not question the tests that I send your way. Rejoice that I test you and want to find you faithful. Rejoice that I know you by name, and you are Mine. Rejoice that I have chosen you from the beginning. You are My Beloved, and I will mold you into My Image. I will make you a new creature. If you are continually in prayer, then you will continually know what I want you to do and the direction you must take. My Children need to be listening to My Voice in these last days, so you can hear when I tell you to move. If you do not obey, you will be overtaken by your enemies. You will be overtaken and suffer loss. You will be given pain and suffering. You must be praying in My Spirit, and allow My Spirit to guide you. You must listen every day to My Voice. If you are in the things of the world, you will not hear My Voice and miss the opportunity to escape. Be brave. Be strong. Be courageous. I will help you stand firm. I will be your strength until the very end. Lean on Me, and I will make you stronger than you ever thought you would be. I AM faithful to the end.

343

You should continue to work out your salvation.

Phil 2:12 Continue to work out your salvation with fear and trembling, for it is YHUH who works in you to will and to act according to his good purpose. Ps 2:11 Serve YHUH with fear and rejoice with trembling. (Rev 3:5, Matt 7:22-23)

My beloved, continue to press towards the goal of obtaining eternal life. This is the only treasure that you would work towards. Men of the world cast their eyes on gold and silver. They want to be wealthy and have power. My children know that this life is temporary and will soon pass away. They want to build up treasures in My Kingdom what will not pass away. You should continue to fear Me and walk in My Ways knowing that I will punish you for rejecting My Laws and doing as you please. You should rejoice that I have given you so much and want to continue to please Me. You must not see the world as men see the world. You must only focus on My Will for you. You must not long for what others of the world want. Even when all around you are not serving Me, you must serve Me and do as I tell you to do. I will reward you greatly for your sacrifices. You are here to be transformed into a new being. You will emerge a glorious being as your fleshly robe falls away from you. Your purpose here is to be found worthy of entering into My Kingdom. You must pass the test. My angels look in amazement at what you will become. You will become My First Born Heir into the Kingdom. I will give all I have to you. You will rule with Me and have authority over all My Kingdom. You will be given keys to the secrets of the universe that not even My angels know. You are My Treasure and I watch over you daily to protect you and keep you safe. Set your eyes on the goal in this life, and do not lose focus on what is important here. I will help you overcome.

344

You should do everything without complaining.

Phil 2:14 Do everything without complaining or arguing, so that you may become blameless and pure, children of YHUH without fault in a crooked and depraved generation, in which you shine like stars in the universe. Ex 16:8 Also Moses said, "This shall be seen when YHUH gives you meat to eat in the evening, and in the morning bread to the full; for YHUH hears your complaints which you make against Him. And what are we? Your complaints are not against us but against YHUH." Lam 3:39 Why should a living man complain, a man, about the punishment of his sins?

My beloved, do not complain about your life. I have given you this life and what happens to you will change you into My Image. When you have to face difficult situations rejoice and be glad that I found you worthy to face these difficult times knowing that I am perfecting you for the Kingdom. Rejoice and be glad every-day that you live, and I will bless you and keep you close to Me. I do not like complainers. I do not want to hear your complains against Me. Even when you are complaining to others about your life, you are complaining to Me about what I have given you. You must accept what comes your way and see them as chances to overcome and pass the test. If you can trust Me through the hard times in life and not complain, then you have learned to have complete faith in Me. Not every man is able to focus on Me and trust Me. So many are blinded by the things of the world and how they can obtain them. Material things will pass away, but the spiritual things will be made known to all. Men of the world will be filled with terror once they see My Kingdom revealed. You will rejoice and be glad. They will be terrified, because they know that judgment is coming. Continue to walk in My Ways, and do not allow the hardships of life to overtake you. Rejoice in all things, and I will bless you with peace.

345

You should renew your mind.

Rom 12:2 Do not conform any longer to the pattern of this world, but be transformed by the renewing of your mind. Then you will be able to test and approve what YHUH's will is-his good, pleasing and perfect will. Col 3:10 And have put on the new self, which is being renewed in knowledge in the image of its Creator. Titus 3:5 He saved us through the washing of rebirth and renewal by the Holy Spirit. (Eph 4:22-24, Deut 18:9, Ex 23:2)

My beloved, I want you to be careful about what you see with your eyes and what you listen to with your ears. I want you to keep yourself pure and righteous before Me. Only when you shut out the things of the world will you be able to renew your mind. You must meditate on My Words every day. Read My Words and allow My Words to cleanse your mind and replace the evil thoughts with good thoughts. As My Words penetrate your heart, your heart will begin to change and you will begin to love others and have compassion on them. You will see others as I see them. The people around you need your love and encouragement. They are torn down by the world. All around them are people who want to criticize and break them down. You are a ray of hope when you come to them with love and compassion in your heart. Your love can heal them and restore them. You will become a haven to them-a place to turn in times of trouble. You will teach them how to turn to Me and establish a relationship with Me. You will turn them from evil to good. You will be a light that allows them to see the Truth before them. You must be ready to help those around you. You must be ready to be My Servant. If you will allow Me to cleanse your mind and make you pure through My Words and My Spirit cleansing you, then you will be successful and prosper. You will continue to struggle with your flesh and fall under it, if you do not allow Me to cleanse your mind. You must put aside all the evil things of this world and focus on Me. Read My Words and absorb them. If you do not understand My words, then call on Me to give you understanding. I will open up Light from Heaven and enlighten your eyes. I will heal and restore you and make you whole. Call on My Name, and I will come to you.

346

You should work hard for YHUH.

Col 3:23 Whatever your task, work wholeheartedly, as serving YHUH and not men. Prov 14:23 All hard work brings a profit, but mere talk leads only to poverty. (Eph 6:7-8, Mal 3:18)

My beloved, I am your Master. I am the One you are working for. I tally your rewards and your punishments. I am the One that knows what you need when you need it. I will give you the task that will make you strong and mighty. You do not work for a boss. You do not work for a company. The job you have has been chosen by Me to form you. If you are unhappy at your work, look at the source of the unhappiness. Do I want you to leave this job and get another job? Are you unhappy because you are not doing your best? Are you unhappy because of the people you work with? Is the job itself not fulfilling to you? If the people around you are causing you to suffer, then remember that you are here to be a Light to these people, and this is your most important task. Love them and be kind to them and be giving, and you will see a change in their attitude towards you. If your boss is hard on you, then suffer under him and learn from him and allow this to form your flesh. I will reward you for your faithfulness to serve him. If your job is unfulfilling, then call on My Name and I will open your eyes to how it can become fulfilling by giving you a different way to look at it, or I will show you another job that will bring you satisfaction. Do not be afraid to look for another job, but leave your job in good faith treating all the employees with kindness and giving your boss a good testimony of your hard work. If you do leave a place, make sure that I am guiding you. Do not allow your own flesh to drive you out of a place where I have placed you. Do not leave a job or company unless I tell you to go. Look for a sign. Ask me to show you clearly what you must do, and I will help you. I will open a door for you, and you will know that it was opened by Me. Work hard and be faithful, and I will bless you greatly.

347

You should dress in modest clothing.

1 Tim 2:9 In like manner also, that women adorn themselves in modest apparel, with shamefacedness and sobriety; not with braided hair, or gold, or pearls, or costly array; But (which becomes women possessing righteousness) with good works. 1 Peter 3:3 Your beauty should not come from outward adornment, such as braided hair and the wearing of gold jewelry and fine clothes. Instead, it should be that of your inner self, the unfading beauty of a gentle and quiet spirit, which is of great worth in YHUH's sight. (1 Sam. 16:7, Prov 7:10)

My beloved, what you wear is a direct reflection of your heart. If you desire to wear revealing clothes or clothes that are too tight, then your heart is filled with darkness. You cannot see that you are causing others to stumble by lusting after your body. If you think it is stylish to dress like the world dresses, then you want to follow after the world. You must want to follow after Me. Make sure that you look at yourself in the mirror and see if you are exposing your flesh in a matter that would cause others to sin. Look at your dress with My Eyes and see how I would want you to dress. Are you drawing attention to yourself or to Me? You are supposed to be My Hands and Feet. You are supposed to be a Light to the world. How can you be a Light if you are dressing like the world? How are you different from others? You must dress modestly and hold a high example for the other believers around you. They may be weak, but you can help them become strong. Turning away from the world is never easy in the fleshly body, but the more you turn towards Me the more I will help you turn. As you draw closer to Me you will be able to see with My Eyes, and sin will become apparent to you. You will want all men to look at you and see Me. You do not have to adorn yourself with gold and silver and costly clothing. Do not spend all your money on yourself, but give to those around you. Clean out your closet, and give to the poor. You do not need an extensive wardrobe. You need a pure heart and loving ways. Rejoice that you can see the world for what it is-a place to test your faith in Me. Do not fail the test, but rise up and guard over yourself. I will robe you with clothes from on high.

348

You should be content with what you have.

Heb 13:5 Keep your lives free from the love of money and be content with what you have, because YHUH has said, "Never will I leave you; never will I forsake you." Phil 4:11 I am not saying this because I am in need, for I have learned to be content whatever the circumstances. Prov 23:4 Do not wear yourself out to get rich; do not trust your own cleverness.

My beloved, I want you to be content with the things that I have given you. First you must realize that all gifts come from Me. I have given you the things that you have today. I have made a path for you, so you can prosper and have success. If you stay on the path I have laid out for you, then you will always walk in oneness with Me. You will be led by Me, and I will open doors for you that only I can open. I will close those doors that will be harmful for you. I only want you to have the things you need to draw you closer to Me. For some people wealth will turn them away from Me and into the world. For other people they will use the wealth that I give them to give to others and make a difference in the world. For some people having good health will turn them away from Me and they will not depend on Me. For other people having good health will help them to be a ser-vant to others. For some people having power will cause them to take their eyes off Me and not listen to My direction. For other people having power will humble them and they will turn to Me to direct them knowing they have so many under them that depend on them for help. Whatever I give to you is what you need to be successful in this life, so you can help others and draw closer to Me. You are here to overcome evil and walk in love. You are here to be tested and be found faithful to Me while on earth. If you endure to the end and serve Me daily, then you will be found worthy to enter My Kingdom. Your life will be spared, and you will live with Me eternally. Be content with what I have given you, and praise Me daily that I have given you so much!

349

You should pray for wisdom.

James 1:5 If any of you lacks wisdom, you should ask YHUH, who gives generously to all without finding fault, and it will be given to you. Prov 2:6 For YHUH gives wisdom; from his mouth come knowledge and understanding. Dan 2:21 He changes times and seasons; He deposes kings and raises up others. He gives wisdom to the wise and knowledge to the discerning.

My beloved, if you lack wisdom in any area of your life, then call on My Name and I will help you. If you are working in a job and you need wisdom to do better for your employer, then call on Me and I will give you wisdom to be able to excel. If you are having problems raising your children, then call on My Name and I will give you wisdom how to raise your children in the things of Me. Do not be concerned that you may fail. If you feel like you cannot do a task, call on My Name and I will give you the wisdom to understand what you are doing and to excel at the task. If you are in disobedience to Me, then you will be lacking. You are not fit for the job you are doing, because you did not seek Me to show you where to go. I am jealous. I want you to come to Me first in everything, and I will guide you. If you decide to do what you want, then you will suffer loss. You must allow Me to show you what is best for you. You do not know what you need for this life. I know what you need to help you become stronger and overcome the things of the world. I will help you in every area of your life. Do not think that I will not answer you. I love you and want you to be successful. I may put you in a difficult job, so you will call on My Name for help and draw closer to Me. Open your eyes and see what I am doing inside of you to prepare you for My Kingdom.

350

You should lay your hands on the sick and anoint them with oil. You should pray in the name of Yahshua.

James 5:14-15 Is any sick among you? Let him call for the elders of the church; and let them pray over him, anointing him with oil in the name of Yahshua. 15 And the prayer of faith shall save the sick, and Yahshua shall raise him up; and if he have committed sins, they shall be forgiven him. (Mark 16:18, Matt 10:7-8, Mark 6:12-13, 1 Kings 17:21)

My beloved, if there are any sick among you, lay hands on them and ask Me to heal them. Why are many not healed when you pray? A righteous man's prayers are heard by Me, but a man in sin is not heard. If the man you are praying for is in sin, then he needs to repent so he can be healed. If the man has a family curse on him, then he needs to pray and fast to release the curse from him. If a man is healed when you pray, rejoice and be glad that I have had mercy on him. I have heard your prayers and had mercy on both of you. My mercy and grace is unending. I love to pour out mercy on you. Sometimes I use sickness to get your attention, so you will wake up and serve Me. You must be strong and stand firm, and then you can overcome any obstacle, because you will pray and I will help you. If a loved one becomes ill, come to Me first. Allow Me to be your doctor-your healer. Do not go to the world first. Do not go straight to a doctor first, but always come to Me first and ask Me to heal you. If you need to repent, then do so quickly and turn from your sins and do not go down that path again. Be brave. Be strong. You are in My hands, and I want you always to walk in good health.

351

You should pray for the believers.

James 5:16 Confess your sins to one another, and pray for one another, that you may be healed. The prayer of a righteous man has great power in its effects. Jer 42:2 And said to Jeremiah the prophet, "Please hear our petition and pray to YHUH your Elohim for this entire remnant. For as you now see, though we were once many, now only a few are left." (1 Kings 13:6, 1 Kings 13:6, Eph 1:16)

My beloved, pray for those around you that love Me and want to serve Me. Support them with your prayers, and I will support you with My Arms of love. Pray for those who are lost and cannot find their way. I will open their eyes and allow them to see, if they are one of My Chosen Ones who have lost their way while in exile. Pray for those who are sick that I may heal them once they repent of their sins and return to Me. Healing will come to them once they have turned aside from their wickedness. If I have placed My Judgment on them because of their sins, then first they must complete the penalty of their sins, and then they will be healed. If the person has a sickness to keep him humble before Me, then I will keep My Hand on him. He will labor unto Me even while he is sick and suffering. Sometimes I must keep a person humble, so he can continue to call out to Me, and I will feed him Life and Truth from My Words. These are My Servants who I use greatly and must stay humble before Me. Pray that the test I give you will not be too hard for you, and that I will help you as you travel through this life. You will see your test in a different light and be able to walk in it, and not be burdened by it. You will become strong and faithful. You will have life and be able to give this life to others. You will remain in My Presence while you are praying for others, and I will hear you and answer your prayers. If you sacrifice your time to pray for others, I will rain down blessings for you and will open the eyes of the people that you pray for. Continue in your prayers, and I will bless you greatly.

352

You should repay evil with good.

1 Peter 3:9 Do not repay evil with evil or insult with insult. On the contrary, repay evil with blessing, because to this you were called so that you may inherit a blessing. Prov 17:13 Evil will never leave the house of one who pays back evil for good. Ps 38:20 Those who repay my good with evil lodge accusations against me, though I seek only to do what is good.

My beloved, do not say evil words to someone, because he has said evil words to you. Do not lash out in anger to others, because they are angry with you. You must put up a wall of love around you. Absorb their anger and hatred and pour love into their wounds. They are hurting and afraid. Anyone who is angry everyday has many wounds and your love could be anointing oil that heals him. If you are around someone who wants to insult you daily, talk to him and see if you have hurt him in some way. Repent of any sins against him and ask him to forgive you. If you cannot find anything that you have done to hurt him, then pray for him and love him and do kind things for him. Your acts of kindness will be like hot coals on him. He will burn inside when you are loving and kind when he has been mean to you. This will not be easy to do at first, because you live in flesh. You will have to let your flesh be subdued and your love be pushed forth. You can teach yourself to love others and overlook their weaknesses. Humans are not perfect, and they will make many mistakes. Do not allow someone's sin to turn you towards hatred. Forgive quickly, and do not allow the enemy to come into you and bred hatred in your heart. Guard over your heart, and stay pure before Me. If you will continue to do good things even when others do evil things, I will reward you greatly. I will send good gifts to you. I will help you overcome all things. Love conquers all. Love will prevail when all evil falls. I AM Love. Walk in Me, and give My Love to others.

353

You should remain sober and not live in excess.

1 Peter 5:8 Be sober-minded; be watchful. Your adversary the devil prowls around like a roaring lion, seeking someone to devour. Eph 5:18 And be not drunk with wine, wherein is excess; but be filled with the Spirit. 1 Peter 1:13 Therefore, with minds that are alert and fully sober, set your hope on the grace to be brought to you when Yahshua is revealed at his coming. Prov 23:20 Do not join those who drink too much wine or gorge themselves on meat.

My beloved, remain sober and upright keeping your mind fixed on Me and not satisfying the flesh. If you seek to satisfy the flesh, then you will suffer under the weight of the flesh. You will become ill and dissatisfied, and you will have no peace or satisfaction. You will be miserable always trying to satisfy the flesh. You can never satisfy the flesh. The flesh always wants more and more. The flesh is greedy and selfish and cannot be pacified. You must live in the spirit, because you are a spirit being. You are born of Me and wrapped in flesh to help you become strong as you fight against the flesh. You are in a battle every day. You must be stable and not bending. You must remain strong and not give into the flesh. You must see clearly and know what I desire you to do. If you sleep too much, or drink too much alcohol, or work too much and not rest on My Sabbath, you will suffer for your excess. If you eat too much, or if you rest too much and do not work, or if you spend too much money and fall into debt, then you will suffer for your excess. Live in moderation and live according to My Spirit. Be led by Me, and you will stay sound and unmovable. If you live in fear and not love, you will also suffer loss. You must walk in the fruits of the Spirit and be led by My Spirit, and then you will have the proper medium. You will be sober minded. You will be stable. You will be a Light for those around you. You will walk hand in hand with Me and be at peace.

354

You should mind your own business.

1 Thess 4:11 Make it your ambition to lead a quiet life, to mind your own business and to work with your hands, just as we told you, so that your daily life may win the respect of outsiders. Prov 26:17 Whoever meddles in a quarrel not his own is like one who takes a passing dog by the ears.

My beloved, do not enter into the affairs of others. Allow each person to work out his differences with the person he has a problem with. Do not cast your opinion in the middle of a fight. Stay out of such fights, and try to be the peacemaker. Try to stop arguments, but do not fuel them with your comments. Do not take sides in an argument between two people. Allow them to find a resolution to walk in peace. If a person comes to you and asks your opinion in an argument, be very wise. Do not be drawn into a trap, but act as a mediator to resolve peace. You must learn to live a quiet life not entering into the affairs of others. Do not continue gossip. Do not even listen to such stories. Do not look for something to tell others that may cause dissention between others. You should be looking for ways to build up others, so they can be stronger. If you know someone who constantly wants you to gossip about others with them, stay away from that person. If you know that a group of people are not good for you, then stay away from them. You may work in a place where the people do not know Me and want to slander others and gossip. Stay away from them, and always offer a word of praise or encouragement as an example to them. Do not belittle anyone, but find the good in that person and bring it forth with your words. The person will respond to your praise and rejoice in it. You could be the difference in his life. You may be the only one who brings kind words to him. Think of how great an impact that your words are daily on the lives of others. Allow love to flow from your lips and heal the wounds of others. You are My Hands and Feet. Walk in love and compassion, and be an example to others. Your acts of love will change those around you.

Which Commandments Should I Obey?

355

You should be thankful for all your blessings.

1 Thess 5:18 In everything give thanks: for this is the will of YHUH in Yahshua concerning you. Ps 103:2 Let all that I am praise YHUH; may I never forget the good things He does for me. (Eph 5:20)

My beloved, be thankful for all things that come your way. It will be easy to be thankful for your food, clothes, shelter, transportation, health, children, and marriage. It is not as easy to be thankful for the blessing that comes your way to form you into My Image. Sometimes you look at them as hardships and cry over them and ask Me to take them away from you. The hardships are blessings. The trying times are blessings. You should be thankful that I love you so much to form you into My Image, so you can be found worthy to enter My Kingdom of Light. If you are not found worthy, then you will go to the Lake of Fire and be consumed. You will be no more, and the memory of you will be gone. If you walk hand in hand with Me and want to serve Me and love Me and be obedient to Me, then you will be counted worthy to enter My Kingdom. You will be ready to rule with Me. You will be joint heirs with Me and have authority over many. You must first be tested, so you will become strong and mighty and can overcome the enemy. If you fall to the enemy every day, then you have no victory. You must rise up and have victory, and be considered faithful to Me. Do not fall into sin every day, but rise up and serve Me with all your heart, so I can bless you and prepare you for the coming days. The days ahead are dark and filled with much evil. If you cling to Me, I will guide you through the darkness, and you will not be deceived even in the darkest of days. Rejoice that I love you so much to not give up on you, but to continue to form you and mold you and make you the complete person that will be worthy of bearing My Name. Your name is written in My Book, and I will transform you until you are ready to take on this name and walk in it. Do not give up, but give thanks in all I bring to you. Rejoice that I love you so much.

356

You should test the spirits.

1 John 4:1 Beloved, do not believe every spirit, but test the spirits to see whether they are from YHUH, for many false prophets have gone out into the world. 1 Thess 5:19 Do not put out the Spirit's fire; do not treat prophecies with contempt. Test everything. Hold on to the good. Avoid every kind of evil. (Jer 23:16)

My beloved, there are many who walk in lies and want to deceive My Children. Be careful to watch for these people. Test everyone by looking at his life. Does he bear the fruits of the spirit? Does he walk in love? Is he humble? Does he give to others or does he build up wealth for himself? You must test the person who speaks the words that you hear. Then you must test the words you hear against My Words. Do these words line up with the Scriptures? Can you find evidence of this in My Scriptures? If you cannot find this doctrine in My Scriptures, then cast it away from you. Even now you have lies that have been given to you by your ancestors. You walk in manmade laws and doctrines. Test every doctrine and see if it is from Me. Even if you have walked this way all your life and now you find evidence that this is not true, turn from it quickly and repent. I will forgive you, and show you a better way to live. Many will come saying that they have a better way to walk. Many will come saying that they know the time I will arrive. Many will come saying that they have heard a word from Me. Test all these things carefully. Ask Me to guide you into all Truth. If you call on Me I will keep you from deception. I will keep you from falling into error. I will deliver you from the lies that you walk in now. I will bring Truth to your house. I will point out to you in the Scriptures the Truth, and you will be set free from manmade doctrine. The enemy will no longer have a hold on you. You will be free to worship Me in Spirit and Truth.

357

You should not lose your first love for Yahshua.

Rev 2:4 Yet I hold this against you: You have forsaken your first love. 5 Remember the height from which you have fallen! Repent and do the things you did at first. If you do not repent, I will come to you and remove your menorah from its place. 6 But you have this in your favor: You hate the practices of the Nicolaitans, which I also hate. 7 He who has an ear, let him hear what the Spirit says to the churches. To him who overcomes, I will give the right to eat from the tree of life, which is in the paradise of YHUH. (Jer 2:2)

My beloved, do you love Me with all your heart, soul, and mind? Do you love me with all your being? Have you left your first love for Me? Do you think that I have not noticed? Do not allow the cares of the earth to take you away from your first love for Me. Do not allow troubles to steal your joy, but hold fast to your joy and rejoice that I have found you worthy to call My own-My child-My first born heir to the throne. You will rule with Me-be given a perfect body so that you only do My will because you are one with Me-married to Me-My bride perfect and complete. Rejoice in who you are and praise Me for My wondrous love for you. There is no greater love than I have for you. If you can understand who you are, then you can rejoice all the day and praise Me consistently and not even complain. You will always speak in love for others and never speak evil of others. My beloved, do not lose the first love you received from Me when everyday was a new delight. Press in and hold fast. If you are being persecuted, I will give you strength to overcome. I will give you the ability to remain strong until the end. I will never leave you, and I will give you the gift of eternal life so you can live with Me forever.

358

You should not be afraid to suffer for Yahshua.

Rev 2:8 These are the words of Him who is the First and the Last, who died and came to life again. 9 I know your afflictions and your poverty-yet you are rich! I know the slander of those who say they are Jews and are not, but are a synagogue of Satan. 10 Do not be afraid of what you are about to suffer. I tell you, the devil will put some of you in prison to test you, and you will suffer persecution for ten days. Be faithful, even to the point of death, and I will give you the crown of life. 11 He who has an ear, let him hear what the Spirit says to the churches. He who overcomes will not be hurt at all by the second death. (Ps 31:23)

My beloved, do not be fearful about the coming days. Do not be fearful about coming persecution. If you listen to My voice, I will keep you hidden from coming judgment on this land. It may mean that you will have to leave your home and most of your belongings and take only what you really need to a new land- a new place to dwell. If may mean that some of your family will not listen to My voice and will be left behind. You will have to do what is best for you and your children. You have to be ready to leave when I say leave or you may face prison or execution. You say, "How can this happen in a land of freedom?" You will see great loss of liberty, so be on guard and know that judgment comes to all lands, and only if you are in one of My safe havens will you escape. Only those who are listening will come to Me. If you love your possessions, you will lose them as they gather up you and your family and take you to jail, because you love Me and want to serve only Me. When you refuse to be branded into the world system of trade, you will be executed for My name sake. Rejoice and be glad that only your flesh was lost, and your soul will be saved, and you will live with Me eternally. Do not be afraid of suffering imprisonment, because you suffer for Me and it will be added to your crown of righteousness.

359

You should not renounce your faith in Yahshua.

Rev 2:12 These are the words of Him who has the sharp, double-edged sword. 13 I know where you live-where Satan has his throne. Yet you remain true to my name. You did not renounce your faith in Me, even in the days of Antipas, my faithful witness, who was put to death in your city-where Satan lives. 17 He who has an ear, let him hear what the Spirit says to the churches. To him who overcomes, I will give some of the hidden manna. I will also give him a white stone with a new name written on it, known only to him who receives it. (1 Kings 9:6-7, Deut 28:15, 2 Tim 2:12)

My beloved, if you are faithful to Me and endure to the end and do not give up and renounce your faith even in times of persecution, I will bless you and take you into My kingdom and bestow on you treasures because of your faithfulness. As the end of this place grows to a close, the Evil One presses My faithful harder. He wants to kill My beloved and swipe out all My children, but he cannot harm those who love Me. He cannot touch My faithful unless I allow him to do so for the sake of My glory. Many of My children want to lay down their life for Me, so My Name can be glorified. Some call on My name for protection against the Evil One, and I will protect them. Do not live in fear, because My power of protection is strong. I kept My servant David safe from his enemies, and I can do the same for you. If you are put in a situation where you are asked to renounce your faith or suffer death, then I will give you the strength to stand and you will be rewarded for your faithfulness to Me. If you renounce Me so you can live, then you have lost your life instead of gaining Me. Do not think that I do not hear your confessions and not think that others do not see, but a multitude of onlookers see your confessions of faithfulness to Me. Be strong and be led by My Spirit, so you can be protected even to the very last day of the Great Tribulation.

360

You should be doing more today for Yahshua than you did at first.

Rev 2:18 These are the words of the Son of YHUH, whose eyes are like blazing fire and whose feet are like burnished bronze. 19 I know your deeds, your love and faith, your service and perseverance, and that you are now doing more than you did at first. 25 Only hold on to what you have until I come. 26 To him who overcomes and does my will to the end, I will give authority over the nations. 27 And he shall rule them with a rod of iron; as the vessels of a potter shall they be broken to shivers: even as I received of my Father. 28 And I will give him the morning star. (*Yahshua*) (Job 17:9, Ps 92:14)

My beloved, hold fast to the truth you have now, but continue to search for more truth while you can. The Evil one will cut off all truth and will allow no one to learn the truth, but he will search everywhere and pervert truth and make it lies. That has been his plan from the beginning. He has taken the scriptures and where he could, he changed the meanings of words so deception could come to My people. He has perverted My days and times. He has perverted My Sabbath and changed the day to Sunday. He has taken away My feast days in the churches. He has the people calling themselves followers of Christ-Christians and they do not even know My ways, because they have been taught to forget My laws and don't think about My commandments. How can you throw out My words? How can you change My ways? Who gave you authority? Who made you ruler of the universe? Who are you but dust? No, you should follow My laws and hold fast to My feast days and show love to those around you. Men will come to deceive you, but you must beware and be on guard. Hold fast to all My teaching. Do not allow men to argue with you, but turn aside and do not enter into such wickedness. Don't argue with pagans who love their deception and want to walk in man-made laws and not search My words for My laws. Hold fast to the truth because the days are dark and the Evil One wants to deceive you.

361

You should pray for strength to stand in these Last Days.

Rev 3:1 These are the words of Him who has the seven spirits of Elohim and the seven stars. I know your deeds; you have a reputation of being alive, but you are dead. 2 Wake up! Strengthen what remains and is about to die, for I have not found your deeds complete in the sight of YHUH. 3 Remember, what you have received and heard; obey it, and repent. But if you do not wake up, I will come like a thief, and you will not know at what moment I will come to you. 5 He who overcomes will, like them, be dressed in white. I will never blot out his name from the book of life, but will acknowledge his name before my Father and his angels. (Is 35:3-4, Ps 138:3)

My beloved, awake and strengthen what remains before you wither and die. Awake and rejoice, and do what I have shown you to do. Complete the work I have shown you to do. Do not give up. There will be resistance, so be strong and endure. Be strong and go forward. Do not dirty your hands in the things of the world. Do not soil your clothes by walking in the filth of this world. It is like feces on your clothing and you stink and are defiled, so stay far away from the things of the world-anything that is sexually immoral such as movies, TV, books, or pornography. You cannot look into these things and remain clean. You must remain clean before Me, or I will blot your name out of My Book of Life, and you will not enter My Kingdom. Be brave and strong and do what is right in My eyes, and you will enter My kingdom of Light. You will be able to wear white and walk in My Presence. You will be given special gifts, because you endured your time of testing on Earth. You will be able to arise from your sleep of death and be given eternal life with Me. Be ready, because I come at a moment when you least expect it. You will know the season and the time, but the moment I come is reserved for My Father. Only He knows when He will arrive, so finish what I have told you to do. Complete what you have started, and walk in righteousness till I return.

362

You should endure patiently until the end.

Rev 3:7-10 Since you have kept my command to endure patiently, I will also keep you from the hour of trial that is going to come upon the whole world to test those who live on the earth.11 I am coming soon. Hold on to what you have, so that no one will take your crown. 12 Him who overcomes I will make a pillar in the temple of YHUH. Never again will he leave it. I will write on him the name of YHUH and the name of the city of YHUH, the new Jerusalem, which is coming down out of heaven from YHUH; and I will also write on him my new name. (2 Tim 2:12, James 5:8, Is 66:22)

My beloved, hold fast to Me. Cling to Me and love Me and you will remain with Me eternally. I will cast aside all the others who gave up in the last days and did not hold onto their love for Me. They will not be allowed into My kingdom. They have lost the opportunity to wear the crown of eternal life. They are lost in darkness. They are no more. Their voice will be gone and forgotten. They will cease to exist, but you will reign with Me eternally. You are a child of the king–My child, and you are a royal child who inherits the kingdom of his father and receives all his riches and shares in all his power. You will rule over nations. You will teach others about Me-who do not know Me or My ways. People not yet born, you will go to and help them learn about Me. You will be like a mother to these little ones. They will receive gladly, because the Evil One is gone, and no more will he torment My children who love Me. The Evil One thinks he can change My plans, but he is wrong. My plans are set in motion, and no man can change them. I change the plans of men to fit My plans, so time ends at exactly the moment I want it to end and the fullness of the Earth has been complete. The Earth will be burned with fire and destroyed, but I will build a new heavens and Earth. I will restore My kingdom on Earth, and My children will rule nations in My name.

363

You should not be lukewarm.

Rev 3:15 I know your deeds, that you are neither cold nor hot. I wish you were either one or the other! 16 So, because you are lukewarm-neither hot nor cold-I am about to vomit you out of my mouth. 17 You say, 'I am rich; I have acquired wealth and do not need a thing.' But you do not realize that you are wretched, pitiful, poor, blind and naked. 18 I counsel you to buy from Me gold refined in the fire, so you can become rich; and white clothes to wear, so you can cover your shameful nakedness; and salve to put on your eyes, so you can see. 19 Those whom I love I rebuke and discipline. So be earnest, and turn from your sins. 20 Here I am! I stand at the door and knock. If anyone hears my voice and opens the door, I will come in and eat with him, and he with Me. 21 To him who overcomes, I will give the right to sit with Me on my throne, just as I overcame and sat down with my Father on His throne. (Jer 7:15, Hos 7:13)

My beloved, either you stand up for Me and confess Me as your Elohim or you say, "You are not my Elohim." Do not waiver between the two by saying that I AM your Elohim, and then live as the world lives. No, I will vomit you out of My mouth. You will not disgrace Me in such a way by saying you serve Me, and you don't. You are an abomination to Me. You sicken Me. I would rather you say, "I do not serve Elohim" and go on your way of the world and not even desire to come back to Me. How can you taste of My fruits and reject Me? You are worse than someone who has never tasted of My Fruits. If you love Me, you will serve Me and you will obey all My commandments. The world will grieve you and you will not desire to look at their wickedness. If you love Me, turn off your TV, movies, books of worldliness and corruption, and look no more to what they do. You watch the news of the day and see how man is lost and how he fights against My hand. I bring judgment on the land, and man can do nothing. I bring My sword to kill, and man can do nothing. I send pains upon the earth, and man can do nothing. You cannot change the future or the course it will take. The Earth will be destroyed and all its inhabitants. Only My children will survive. Make your choice. Either serve me with all your heart or don't. Do not be lukewarm.

364

You should not be a coward but an overcomer.

Rev 21:1-6 He said to me: "It is done. I am the Alpha and the Omega, the Beginning and the End. To him who is thirsty I will give to drink without cost from the spring of the water of life. 7 He who overcomes will inherit all this, and I will be his Elohim and he will be my son. 8 But cowards, traitors, perverts, murderers, the immoral, those who practice magic, those who worship idols, and all liars-the place for them is the lake burning with fire and sulfur, which is the second death." (Is 35:4)

My beloved, you must be brave and courageous and not a coward. You must not give up under hardship, but endure until the end of your days on Earth. This is a temporary place for you, but I AM preparing a place for you so you will no longer wear your robe of flesh. You will emerge in your new spiritual body where no pain, sadness, tears, or grief will harm you. You will rejoice all the day in My Presence. I will be in your midst all the time, and there will be no distance between us as there is now. You have the flesh that keeps us a part, so you cannot see the spiritual realm. You accept who I AM by faith even though you cannot see Me. No man can see Me. Soon all the walls will be torn away, and you will walk in a spiritual realm. You will be able to have power to reign with Me. You will have authority over all others, because you are My child. Do not be fearful and cowardly, but be bold and brave and stand firm until the end. Those who give up will go to the lake of fire. Only those who remain true to Me-faithful to Me-do not deny My Name-continue to confess their love for Me will be counted worthy to be given the gift of eternal life and live with Me forever. Be brave and do not seek the things of the world. Call on My name for strength, and I will deliver you from the Evil One.

365

You should wash your robe and prepare for Yahshua's coming.

Rev 22:12 "Behold, I am coming soon! My reward is with Me, and I will give to everyone according to what he has done. 13 I am the Alpha and the Omega, the First and the Last, the Beginning and the End. 14 Blessed are those who wash their robes, that they may have the right to the tree of life and may go through the gates into the city. 17 The Spirit and the bride say, 'Come!' And let him who hears say, 'Come!' Whoever is thirsty, let him come; and whoever wishes, let him take the free gift of the water of life." (Ex 19:10)

My beloved, you must be clean before Me. You must cleanse yourself from the things of the world before you can enter My kingdom. You must be white before Me with no filth on your robe or your hands and feet. You must be able to walk away from the world and not be soiled by it. If you are grieved over what you see on TV, movies, games, books, computers-all the portals that the enemy can use against you, then close the portals in your home. Close off the entryways that the enemy can sneak in and destroy you and your children. If you close the portals, you close the filth from pouring into your house. Do not support Hollywood by going to see movies. Do not rent movies or view movies that are offensive to your eyes. Cut off your TV cable and monitor closely your computers. Guard your children by putting guards on your computer and TV. Be very careful to keep the filth of the world from your children. If you are not very careful, how can you keep from making your robes dirty? You must not allow the enemy to come into your house-your sanctuary from the world. Your house should be a house of peace not filled with the world. Prepare yourself. Cleanse yourself and get ready, because I AM coming soon to collect My bride. I will have the marriage supper, so I can be at one with My people at last. I will place them in authority, so they can rule with Me. Get ready. I AM coming soon!

www.ingramcontent.com/pod-product-compliance
Lightning Source LLC
Chambersburg PA
CBHW070338090426
42733CB00009B/1224